# Voodoo Queen

# Voodoo Queen

## The Spirited Lives of Marie Laveau

### By Martha Ward

UNIVERSITY PRESS OF MISSISSIPPI    JACKSON

www.upress.state.ms.us

The University Press of Mississippi is a member of the Association of American
University Presses.

∞
Library of Congress Cataloging-in-Publication Data
Ward, Martha.
  Voodoo queen : the spirited lives of Marie Laveau / by Martha Ward.
    p. cm.
Includes bibliographical references and index.
  ISBN 1-57806-629-8 (alk. paper)
  1. Laveau, Marie, 1794–1881. 2. Voodooism—Louisiana—New Orleans—History—19th
    century. I. Title.
  BL2490.W37 2004
  299.6'75'092—dc22                                                    2003018292

British Library Cataloguing-in-Publication Data available

This book is dedicated to Madame Marie Laveau
and Mam'zelle Marie Laveau, and to the hope of mercy,
racial justice, and the protection of all our children.

SO BE IT.

# Contents

# *Introduction:*
# *At the Beginning*

It is a prime-time story when free women of color use their spiritual gifts to confront suffering and injustice, and white men in power accuse them of witchcraft. Marie Laveau, the legendary founder and priestess of American Voodoo, was in real life two women with the same name—a mother and her daughter, both Creoles of New Orleans. Yes, they worked their magic on a city's soul, and year after year thousands of visitors make pilgrimages to the famous tomb said to hold their remains. Yet, until now, the story of their spiritual and historic lives has been unavailable, and the legends of sorcery and evil deeds that encircle them have gone unchallenged.

Hysterical reporters in the nineteenth century accused the Laveaus of wizardry, heresy, and dancing naked with snakes. Marie the First, the mother, healed those with yellow fever and cheated the hangman's noose with her magical powers—or so it is said. Her daughter, Marie the Second, hypnotized the police force and cured domestic violence. The gossips still swear that they knew how to make white women roll on their bellies, work *gris-gris* on judges in murder trials, and cause husbands to disappear forever. Wealthy white New Orleanians insisted that the wily Maries operated a street-level system of intelligence through which they gained information and exerted backstairs power over those who stood in their way.

The Laveau women were guilty as charged. Both women led dangerous, secret lives—but not because of midnight ceremonies in graveyards. They were free women in a slave society, French Catholics in an Anglo-Protestant nation, and Creole leaders in the largest and strongest community of color in America. They were *gens de couleur libre*—free people of color. Both loved

Figure 1. The tomb of the Widow Paris (© Michael P. Smith, New Orleans)

men they could never marry. Their families, already linked in illegal love, defied their church and the law to help slaves escape and blacks, bond and free, to assemble and dance together in defiance of the law.

The Laveaus led colorful lives in one of the most colorful cities in the world. Their woman-centered story began in 1803 just as ill-bred foreigners from a nearby, new nation called the United States purchased their territory from France. It spanned the golden years of Creole culture and the glittering but dangerous life of antebellum New Orleans, then moved into the traumas of Civil War. The death of the first Marie Laveau in June 1881, and the disappearance of the second at the end of Reconstruction in 1877 parallel the passing of Creole life. Their embodied visions of justice and mercy died with them.

Voodoo was not just a religion—it was the raw edge of survival. People dropped dead on the streets as epidemic plagues consumed the city. Slave-sale houses ringed the French Quarter, and public executions drew Mardi Gras–size crowds. White men with power played racial politics for keeps— but they could not collect the garbage or bury the dead. When things went wrong in the neighborhoods of New Orleans, the civil authorities blamed the Voodoos.

New Orleans is a place where you invite the dead to your parties, where the smells of a spicy gumbo and the sounds of a jazzy backbeat fill the air. The city was a crucible of transformation that forged a vibrant Creole culture—a New World people whose ancestors were French, West African, Spanish, Central African, Catholic, Native American, and who had pinches of many other groups or nations added like spice to a good gumbo, people who created a unique collective culture from the ingredients they had on hand. Voodoo, jazz, the region's world-famous cuisine, and the dancing ironwork that graces the city's architecture have Creole roots. The "spirit of New Orleans" that attracts millions of visitors to the smells, tastes, sounds and sensory richness of the fabled city is in large measure the legacy of Creole culture.

*Isn't Voodoo dangerous? What happens to you if you tell its secrets?* White friends whisper questions like these to me when I meet them on the street or attend dinner parties at their homes. "Aren't you afraid of Voodoo?" they ask. "You don't believe in Voodoo, do you?" An African American neighbor looked around carefully before he announced, "Me, I don't have nothing to do with that Hoodoo stuff. It's some powerful to mess with. You take care, hear." A state librarian begged me to write a biography of a woman with more quality and substance than she thought Marie Laveau had. A New Orleans historian dismissed my quest, "It's merely folklore"; and another colleague remarked, "Oh, women's history."

The two most common concerns I hear are these: First, Voodoo is evil, satanic, demonic. A person who trashes or trifles with power like that can get hurt, the voices warn. Second, people caution me that no reliable sources of information about Marie Laveau are available. Either they never existed or they have been stolen, destroyed, or spirited away. Materials from the official histories pay little attention to women, particularly women of color; and the Laveaus—in common with many women of their century—left nothing in writing. Yet Marie Laveau in her many reincarnations rules the imagination of New Orleans. For many, she is still a member of the community; they consult her for problems and visit with her on her special holidays—the Feast of All Saints in November and the Eve of St. John the Baptist in June. To some the Maries were like Moses—a magician who led his people out of bondage. Marie as a still-living ancestor continues to visits the citizens of the city in their dreams and visions.

The archives and libraries of Louisiana are national treasures. So are the archivists and librarians. But Marie Laveau seekers and undergraduate term paper writers frustrate them. They will tell you when you ask, as I sheepishly have, that very little is available and few find what they expect to see. Many records of baptisms, marriages, and burials for Catholics of color were closed throughout large parts of the twentieth century. A librarian at the Louisiana Division of the New Orleans Public Library sighed, "If it has Marie Laveau's name on it, it just disappears."

In the Louisiana Historical Collection, the head archivist showed me a mutilated copy of the city directory. Someone had carefully razored out an entry that identified a family as "free people of color." She told me about a visitor who read the archival records and asked what the designation "f.w.c." meant. When the woman realized that her ancestor had been a free woman of color, she fainted. Race remains the best reason for secrets and conspiracy in the Crescent City.

Other kinds of warnings appeared. These cautions came from the front of a set of business records in the Office of Conveyance: *"Whole Volume: Tight Binding. Faded Copy. Book in Poor Condition. Difficult to Film. Torn Pages. Missing Pages. Covered material. Soiled Copy Throughout Volume."* The original is too fragile to use. Microfilm technologies cannot improve what is yellowed, chipped, stained, or gone forever. The warnings in the documents, however, omitted the dangers to researchers of hard chairs, aching eyes, and screaming neck muscles.

At the end of the book I have thanked a long list of people without whose support, technical assistance, and encouragement I could never have written this book; I have also added a chronology of the priestesses' lives and the scholarly citations and notes that provide the bones for a spiritual biography, fleshly "proof" of the priestesses' existence. There, for example,

I cite official documents I have found. But the Laveaus manipulated many of them for severe and secret purposes known only to themselves, and even authentic "historic facts" and "anthropological analysis" will not add up to the "truth value" of their lives. So I have had to listen to and repeat the rumors, hearsay, and slander about the Laveaus that still circulate. Creole conversation that shades into gossip is called *gumbo ya-ya*, part of the moist air people breathe in New Orleans. I have wandered historic neighborhoods, signed up for guided tours, attended Voodoo rituals, and haunted cemeteries, ceremonies, and church services. Out of the corner of my eye, I have watched for signs of the spirits the Maries called into the city. I have relied on dreams, intuition, a hyperactive imagination, and funky Voodoo luck. From time to time I have stood in front of the Laveau tomb in St. Louis Cemetery One and talked with her. Marie laughs when I ask, "What really happened?" "Who knows the whole story," she says, "and maybe it's better that way."

Why, a sensitive person might ask, is a white academic and anthropologist writing about women of color dead over a hundred years? The first reason—New Orleans is a magnificent and inclusive city, and I have loved her longer than I ever loved a man. And the second—in the mid-nineteenth century, police raided Voodoo gatherings in New Orleans on the pretext of "illegal assembly." The next morning, newspapers carried shocked stories of the white women who danced at the gatherings. "Blacks and whites were circling round promiscuously, writhing in muscular contractions, panting, raving and frothing at the mouth. But the most degrading and infamous feature of this scene was the presence of a very large number of ladies, moving in the highest walks of society, rich and hitherto supposed respectable, that were caught in the drag net. These facts are beyond controversy, and the scandal, attested by thousands, was made the subject of town gossip for many a year."

The magistrates turned the nameless white women over to the authority of their husbands or fathers; they remanded enslaved women to the mercies of masters or mistresses. Women of color, though fined and harassed, went free. Another writer complained that white women sought counseling and bought charms or powders from women of color—"neurotic and repressed white women were especially easy victims of the Voodoo doctors."

So I, merely an aging storyteller, claim whatever privileges those anonymous white women had. I accept the labels they carried: race traitor, class defector, religious heretic, neurotic, repressed, and out-of-control female. The most famous song in New Orleans begs a favor from the spirits:

> *O Lord, I want to be in that number, when the saints go marchin' in.*

What does one need to know before reading this book?

〜 The many meanings of Creole: People come to New Orleans from all over the world to eat in the famous Creole restaurants of the city. They try remoulade sauce, turtle soup, fried oysters on French bread, crayfish bisque, shrimp creole, and many other tasty dishes, and they ask, what does Creole mean? I tell them that Creole is something or someone who was born and bred in the New World, something or someone who owes more to the unique environmental and social conditions of south Louisiana than to Africa or Europe. Creole is a handy adjective for things native to Louisiana, things of value, like Creole tomatoes or Creole cream cheese, the delicious ingredients in Creole cuisine. I say that Creoles came in every color in the social rainbow, and, in the main, were French-speaking Catholics who tended to marry each other when they could, and, when they couldn't, invented imaginative solutions to be together and to care for the babies born to them. In Marie Laveau's time, Creole was a culture more than a color, a culture with distinctive music, cuisine, clothes, and drinking habits.

The question "who is a Creole?" may provoke pained or angry responses among people who have lived in New Orleans for generations. One group says that a Creole is someone whose ancestors came to the colonies from France or Spain, who was born in Louisiana, and who may be light-skinned and "black" as well. A second group of Creoles agree with all but the last part. They insist that Creoles never had any African relatives— they swear this on the graves of the very ancestors who owned slaves, kept a second "wife" as mistress, and fathered mixed-race children. Creoles of color, by contrast, often say that African American is too confining a social category for them. Like Marie Laveau, they have four grandparents, eight great-grandparents, and sixteen great-great-grandparents—one of them may have come from Spain or Senegal, one from Benin or Belgium, and another from one of the many Indian nations already living in Louisiana. Many Creoles wish to know about and pay homage to all their ancestors.

⌒ Most people, places, or things in New Orleans have an alias. They are a.k.a.—"Also-Known-As." Proper names had many different versions, alternative names, and beautifully eccentric spellings. In the nineteenth century, for example, many journalists and writers used the classy French spelling—Voudou. I chose the contemporary American spelling—Voodoo—but I make certain to capitalize it as the name of a major religious tradition. To complicate matters, I have found at least eight Marie Laveaus, spelled in a number of imaginative ways. The first Voodoo queen had a grandmother, a half-sister, an aunt, a sister-in-law, and a next-door neighbor with the same name in different spellings—each woman had other names as well. Marie the First named all three of her daughters Marie. Marie the Second used her mother's trademark name when she pleased, but some legal documents use a different one. Women of color did not always adopt a father's name, and the sexual politics of the time prohibited many from having legal husbands. Moreover, Marie was—for obvious religious reasons—the most common woman's name in the city. It is little wonder that researchers and reporters alike are hopelessly confused.

⌒ Voodoo begins with people—usually women—who feel the tug of the spirit world. They say: *The spirits choose whom they will. They enter into my body and my soul. They bring blessings for all of us.* In common with all religions, Voodoo is a way to explain the unexplainable, to move the immovable, and to find power or agency in a dangerous world. But women like the Laveaus who take charge of their bodies, their houses, and their gods threaten the political powers. Voodoo draws fire.

⌒ New Orleans Voodoo is not the same thing as Haitian Vodou, and neither resembles Hollywood "voodoo." Voodoo, Southern Hoodoo, and their sister religions are the intense fusions that happened when the people of the African Diaspora met Catholics and colonists in the New World.

In New Orleans its practitioners were generally called "queens," "doctors," "workers," or fortune-tellers.

∽ In Louisiana, parish means what county does in the rest of America, and bayou means a small creek or river. In New Orleans, *Faubourg* is a neighborhood, and an *armoire* is a large, freestanding wardrobe with doors and shelves; even elegant houses lacked closets. No one can reckon the conventional directions—North, South, East, or West—because the below-sea-level city is ringed with levees that block the horizon. So citizens gauge where we are relative to the Mississippi River. Regardless of its broad curves or the direction it actually takes, it flows downriver or south to the Gulf of Mexico. Upriver is the opposite direction or north regardless of the readings of a compass or a map.

∽ A *picayune* was a Spanish coin used for small purchases. That's why it became the name of the longest-published newspaper in New Orleans—the *Picayune*.

∽ The color white is not always what it seems to be. Watch for white handkerchiefs, handmade altars, homemade gumbo, and light summer dresses.

∽ Spirits of many kinds appear in this biography whenever they feel like it. Such creatures are the experiential reality—alive in every sense of the word—of vast numbers of people on the planet. It will do no good, therefore, to question me or other humans in the book about our "beliefs." New Orleans is a high-spirited place. Mardi Gras is a spectacle of parades and balls named after mythical beings, gods, goddesses, and creatures of a cross-cultural imagination that has no rival in America. Bourbon Street is famous for another kind of possession—the spirits of alcohol. A local television station named itself "the Spirit of New Orleans." Hollywood calls the city the "Big Easy"—a local phrase for getting high, getting off, or getting in the spirit.

∽ Marie Laveau, both mother and daughter, was a conjure woman. *Conjure* is the "magical means of transforming reality." Conjurers see and understand things most people cannot. They exist in two realities, use two kinds of consciousness—one for consensual realities and the other for the spiritual realms. Thus, a conjurer, like all mystics and visionaries, is two-headed.

$\sim$ New Orleans Voodoo is no more satanic or evil than any of the world's religions. The accusations about human sacrifice, cannibalism, or devil worship are figments of fevered white imaginations and a mean-spirited way to turn women of color into the Other. In place of such superstitious hype, I offer far more dangerous, hair-raising, melodramatic, and magical tales.

# Voodoo Queen

# Chapter 1

## Who in Heaven or Hell, Africa or France, Was Marie Laveau?

WHEN CREOLES DIE, THEY GO TO PARIS.—NEW ORLEANS PROVERB

The drummer started a slow beat; a trumpet made from an animal's horn sounded four long notes. The gathering had begun. As Marie Laveau crossed Rampart Street and neared Congo Square, the multi-leveled roofs of the French Quarter and the spires of St. Louis Cathedral rose behind her. At the entrance to the dance plaza, she passed market women selling their wares—pecan pies, spruce beer, Louisiana rum, and pralines filled with peanuts, coconut, or popcorn. Marie had left the corsets, petticoats, and heavy undergarments she wore to church that Sunday morning at home. In their stead, she chose a loose, low-necked cotton dress that permitted easy movement in the subtropical humidity and allowed the Great Serpent Spirit to enter and use her body. Her gold earrings and bracelets flashed in the sun, and her *tignon*—a vividly colored madras handkerchief wound as a turban—stood high in seven points.

A man who saw her there said, "She come walkin' into Congo Square wit' her head up in the air like a queen. Her skirts swished when she walked and everybody step back to let her pass. All the people—white and colored—start sayin' that's the most powerful woman they is. They say, 'There goes Marie Laveau!'" The policemen stationed at each of the four gates to Congo Square watched the crowd part as Marie Laveau passed. They were waiting for her.

In every decade after the founding of New Orleans in 1719, the city fathers—first French, then Spanish, and after 1803, Anglo-American—had tried to control Congo Square and people like Marie Laveau who gathered there. Whites complained about loud music, lewd dances, sexy songs, Voodoo rituals, and the explosive potential of free and enslaved black people who met by the hundreds, sometimes by the thousands, on the old parade ground and market outside the original city walls. The authorities feared slave uprisings and insurrection. They worried that free people of color, whose numbers and prosperity grew with each passing year, planted ideas of liberation in the hearts of enslaved people.

The civil authorities established curfews—Sundays at sunset—and fired a cannon to signal the end of the gatherings. So citizens of color made up satirical songs that mocked the guns. The city fathers planted trees to obstruct the dance ground, and the Voodoos, under the leadership of the Laveaus, offered an array of social and benevolent services beneath their branches. With each new plan to limit the gatherings, white officials changed the name of the square. But people of color persisted—to them, it was and always would be Congo Square.

In 1843, after decades of futile attempts to contain the dances, authorities built an iron fence around the Square, placed a gate on each side, and closed it on Sunday afternoons. Within two years, the community of color forced the city administrators to reopen the dance plaza; according to persistent legends Marie Laveau the elder provided both the spiritual assistance and the political pull to make it happen. Still fearful of the power of free assembly, however, the city council ordered police to stand guard at the four gates of Congo Square every Sunday afternoon.

A number of black men claimed they had witnessed what Marie Laveau did in response to the ordinance. One said, "People complained about her and policemens were stationed at the gates. When Marie saw those policemen, she looked at them, never said a word, and walked right in. She just mesmerized those men and a lot of other people, 'cause they never said a word or tried to harm her." Another man said, "Marie Laveau brought the people into the square with her unmolested by the policemen. She hypnotized them and they could not do anything." Black men swore she "fixed" the authorities on those Sunday afternoons in the decade and a half before the Civil War: "Sometimes them policemens tried to keep Marie Laveau out, but she jest hypnotized 'em and walked in. She could do that to anybody what got in her way. I seen her make polices get down and bark like dogs." When Marie Laveau's magical spells, commanding presence, or strategic bribery had taken hold, the police relented and joined the crowds to watch her perform.

Marie slipped off her shoes and walked to the center where magical lines from the four corners and the four gates intersected. As was her custom, she knelt on the ground and rapped three times. The crowd loved the one-two-three rhythm and shouted it with her—*Father, Son, and Holy Ghost. Faith, Hope, and Charity.* Then from a box near her feet, she lifted a fat snake. The earth-toned creature—probably a Louisiana *Coluber*—was not poisonous, but it stretched twelve to twenty feet and entwined itself in undulating coils about the body of the priestess. Those who witnessed the performances were fascinated and frightened. "Marie danced with a snake and hypnotized everybody. No one knew what to do to prevent this act."

Marie signaled the band and began to move with slow, sinuous grace. Bare soles flat on the packed earth of Congo Square, she shifted her weight from one ankle to another, then to her knees, thighs, hips, torso, and up to her shoulders. Her feet never lifted from the ground; she swayed in waves like the movement of snakes. Other women joined her and danced within their own tight circles or rings, some no larger than ten feet in diameter. Many waved white handkerchiefs "extended by the corners in their hands." Men with bracelets of bells on their calves danced in circles around the women. Sometimes they balanced bottles of rum or other spirits on their heads. They mimicked fighting and leaped into the air in displays of gymnastic ferocity.

Other men sat astride large drums, handmade from wooden barrels and covered with animal skins, or held small ones between their legs. They beat with fingers, fists, feet, and the shank-bones of oxen or horses. The music began with "slow, slow vehemence on the great drum and fiercely and rapidly on the small one." Others in the band played tambourines, gourd rattles, three-reed pipes; they stroked an animal jawbone with a metal key or strummed a four-stringed, African-inspired banjo. The songs of dancers and chorus joined them—a "long-drawn human cry of tremendous volume, richness, and resound, to which no instrument within their reach could make the faintest approach."

The most popular song in Congo Square was the *Calinda*, a sensual song and dance complex that most onlookers associated with Marie Laveau and the secrets of Voodoo. The verses varied, but the chorus remained the same— *Danse Calinda, boudoum, boudoum! Danse Calinda, boudoum, boudoum!* White writers or travelers who heard the song in Congo Square wondered, how could anything so provocative be religious? One observer complained that "Nothing is more dreaded than to see the negroes assemble together on Sundays, since, under pretense of Calinda or the dance, they sometimes get together to the number of three or four hundred and made a kind of Sabbath. It is in those tumultuous meetings, that they sell what they have stolen to one another and commit many crimes. Likewise they plot rebellions."

Africa lived again in Congo Square on those Sunday afternoons six decades before the Civil War. In 1808 a traveler to the city saw "twenty different dancing groups of the wretched Africans, collected together to perform their *worship* after the manner of their own country." Another saw people dance "a rapid jig" to exhaustion, then sink to the grass, and accept water and refreshments from fellow dancers. "All is hilarity, fun, and frolic. Every stranger should visit Congo Square when in its glory." But a third complained, "I have never seen anything more brutally savage, and at the same time dull & stupid than this whole exhibition."

The dancing rings in Congo Square were reunions of African nations that the Diaspora and the Atlantic slave trade had dismembered. A Bambara man with face tattooed from temples to neck, wore an amulet that marked him as someone from the mountain villages of the high Sudan. There were "tall, well-knit Senegalese from Cape Verde, black as ebony, with intelligent, kindly eyes and long, straight, shapely noses; Mandingoes, from the Gambia River, lighter in color ... whose enslavement seems specially a shame, their nation the 'merchants of Africa,' dwelling in town, industrious, thrifty, skilled in commerce and husbandry, and expert in the working of metals, even to silver and gold." One could have seen "rosy-cheeked Foulahs," "tattooed Iboes," groups of warriors, and those from the French Kongo—"serpent worshipers, yet the gentlest and kindliest natures that came from Africa." But, equally striking to visitors and locals alike were the growing numbers and energy of Creoles like Marie Laveau—people born free in the New World, born to parents and grandparents who were both African and European.

On the Sunday afternoons when Marie Laveau herself danced, Congo Square was spirit theater. Marie devoured drumbeat, song, and motion. They drove her from her body, out of her social identity, and into the climax of spirit possession. As the snake curled about her, she called to its soul in song—"Come Great Serpent Spirit. Join us, *Le Grand Zombi.*" The serpent spirit entered her, became who she was; they whirled as one in ecstasy and awe.

| | |
|---|---|
| *L'appe vini, Le Grand Zombi.* | He comes, the Great Serpent. |
| *Pour faire gris-gris.* | Comes to make things happen. |
| *Pour faire mourir.* | Comes to face down death. |

Spirit possession is a visceral, embodied language that speaks of matters too painful, too profound, or too dangerous to be discussed in other ways. It ends in joy too vast to be described, a gift to one's soul as well as a spiritual burden borne on behalf of a suffering community. Spirit possession is sexual, sensual, and intimate; it teaches resistance and bestows the kind of power that faced down the policemen at the gates of Congo Square. It is contagious, and people who catch it or are caught up in it are changed forever. It is shocking and disturbing to those who witness but never experience it. They fear, and rightly so, that they, too, could be possessed.

A black man who saw Marie the First in possession trance said, "When she got in the middle of the Square, she took her snake out of a box and danced with it. When she got through dancin' all the other folks would dance—not before. I tell you, she could make anybody do anything and sometimes she made 'em do terrible things. She made wives turn on their husbands and run off with other men. She made fine white ladies lie on the ground and roll their bellies." A white man who attended the gatherings in Congo Square at their height wrote, "Now for the fantastic leaps! Now for frenzy! Another pair is in the ring! What wild—what terrible delight! The ecstasy rises to madness; one—two—three of the dancers fall—*bloucoutoum! boum!*—with foam on their lips. The musicians know no fatigue; still the dance rages on. No wonder the police stopped it in Congo Square." Newspaper reporters in the nineteenth century who attended Voodoo events wrote shocked accounts of what they had seen. "The sudden entrance of a flaxen-haired white girl who whirled around the room in the arms of a negro blacker far than the ace of spades" stunned one journalist. Yet he made the gift of ecstasy visible—"her pallid wanton face actually beamed with exuberant levity. Even the negresses gazed at her with a look of wonder." The personality, ego or consciousness of the young girl dissolved into unity and the universe—"set adrift on the rapids of depravity, she had reached the center of the vortex."

People who return from possession trances compare their experiences to the glow after great lovemaking, the knowledge of truth that comes in childbirth, or the welcome visit from a beloved, long-dead relative in a dream. A white woman visiting New Orleans happened upon a church service where she saw "enchantment" performed. An entranced woman walked through the congregation with outspread arms, then sank to her knees on the platform by the altar and grew still. As the woman regained her consciousness, "she talked to herself in a low voice, and such a beautiful, blissful expression was portrayed in her countenance, that I would willingly experience that which she then experienced, saw, or perceived. It was no ordinary, no earthly scene. Her countenance was as if it were transfigured."

No white traveler or journalist claimed to have seen either Marie Laveau dance in spirit possession at Congo Square. But many believed she reigned there as queen; as one said, she had a "natural supremacy, and ruling over superstitious fears and desires of every fierce and ignoble sort, she wields no trivial influence." By contrast, black men who were children in the 1840s and 1850s assured interviewers from the Federal Writers' Project, a Depression recovery program in the 1930s, that they had seen Marie Laveau the First's performances in Congo Square in the tense years before the Civil War. They claimed that *Danse Calinda, boudoum, boudoum* was a musical metaphor that mocked the cannons fired at sunset, scorned slavery, and paid tribute to the delicious dangers of the music and dancing in Congo Square on Sunday afternoons.

Marie the First was in her early forties in 1843 when city authorities closed Congo Square. She was the practicing priestess whom black men swore they saw mesmerize the policemen stationed there. In the prime of her priestly powers, she lived within earshot of the square and had been a regular visitor through its peak years in the 1820s and 1830s. Her daughter, Marie the Second, was eighteen, and beginning to build her own spiritual powers within Voodoo circles.

When the two priestesses danced in Congo Square and at other places in New Orleans, they shouted—*Voudou, Voudou*. Through the sacred word, a widespread African name for spirit or deity, they invited or invoked the spirits to enter their bodies, to be incarnated in them. After 1820 local newspapers used the word to describe the social group—a cult of primitive superstition, idolatrous rites, and snake worship, they insisted. Regardless of the low value placed on the religion by members of the press, practitioners, then as now, tell us that the word *Voudou* in all its spellings translates best as "those who serve the spirits."

～

Marie Laveau's color—people said—was red, yellow, brown, black, golden, rosy brick, peach, banana, apricot, light, bright, fair, and high. Her color, the so-called social fact around which cultural life in New Orleans revolved, depended on who was looking at her. Although none agreed on tones and tints, everyone agreed that Marie Laveau, like her Creole sisters of color, was exceptionally beautiful. Travelers and tourists raved about the Creole women they encountered in the streets, churches, and ballrooms of New Orleans. In 1842, an English visitor noticed dark, liquid eyes, coral lips, pearly teeth, and "long raven locks of soft and glossy hair." He said that Creole women walked in such an elegant manner, one might mistake them for the goddess Venus. Other visitors described free women of color as "exotic" and "exquisite."

Beautiful and multihued, both the Marie Laveaus were a mixture of races and cultures—white, black, and red, French, Spanish, West African, Central African, and Native American. Marie the First was born in 1801, at the beginning of the nineteenth century and the American regime in New Orleans—a century after the founding of the New World colony of Louisiana. In 1803, when she was still a toddler and a citizen of Spain, and briefly of France, a foreign nation called the United States of America purchased her city and the immense river-centered territory it dominated. For the rest of her life, she was an involuntary American citizen who spoke French and who looked to Paris, not New York or Washington, for her cultural compass. Marie was the spiritual child of the Diaspora, the vast involuntary movement of African peoples across the Atlantic to the Americas, as well as the Mediterranean-style Catholic Church into which she was baptized. Above all, however, Marie Laveau was a Creole.

Travelers were right to gossip about the sexual lives of Creoles. Marie Laveau's color—whatever it was—came from a century of convoluted colonial contacts that began in 1699 when a small group of Frenchmen laid claim to the territory of Louisiana. They met and married Native Americans already settled on the marshes and waterways, people who knew about the local climate and ecology. Twenty years later the Frenchmen began to bring Africans into the little colony to meet their growing labor needs. The majority of the African founders of the colony of Louisiana came on one of the twenty-three ships the French chartered from 1719 to 1743. Each ship sailed directly from West Africa, which meant that—contrary to common assumptions—most Africans in Louisiana did not pass through the Caribbean first. The majority of the 5,989 people on board those ships were from the Senegal River basin. They brought Bambara culture from their homeland and spoke the same or related languages. Africans brought extensive knowledge of tropical agriculture, irrigation, metallurgy, marketing, and medical care geared to the climate.

The next largest group of Africans in colonial Louisiana came from the Kingdom of Kongo in central Africa. A French ship carried 294 Kongolese people to Louisiana in 1720; much later, large numbers of people from Kongo landed in St. Domingue, now called Haiti, on the eve of its great slave insurrection, and, after that rebellion, made their way to Louisiana. The ancestors of many people of color in New Orleans were Kongolese, many already Catholic. The *gumbo ya-ya* says that Marie's mother's mother came directly to Louisiana from the Central African kingdom and passed on spiritual customs to her daughter and granddaughter that resemble those of the *ngangas* or mediums, priestesses, or shamans of widespread religious movements in Kongo. *Ngangas* were diviners or fortune-tellers, dream-interpreters; they were visionaries and trance experts who used drumming, dancing, and rhythmic chanting or clapping. *Ngangas* addressed social problems like love and luck. They knew that jealousy, greed, and the anger of others were curses that caused its victims to suffer. *Nganga* sounds like "wanga" or "ouanga"— words often used as synonyms for Voodoo in New Orleans. Both Marie Laveaus and their peers were called "wangateurs."

Africans in this new world were not simply empty creatures waiting or willing to be filled up with European "civilization." Some stayed in touch with shipmates or lived near each other in the plantation or parishes of the colony. A few were reunited with family members who moved from Africa as free people of color to be near their enslaved relatives. Others came with or quickly established family groups. Many Africans achieved their freedom within a few years of their arrival; some became prominent property owners within a generation. Free people of color were not Southerners; New Orleans was not the American South. Slaves were not always black, and blacks were not always slaves.

Throughout the colonial period, Europeans were neither safe nor in full control. The hapless colony, a distant fragment of France, lacked food and medicine. Frenchmen took African and Native American women as slaves, companions, employees, and in many cases, as wives. Without them, the men would have died more quickly and in even greater numbers than they did. The women knew "home health care"—herbs and teas, poultices and bandaging,

diagnosis and treatment. They could produce food from the ground up, prepare meals, and provision a family. In return, many women negotiated safety,
protection, and freedom for themselves and their children. Some women
inherited property, established their own businesses, and set up their own
households. They bought themselves and their family out of bondage, forged
a degree of personal freedom that European women of the period could not
imagine, and set a high standard of leadership for Marie Laveau.

By the time Marie Laveau was born at the end of Spanish and French
control and the beginning of the American national period, approximately
20 percent of the eight thousand citizens of the city were free people of color.
In each generation in the century of colonialism, European, African, and
Native American parents produced babies with a variety of social and physical
characteristics, multicultural, multiracial offspring who lived under a variety
of mean-spirited racial names like "Quadroon," "Mulatto," or "Octoroon."
Through time the calculation of degrees of arbitrary and useless genealogical
relationships became burdensome and embarrassing. Like Marie Laveau,
the children and grandchildren of the colony's complicated marital and sexual histories began to identify themselves simply—"*Je suis Créole.*" I am Creole.

～

Marie Laveau the First lies buried—presuming we trust one set of documents and oral traditions but not others—in a tall, well-marked tomb in
the oldest graveyard in New Orleans. When friends and relatives visit,
I take them on a guided tour of Marie's life; we begin in the city of the
dead—St. Louis Cemetery One on Basin Street. As we pass through the
iron gates, the guides for the French Quarter walking tours are already lec-
turing their charges at her tomb. No matter what time of the day I visit,
someone has already left gifts for Marie—flowers, candy, wine, gum, salt,
coins, food, plastic Mardi Gras beads or other offerings. Once I found
a sealed bottle of Southern Comfort and a Barbie doll, another time the
bride and groom from the top of a wedding cake.

More compelling than gifts, however, are the X marks that cover the stucco
sides and marble front of the famous tomb. Despite frequent cleanings,

the signs, often in groups of three, appear as if by magic. Tour guides say they signal wishes, requests to Marie Laveau for special favors. Sometimes tour guides instruct their clients to knock three times, turn three times, and make a wish. Others, not so respectful, allow tourists to mark on the tomb in the name of favors sought. Everyone who sees the marks asks what they mean. My theories may not satisfy everyone. People around the planet understand that where two lines cross, men and women may meet the spirits. The sign of crossed lines within a circle is widespread in Africa—in the Kingdom of Kongo, for example. The cross and crucifix of Christianity are close relatives in this ancient human tradition. One day in the New Orleans Notarial Archives, I turned the thick crackling page of a document and found Marie's own X on a handwritten page, a record that secured freedom for a woman of color and her children. Marie the First signed legal documents with this time-honored signature mark, a declaration of faith that the written sign sealed her intentions for the notary who witnessed the document and sent them the spirits who made such matters happen— her legal mark looked exactly like those on her tomb.

The brass plaque that cemetery preservation activists attached to the front says that "this Greek revival tomb is the reputed burial place of the notorious voodou queen," and that Marie Laveau was the most widely known of many practitioners of the "mystic cult." Some tour guides hint that they know where the "real Marie Laveau" lies—and it is not in St. Louis One. Their confusion is understandable. The two Maries are difficult to tease apart; furthermore, the disappearance and disputed gravesite of the second haunt all accounts of their already puzzling lives.

When my guests and I leave the walled cemetery, walking past Congo Square, renamed and renovated once again, I feel the ghosts of the buildings and streets as the Maries knew them in their time. As they did, we enter the French Quarter and stop in the first block of St. Ann Street. The house on St. Ann between Rampart and Burgundy that the Laveaus made famous no longer exists, and no one who ever visited it is still alive. But once, we could have glimpsed its red tile roof peeking up beyond the high fence in front; we could have peeked through the holes in the fence, like neighborhood children did, and watched Marie Laveau twine a snake about her body.

Visitors—and there were many—entered a large front yard with room enough for dancing, domestic animals, and a profuse garden of vegetables, fruits, and flowers. A pomegranate tree shaded the house; wide-leaved fig trees and bananas plants as tall as the roof produced sweet fruit that children loved. Honeysuckle vines offered both a pleasant aroma and the Creole cure for sore throats. Members and guests of the Laveaus' household walked up three wooden steps, which one of the women of the family scoured with red-brick dust each morning, and entered the first two rooms of the house from the side gallery or porch under the long overhanging roof. Beyond that apartment was another gallery, and a second set of rooms with a separate entrance. A former neighbor told a curious interviewer decades later, "When Marie Laveau's son-in-law died, she built a raised addition to the rear." She remembered how she and many children grew up playing at the Laveaus' house. "Child, I wish I had a nickel for all the times I was in that yard."

When the last Laveau died, family members who wanted no part of their Creole legacy sold the property, and the new owners tore down the house. All that remains is a persistent story of how the queen of the Voodoos came to possess it. It seems that a man from a prominent and wealthy white family came to Marie Laveau the First. The police had arrested his son for a serious crime; the evidence against the young man was compelling. The father begged her to prove his son's innocence and obtain his release. Marie walked to St. Louis Cathedral each morning at dawn; some versions of the story say she prayed there for three days, some say seven, and others nine. As she knelt at the altar rail, she placed three red-hot Guinea peppers in her mouth and held them there for several hours. Then she walked to the seat of government, the Cabildo, next door to the church, and deposited the peppers under the judge's chair. The judge dismissed the young man's case, and the grateful father rewarded Marie Laveau with the house on St. Ann Street—or so the *gumbo ya-ya* claims.

The story may be a timeless moral tale about a free woman of color who bettered herself through good magic or "white" magic performed in church, and who received a house from a grateful white man. Some conclude that prayers, Voodoo spirits, and scorching Guinea peppers have the power to influence court proceedings. Others believe that kneeling in St. Louis Cathedral was only a ruse, a front; Marie the First had privileged information about the case and contacts in the police department; she knew the judge, some say. I tell my visiting friends that any or all of these deductions may be true, but the only historic fact is this: Marie moved her family into the St. Ann Street house in the fall of 1832.

When we leave the ghostly remains of the Laveau home behind us, I guide my guests to popular Voodoo museums and shops in the French Quarter. I tease them; nice people and ethical practitioners are not supposed to wish overdrawn bank accounts on their ex-spouses, vaginal itch on a whining in-law, or impotence on a faithless lover. We do not resolve quarrels, jealousies, betrayals, or the sight of another's success with hurtful magic. Nonetheless, the wish to "fix" other people remains a temptation. So "voodoo dolls" have become a staple of the popular and mercantile imagination, yet no evidence exists that the Laveaus ever made or used them. Tourists buy mugs or posters that say "Voodoo Unto Others before They Voodoo Until You." They sign up for haunted house and ghost tours that feature the Marie of legends. Although no reliable photographs, paintings, or engravings of either Marie exist, a woman like her often visits locals, even tourists, in visions or in waking dreams. Such images circulate on postcards, books, and candles and conjure up Marie's memory.

French Quarter streets were designed for horse-drawn carriages and foot traffic. In the Laveaus' time, carts called "Black Marias" carried prisoners to jail and the dead to the morgue. Today plastic flowers decorate the animals and carts that transport tourists amid delivery trucks and taxis. As we weave our way through the noisy traffic past the antique shops of Royal Street on our way to the Pharmacy Museum on Chartres, I tell my friends about the third woman in Marie Laveau's story—Philomène, daughter of one queen and sister of another. Philomène was keeper of the keys for the family legacy; she kept their secrets so well that succeeding generations take her lies as truths. When her famous mother, Marie the First, died in June of 1881, Philomène spoke with a reporter from the *Picayune*—a paper favorable to Creoles and to Catholics. He rendered into English the sweet lament of a French-speaking daughter who loved her mother but wanted to distance herself from the accusations doing Voodoo had brought into her household. "All in all Marie Laveau was a most wonderful woman," the *Picayune* article stated. "Doing good for the sake of doing good alone, she obtained no reward, oft times meeting with prejudice and loathing." The article concluded that, as long as God's sunshine played around her little tomb, the citizens of New Orleans would remember Marie Laveau.

But Philomène's calm statements did not quiet the controversies. The next morning, an angry rebuttal appeared. The editorial writer from the *Times Democrat*—a Protestant, Anglo-American newspaper—damned the *Picayune*. Marie Laveau was no saint. Somebody, they claimed, had been "stuffing our contemporaries in the matter of the defunct Voudou queen." The newspaper denounced her—"she was, up to an advanced age, the prime mover and soul of the indecent orgies of the ignoble Voudous; and to her influence may be attributed the fall of many a virtuous woman." The sarcastic article ended with a single exclamation—"puah!!!"

The *Times Democrat* was correct. Philomène had given the *Picayune* reporter a less-than-factual version of her mother's life. She claimed, for example, that her mother had been ninety-eight years old when she died—an assertion which, if true, made Marie the First only eight years younger than her own father, and concentrated her child-bearing years between the ages of forty-five to fifty-five. Philomène gave false information about her father's military service and misrepresented the family's genealogy. Her obituary is responsible for one of the most glaring exaggerations about Marie Laveau's life—the number of children she and Philomène's father had. Hardly a "fact" about the family corresponds to historic records or common sense reckoning. But Philomène's obituary has become the mythic standard for her mother's life.

As long as Marie the First, Marie the Second, and Philomène were alive, newspaper reporters tried to find them—with mixed results. After their deaths, journalists recycled the tired, old stories of beheaded chickens, midnight sacrifices, and ghostly graveyards. Then, in 1935, at the peak of the Great Depression, the United States government employed otherwise unemployed writers throughout the country to collect folklore—tales, stories, supporting records, accounts from slavery times, and other materials about the lives of ordinary people unique to their region, records that would otherwise disappear with time. As a small part of the massive recovery programs, the administrators of the Works Progress Administration or WPA created a unit in each state called the Federal Writers' Project. The crown jewels of the men and women in Louisiana are hundreds of interviews they recorded and testimonies they collected from 1935 to 1943—in particular, eyewitnesses to Voodoo celebrations and personal friends or former enemies of both Marie the First and the Second.

The leaders and writers of the WPA Project started with Philomène's obituary for her mother and the hostility that surrounded the family in the media of their time. They quickly became obsessed with their search for the Voodoo queens—it is fair to say they were possessed. Robert Tallant was a reporter for a local newspaper and aspiring novelist when the head of the WPA Writers' Project hired him to prepare some manuscripts for publication. From these sources and his own prejudices, he compiled a "nonfiction" book he called *Voodoo in New Orleans*; it has been in print since its original publication in 1946. Some citizens of New Orleans told the staff of the WPA Federal Writers' Project that Marie and her followers were sorcerers and witches who sold their souls to the devil in return for power or changed little children into black cats, and Robert Tallant promoted their viewpoint in his book. Because of Tallant's book, many people think that the "voodoos" were devil-worshipers who added Catholic statues of saints, prayers, incense and holy water to their sacrifices of snakes, black cats, and roosters in rituals of blood drinking and group sex.

The citizens of New Orleans who spoke to the interviewers from the Writers' Project disagreed with each other at every turn. Marie Laveau was dark-skinned; no, she could have passed for white. She was rich; she died broke. Her ghost flies around and slaps people; her gentle spirit is at peace. People of color swore that Marie Laveau arranged their loved ones' release from prison through the sheer force of her personality. White people retorted, Marie Laveau was an infamous enchantress who subverted justice with black magic. Yes, people admitted, she crossed class, caste, and color lines; but some questioned the social worth of such transgressions. Many citizens acknowledged that she was a trance-dancer, a psychic, and a medium—yet that meant spiritual mastery to some and eternal damnation to others.

New Orleanians agreed on only two points—both Maries were beautiful, and each one wore a *tignon*, a Creole turban, sometimes called a "madras" because the brilliantly colored cotton fabric Creole women favored came from India. Old men who reminisced about a sensuous, sexy woman with a fine, fine figure, had seen Marie the Second in the years she brought her own brand of glamour and controversy to the city.

"Marie Laveau? Sure I remember her. My, the way she did dress at her jamborees! She was well built and her lips were large and red like ladies make them now with lipstick, but hers were just naturally red. She wore a madras on her head. She had nice ways for everybody. She held her head high and walked a straight, proud walk."

"When I remember her it was around 1870 and she was about forty years old, but looked younger," said another man. "She was light and could have passed for a Spanish lady. The mens used to go crazy lookin' at her. She had the reddest lips I ever seen in my life. She wore a *tignon*, with little curls hangin' down around her face, and she always had big gold hoops in her ears. She wore blue dresses that had big skirts and a shirtwaist buttoned straight down the front and come in tight in the middle; it sure showed off her bust." Marie also loved fine jewelry and "always wore diamond rings, large oval eardrops, a handsome brooch, a diamond horse-shoe, and a plain gold bracelet."

Women did not remember Marie the Second in the same manner. "Marie Laveau? Who, that she-devil, that hell-cat Marie Laveau! Of course I remember her," screamed an old friend of the family. "What she look like? She wore always a madras handkerchief tied around her head. There were two curls, one on each side of her face. She walked like she owned the city. She could call spirits out of your house. She would make pictures come off the wall."

One eighty-seven year old woman could not be bothered to denounce the priestess. "I don't know nothing 'bout Marie Laveau," she vowed when the interviewers from the WPA Writers' Project knocked on her door. "And my iron's gettin' hot."

In 1786 a newly appointed Spanish governor, Estevan Miro, published a manifesto, a "Proclamation for Good Government," that forbade free women of color to wear veils, bonnets, jewels, or ornaments of value, to adorn their hair with feathers, or to show their curls. He ordered free women of color to cover all their hair with a handkerchief or bandana—the symbol of working, domestic, and enslaved women. The governor's edict, however, was largely symbolic. So were women's responses. Creoles of color turned their *tignons* against their colonial masters. Stylish and flattering turbans grew from simple handkerchiefs. Some women tied the points in front, some in back, or onto the side. The headdresses grew taller; some *tignons* had seven points and forbidden curls soon framed innocent faces. Travelers often reported that *tignon*-headed free women of color moved through the city as though they owned it.

Marie the First was destined by birth to wear the *tignon*, the legacy of resistance for women of her class and color. But Marie the Second was born in 1827, well into the American administration. The Spanish governor with his jealous rules was long dead, and the American authorities who took over in 1803 never cared about women's head coverings; they had their own sumptuary markers for race and class. Nonetheless, Marie the Second wore a madras *tignon* from which her curls peeked defiantly long after the turbans went out of fashion; she wore them in the traumatic times before and after the Civil War. And she wore them when she twirled and twisted in spirit possession at the lakefront beaches after an enemy army and racial apartheid had entered New Orleans. Marie the Second sported a bright *tignon* to signal her status and identity. She flaunted her turban, gold jewelry, and a proud walk that announced to all who saw her—I am not white, not slave, not black, not French, not Negro, not African American. I am a free woman, a Creole of New Orleans.

By the time I finish Philomène's strangely slanted obituary for her mother, the stories people told the WPA Federal Writers' Project, and Marie the Second's defiance of race-bound rules, my friends and I have found a place to sit at the Café du Monde beside the levee of the Mississippi. We order cups of chicory coffee and several plates of *beignets*, square fried donuts covered with powdered sugar; we watch the tourists. Finished, we walk along the iron-fenced edges of Jackson Square, admire the red-brick apartment buildings that flank the upriver and downriver sides of the old plaza, and pass psychics who will tell our fortunes for a fee. Jackson Square with St. Louis Cathedral on one side and the levee of Old Man River on the other is, for me, the most perfect urban space in the New World. At the stone steps of St. Louis Cathedral, we stop; before we enter and light candles in the hushed sanctuary, I end the informal tour with the legend of the spiritual bargain Marie struck with her parish priest and confessor.

Everyone in her time and in the century to follow knew that Marie the First was a practicing Catholic. They understood that she attended Mass at the cathedral on Sunday morning and danced to possession with a great snake in Congo Square that afternoon. To sustain her double religious lives, it is said, Marie Laveau made a deal with Père Antoine, the saintly pastor of St. Louis Cathedral and the former head of the Spanish Inquisition in Louisiana. Marie guaranteed that worshipers flocked to his church in an anticlerical age and that Catholics observed annual feast days and the sacraments of marriage, baptism, and Holy Communion. For his part of their bargain, Père Antoine allowed the Voodoos a gracious ceremonial coexistence and ecclesiastical assistance in such delicate matters as births out of wedlock or marriages across sensitive social lines. Marie and other women of color could dance with *le Grand Zombi*, defy the racial rules of the American administration, and make magic to find husbands or rid themselves of them; they could dance, build altars in the side aisles, chant and drum—just fill my church on Sunday and feast days, he asked in return.

When my friends and I have paid our respects to the spirits of Marie Laveau and Père Antoine, we push open the heavy doors of the cathedral and walk outside into bedazzling tropical light; we can hear a band playing the music that makes New Orleans unique, songs of saints and sin and spirits; and a few people in the crowd in front of the church are dancing.

"Marie Laveau, leader of the spiritual bands of Voodoo, and her mentor, Père Antoine, Catholic priest and saint of the people," I say to my guests, "sealed their pact on these steps."

# *Chapter 2*

## Catholic in the Morning, Voodoo by Night

On the Saturday afternoon before Palm Sunday in the spring of 1819, a group of women like the young Marie the First, then seventeen years of age, carried three boxes of graduated sizes into St. Louis Cathedral. They stacked them up in the downriver aisle, lifted a heavy painted arch to the top, and nailed it in place. When the construction was complete, the women covered the platform with a shimmering white cloth. On two of the stepped sides of the shrine they placed wax dolls about the size of a five- or six-year-old child and draped silver banners about the dolls' scarlet-robed shoulders. Beside the statues they set vases filled with bright bouquets of silk flowers and arranged four rows of candles.

Then, in the quiet of a cathedral afternoon, in the style of adoration that Spanish Catholics had polished for centuries, the workers raised a statue of *Maria la Madonna* to the top of the altar. The image, about two feet high, was "dressed in black velvet," wrote a visitor who saw it, and "her robe was drawn out on each side & fastened to the back of the niche so as to give the whole figure a triangular shape. A silver embroidered cross extended from her chin to her feet, & at each ear she had a large silver shell."

The following morning, the visitor, a Philadelphia architect who came to New Orleans to complete renovations to St. Louis Cathedral and build waterworks for the city, attended the Palm Sunday Mass, and admired the altar and the statue of the Virgin there in place. To his dismay, however, he found the sanctuary was "exceeding crowded, & calculating 1½ square to each individual, not less than 1,500 persons can have been present." The majority of churchgoers that morning were women—women of color in bright *tignons* and a smaller number of white women in frilly bonnets—hundreds of women like Marie Laveau clustered about the altar, filling the aisles. Two other qualities of the service at the start of Holy Week startled the architect—banks of candles, the major illumination in churches of that time, burned supernaturally bright, and the music was sadly disappointing. There was no organ, no hymns, and the choir that "chanted the service were the loudest & most unmusical that I ever heard in a church." They sang "in the most villainous taste imaginable, something between a metrical melody & a free recitative, it is not easy to conceive anything more diabolical."

At the end of the triumphal service, Père Antoine handed long branches cut from palm trees native to Louisiana to all those who attended the service—certainly the visiting architect received one, and in all likelihood, Marie Laveau, her mother, half-sisters, Voodoo elders like Sanité Dede, and their Creole friends did too. Carrying her palm branch, a blessing for the year to come, Marie would have walked out into the sunlight of the parade ground in front of the cathedral where four years earlier the city had celebrated victory at the Battle of New Orleans, and had honored its hero, General Andrew Jackson, the gangly, Protestant frontiersman who had saved the city from a British army bent on rape and pillage. Beyond the square she could have seen a forest of masts; ships from around the globe anchored at the levee of the Mississippi that disgorged cargo from every nation and exotic diseases that periodically wracked the city. Then ship masters ordered dock workers to load cotton bales and sacks of sugar for the outbound voyage. The square was filled with people on Palm Sunday as it was each Sunday—nuns in black habits and white headdresses, pirates in leather and feathers, sailors, drunkards, gamblers, and hundreds of refugees from the successful black revolution that swept the island of St. Domingue in the Caribbean, once France's richest and most populated colony, which was, by the time of the Louisiana Purchase in 1803, the new nation of Haiti.

Marie may have met her father and her fiancé on the square—Creole men attended church mostly for baptisms and weddings. They could have walked through the crowds, greeted friends, and then stopped in front of Rose Nicaud's coffee stall on the downriver corner of the parade ground and ordered coffee and *beignets*. Rose brewed her own special blend of chicory coffee and poured it into thick mugs with equal amounts of hot steamed milk. She bought herself and her family out of bondage with the recipe— her coffee was so good that Creoles called it the "benediction that follows prayer."

～

Marie Laveau was a member in high standing at St. Louis Cathedral—the centerpiece of the French Quarter and one of the most graceful cathedrals of the New World. Marie herself and her children were baptized there; she married at its altar—these are matters of sacramental record. Not everyone, however, was impressed with the quality of Marie's devotion to her church. White men said she corrupted the faith, that she was blasphemous and turned the veneration of the Virgin Mary into a sacrilege. In contrast, Marie's daughter Philomène insisted, "besides being charitable, Marie was also very pious and took delight in strengthening the allegiance of souls to the church."

Marie Laveau's confessor and Catholic mentor, Père Antoine, was two different men in the same body; in the language of conjurers he was a two-headed man. The first, Padre Antonio de Sedella, had arrived in New Orleans twenty years before Marie was born. Although he was the nominal leader of the Spanish Inquisition in Louisiana, he carried out none of the persecutions of women or so-called heretics that marked his colleagues' activities in Europe and other parts of the New World. Instead, he got into trouble with his male peers, his superiors and the secular authorities; they called him "the scourge of the Church," a conniving plotter and rebel, and "a law unto himself." As a cleric embroiled in parochial politics, Sedella is easily forgotten.

But something happened. A conversion experience—someone he met, perhaps an experience of spirit possession—transformed the Spanish monk Padre Antonio into Père Antoine, a Creole saint who lives in legend and blessed memory in New Orleans. Marie the First was Antoine's disciple, coworker, devoted parishioner, and best friend to the priest whose church she allegedly promised to fill. They visited prisoners in the crowded, filthy jail next door to St. Louis Cathedral and prayed with those about to be executed. Philomène said that her mother "knew Father Antoine better than any living in those days—for he the priest and she the nurse met at the dying bedside of hundreds of people—she to close the faded eyes in death, and he to waft the soul over the river to the realms of eternal joy."

Père Antoine cut a remarkable figure in a city full of exotics. Portraits of him show his beaked nose and fierce, enigmatic eyes. A curly white beard emerged from his neck below a heart-shaped face and a monk's tonsure. He wore monastic garb—open sandals and a long, brown-hooded robe tied with a thick cord at his waist. When it helped his fierce campaigns against the slavery system, he cloaked himself in his vows of poverty and scorned civil authorities. Père Antoine used his office as pastor of St. Louis Cathedral and whatever spiritual contacts he had to influence court cases and to win freedom for women of color and for their children.

The good father's critics gossiped about him just as fiercely as they later gossiped about Marie Laveau. They accused him of adultery because his "Mulatto" housekeeper had too much freedom and a son who—it was said—looked too much like Antoine. They accused him of debauchery because he gave money to single mothers with children. They claimed—and the sacramental records of the Cathedral prove this charge—that Antoine performed baptisms and burials for people whom secular authorities and his superiors had forbidden him to bless. It was also claimed—but cannot be proved—that he performed wedding ceremonies for mixed race couples forbidden to marry under state laws. Priests assigned to New Orleans protested having to perform baptisms, marriages, and burials for prostitutes, concubines, Freemasons, and citizens who wanted to keep a mistress or get a divorce. They muttered that the city under Antoine's spiritual leadership was the "new Babylon," or the "sewer of all vice and refuge of all that is worst on earth."

People in New Orleans gossiped that, in addition to favoring people of color and Voodoo women, Père Antoine was a Freemason, a secular brotherhood traditionally hostile to Catholics, especially the clergy. It is true that Antoine welcomed the Masons, offered them sacraments, allowed them to display their ceremonial regalia in the Cathedral, sanctioned their secret initiation rituals, and insisted that priests accompany all coffins with masonry symbols on them to the cemetery. Yet no one gossiped about the religious professionals who probably influenced Marie Laveau the most, the women who taught her the prayers and the Christian theology she turned into Voodoo—the nuns of the Ursuline order.

Although French royal policy and the *Code Noir* or "Black Laws" of 1724 instructed European Catholics to baptize newly arrived Africans as soon as possible, there were no seminaries and too few priests to provide spiritual direction or religious education in Louisiana. The only Catholics to answer the call to educate Africans and Creoles in matters of faith were a group of privileged French Catholic women who arrived in the struggling colony in 1727—they designed and implemented the first educational system in Louisiana. The Ursulines enjoyed a striking degree of economic independence, much more than most white women of their time had. They inherited property, managed their community resources, and made most decisions free of male authority. They built a community of Catholic mothers and a convent where women of every race, class, and nationality could find refuge and support.

From the time she was born, Marie heard the Ursulines pray. In common with most young women of her class, she had learned the *Catechism*, a call and response, question and answer lesson about the principles of faith and spirituality, at the knees of the self-reliant nuns. When they asked her, "Who is God?" she answered, "God is a Spirit, eternal, infinite, all-powerful, who sees everything, and who made all things from nothing."

"Why do we say that God is a Spirit?"

"Because God has no body, no face, no color, and so one cannot perceive Him with their senses. God is in the sky, in the earth, and in all things."

Marie bore witness to her relationship to God and the spirit world each time she recited the Apostles' Creed, at each Mass she attended, every time she danced in Congo Square—*I believe in one God . . . and in all things seen and unseen . . . in all things visible and invisible.*

Yes, the *Catechism* admits, many things remain a mystery. For example, one member of the Holy Trinity—the Father, Son, and Holy Spirit combined—became a human being. He entered or assumed a human body; although he was still part of God, he had a face, a form, a color, human senses, and a human soul. The Holy Spirit entered and used the body of a woman, his mother, Maria the Madonna, to make this magical transformation of reality possible. This miracle or mystery is called the "incarnation"—which Marie Laveau, as have many others, interpreted as a special kind of spirit possession.

Marie, like everyone in the city, had also seen the Ursuline nuns perform miracles. During the Battle of New Orleans in January of 1815, members of the order watched from their balconies and dormer windows as the smoke rose from the Chalmette battlefield. Through the long night of conflict they prayed, and on their chapel altar they placed a statue of Our Lady of Prompt Succor. Protect and spare our city, the nuns begged her; if you do, we promise to say a Thanksgiving Mass in your honor on the anniversary of victory, forever. When morning dawned, the nuns prepared for Mass. Old men who could not join the troops and women and children of all colors filled the solemn chapel. As the priest lifted the bread and wine, a messenger ran down the aisle. The British were in retreat, the city saved.

In the catechism classes and in sermons at St. Louis, Marie Laveau listened to stories of spirit possession in the Christian tradition. On Pentecost, the fiftieth day after Jesus' resurrection, his grieving friends gathered for a meal. "And suddenly from heaven there came a sound like the rush of a violent wind, and it filled the entire house where they were sitting. Divided tongues, as of fire, appeared among them, and a tongue rested on each of them. All of them were filled with the Holy Spirit and began to speak in other languages, as the Spirit gave them ability."

Marie Laveau and Creoles of color—like their black brothers and sisters in the South—heard about Moses, an African, a shaman, and a visionary leader who worked miracles and led his people out of bondage. When his people needed something to drink in their desert wanderings, he struck a rock with his rod—water flowed. He tossed his rod to the ground—it became a snake, and once again a rod. His community of faith moved with pillars of fire by night and a cloud by day. He talked with an angel in a burning bush. With the spiritual guidance Moses received, he issued elaborate instructions in ritual preparation—oils, spices, perfumes, herbs, and offerings. He taught his people to build altars and made sacrifices. He gave them formulas for spiritual practice, practical laws for getting along with each other in trying times. At the risk of blasphemy, we must note that both Marie the First and Marie the Second developed similar techniques.

The best evidence, however, of how well Marie Laveau learned the lessons of Catholic evangelical education and dedicated them to Creole Voodoo comes from an African American anthropologist and novelist from Florida. In August of 1928, Zora Neale Hurston, a graduate student at Columbia University, came to New Orleans—as hot a place on earth as she had ever been—in search of Hoodoo conjurers and root workers. Hurston entered an intense spiritual collaboration with a "conjure-priest"—a "doctor" who convinced her that he was a grand-nephew of Marie Laveau the Second. To protect him and their secret, esoteric relationship, she called him Luke Turner.

Turner dictated thirty sessions or cases of spiritual counseling to Hurston, formal petitions for help with answers and advice from a spirit. He told her that each person trained in the Laveau tradition passed on the litanies to those they taught—Marie the First learned them from her mother, then taught them to Marie the Second, and Luke offered what he called "the works" to Zora. The narratives are transcriptions of a seance or spirit contact that contain prescriptions or formulas to solve the problems the patient has brought to the practitioner. These works of poetry—the Psalms of Voodoo—contain echoes of the call and response patterns of oratory in the African American community as well as the questions and answers in the *Catechisms* the nuns taught. There are petitioners who wish to cross their enemies and those who wish to be uncrossed. A man whose lady friends speak badly of him, someone who has lost a sweetheart or a business or who has been slandered seeks help. Men and women who cannot keep their friends or are involved in nasty court cases suffer, so they visit their spiritual counselors.

Each prayer—like the one for "The Lady Who Wishes to Cross Her Enemies"—begins with a petition. "O good mother, I come to you with my heart bowed down and my shoulders drooping and my spirit broken for an enemy has sorely tried me." The client offers examples of the trials she has endured at the hands of her enemies and asks for help, "On my knees I pray to you, good mother, that you will cause confusion to reign in my enemies' house, and that you will take their power from them and cause them to be unsuccessful." Then the Good Mother answers in the voice of Marie Laveau, the priestess, and gives the supplicant instructions. The session ends with a blessing and benediction, "Oh my daughter, go you in peace and do the works required of you so that you will have rest and comfort from your enemies, and that they will have not the power to harm you and lower you in the sight of your people and belittle you in the eyes of your friends. So Be It."

Another woman who had "an Empty House"—the kind of house she kept is clear—came with this request. "Oh, good mother, I come to you to ask your help for prosperity. The stranger passes my door and sees me not, neither do they stop nor look into my inn. My house is empty—there is no laughter, nor is there any feast day, neither do they remember me or know me. The clink of gold has not passed my palm for these many days, neither friend nor stranger has brought me gifts. My purse hangs limp from my tassel with no hopes of having it filled. Oh, good mother, I am full of lamentations and the evil spirits live in my house so I beg that you shall hear my prayer and in the fullness of your wisdom give me help."

In Marie's disembodied voice, the Good Mother gave the businesswoman elaborate recipes to cleanse her house—use Essence of Fast Luck, French incense, myrrh, sandalwood, and a little dragon's blood. Honor St. Joseph, St. Roch, and St. Peter. "Do all of these things so that the men folks shall enter and be entertained, and that they shall remain pleased with you and shall shower you with their gold and precious stones so prosperity shall enter into your house and shall drive away care and worry. So Be It."

Several times each day, the Ursuline nuns in their convent, Père Antoine in his cathedral, and Marie Laveau wherever she happened to be in New Orleans, chanted the *Creed*, the *Our Father*, and the *Ave Marie*. These, the greatest prayers of the Catholic church, end with the benediction—*Ainsi Soit-il.* Translated word for word, the French phrase has become the great *Amen* of Voodoo—"So Be It." Inside the *Catechism* that the priests, the nuns, and the future priestess owned, and looked at if not read, were poignant engravings of a vulnerable Virgin Mary standing atop the globe, the earth in her care. At her feet circled a great serpent.

Marie's spiritual life centered on Maria the Madonna, *Sainte Marie*, the Holy Mother, the Virgin Mary, the Good Mother, the Great Goddess of Chance, and the Great One, child of Mother Earth. This woman—a goddess, a female spirit—has many names, many tasks, many faces. In Christian traditions, she conceived a child without intercourse, carried the pregnancy through personal difficulties, and gave birth to a god. She spoke with angel spirits and pondered things in her heart. She comforts mothers whose babies, like those of women in New Orleans, died too young and too often. She witnessed the public execution of her first-born son. In African traditions, she is Oshun, goddess of love; Oya, goddess of lightning and wind; or Yemaya, goddess of the ocean. She appears as Erzulie when hurricanes threaten New Orleans. In this persona she is charming and sensuous, a woman of color who wears her beautiful black hair long. She lives in springs, lakes, rivers, ocean and seas—anywhere there is water—and loves fresh flowers, good perfume, skin lotion, or bath salts. Wealthy, she has her choice of capable, considerate lovers.

She is also the Holy Spirit, the Grace of God, Isis of the South. She is Our Lady of Prompt Succor who protected New Orleans from British invasion in 1815, and who bestows a special quality of mercy—quick and sudden comfort. She is *Notre Dame*—Our Lady, or just "the Lady" who still makes appearances to the citizens of New Orleans. Aaron Neville, brother of Art, Charles, and Cyril of the great musical family of Nevilles, said that she came to him in the 1980s. Aaron was in trouble; in his forties, he was addicted to heroin—"the boy that makes slaves out of men." As he waited to enter a drug rehabilitation program in New Orleans, he sat down at a friend's piano and began to play songs from his Catholic childhood. His fingers ran over the piano keys, and the words poured out:

> Lovely lady dressed in blue.
> Oh, won't you please teach me to pray.
> 'Cause God was just your little boy
> I want to know, please teach me how to pray.

⌒

Sometime between the Battle of New Orleans in 1815 and the birth of her first child in 1827, young Marie, born and baptized a Catholic and steeped in its rituals and prayers, began her lifelong apprenticeship to the spirits of Voodoo and to the memories of Africa bred in her bones. Neither the benevolence of Père Antoine nor the teachings of the Ursuline nuns could lead her through the revelatory crisis or spiritual "opening" that transformed her into a priestess. One did not join a society like Voodoo; one sought and suffered intense initiations at the hands of the spirits. They alone chose who was worthy. On the worldly plane, Marie Laveau needed a mentor or sponsor, someone like Sanité Dede, to reveal the secrets of possession rituals. She needed drummers, a choir, and the dark of night to ascend into Voodoo membership.

No moon shone over the abandoned brick yard just outside the French Quarter as the priestess, band, and chorus prepared to initiate—to baptize in drum beat and dance—new disciples of the Voodoo fellowship. The only light came from the half-opened door that Sanité Dede had opened to the three knocks. The priestess fussed at the slave woman who stood outside, "Thou hast come late tonight, yet thou knowest well we have four *voudous* to make." Dede was also suspicious of the white teenager who accompanied the late arrival and questioned the petitioner.

"I had to bring the young white master," the slave woman begged Sanité, "I don't have a pass. I needed him to get through the police posts."

Dede admitted them to the initiation ceremony; later, the boy grown to manhood told a journalist what happened to him that night. "An entrance was opened at the call of Dede, and I witnessed a scene which, old as I am, no passage of years can dim." The brick shed, some forty by twenty feet, glowed from the light of sconces and the candles on two white-clothed altars. All of the sixty or so participants had white kerchiefs tied around their foreheads. Most of the women had the white one tied over the "the traditional Madras handkerchief, with its five, nay, with its *seven* artistic points, upturned to heaven." The crowd included all ages, every shade of skin, a half dozen white men, and at least two white women the boy recognized.

A black doll wearing a costume painted with signs or emblems, a necklace of snake vertebrae, and an alligator fang encased in silver were tied to a cypress sapling in a container on the altar. Two lifelike stuffed cats sat on either side of a large table between "an old negro by the name of Zozo, well known in New Orleans as a vender of palmetto and sassafras roots; in fact, he had a whole pharmacopeia of simples and herbs, some salutary, but others said to be fatal." Zozo or "Bird," the leader of the band, played a large homemade drum and tambourine. His assistant played a smaller drum; one man twirled a large gourd rattle and another played a banjo. The four initiates, women of color dressed as Marie would have been in *tignons* and loose white dresses, stood in a semicircle in front of Sanité Dede. She sprinkled them vigorously with liquid from a calabash in her hand, speaking softly and moving her hands over them.

At a signal from Sanité, Zozo drew an immense snake from behind the doll. The snake's red and black lozenges glistening in the firelight mesmerized the teenager. Zozo talked and whispered to the snake, then compelled it to stand upright for about ten inches of its body with its head stretched horizontally. Passing the snake over the heads of the initiates, he cried out, as Marie Laveau did in Congo Square, "*Come Voudou, Voudou.*" When the spirits arrived, "a long, deep howl of exultation broke from every part of the shed. Pandemonium was unloosed."

The women or "enchanted ones" did not move their feet from the ground as waves of ecstasy flowed from toes to eyes. One woman danced in a circle not more than two feet in diameter. "She began to sway on one and the other side. Gradually the undulating motion was imparted to her body from the ankles to the hips. Then she tore the white handkerchief from her forehead. This was a signal, for the whole assembly sprang forward and entered the dance. The beat of the drum, the thrum of the banjo, swelled louder and louder. Under the passion of the hour, the women tore off their garments, and entirely nude, went on dancing—no, not dancing, but wriggling like snakes."

As Zozo chanted hypnotically, physical sensations overwhelmed the young white teenager. He went into shock—racial, cultural, and sexual. The opposite of spirit possession is the physical and emotional struggle it takes to stop the flow and surges of feeling. "I had grown sick from heat, and an indescribable horror took possession of me. With one bound I was out of the shed, and with all speed traversed the yard, found the gate open, and I was in the street." Years later he told the reporter that the devil was there in the abandoned brick yard, in those dances with the snake that night.

There is no historical evidence that either the devil or Marie the First was in the brickyard that night, which internal evidence dates to about the year 1825; but the young lad's account of an initiation ceremony fits the trajectory of her life as a priestess. Marie Laveau the First did not invent Voodoo, nor did women like Sanité Dede import the spiritual tradition into New Orleans like cargo off a ship from Haiti. Voodoo was alive and vigorous long before Marie's birth in 1801, well before the American period, which began in 1803, or before the French community of New Orleans welcomed ten thousand refugees from the revolution in St. Domingue in 1809. "Master magic"— techniques of spiritual power and social agency needed to handle dangerous or unpredictable situations—had came aboard the first slave ships. In court cases in 1743 and in 1773, extensive testimonies and the judges' final rulings confirmed both the existence and effectiveness of *gris-gris*—the manipulation of power relationships between masters and slaves, or between men and women, through rituals, amulet bags, chants or spells, even sophisticated poisons. *Gris-gris* is a potion or spell to harm or help someone, a means to manifest your intention. The members of the court never doubted that some people knew how to make the charms work—proof that the concept of magical empowerment was part of the intellectual life of the colony.

Vodou in Haiti and Voodoo or Voudou in New Orleans were not the same, although both crowned their work with master magic and spirit possession. Each spiritual half-sister came of age in very different social circumstances. A black revolution built and exploded in French St. Domingue, creating a new nation. In Louisiana, American racial laws intensified in slow steps that led to a war in which both sides were white, a conflict that tested but did not destroy their country.

The ten thousand French-speaking Catholic Creoles who came to New Orleans after the insurrection that convulsed their homeland, and while Marie Laveau was still a child, mirrored the patterns of gender, race, and class already present in New Orleans—30 percent white, 34 percent free people of color, and 36 percent enslaved people. Their arrival roughly doubled the population of the city of New Orleans. The new French exiles postponed "Americanization" by at least two decades. They magnified "Creolization," and as the mayor said, earned a reputation for "uncommon industry." Most old French families in New Orleans have ancestors from St. Domingue-Haiti.

The French exiles added Caribbean spice to the music, food, dances, and rituals both of Voodoo and of New Orleans. They gave Marie Laveau additional spiritual mentors—women like Sanité Dede, who is a likely candidate for having initiated and trained her. Above all, the "foreign French" émigrés brought young, beautiful Marie a bridegroom.

# Chapter 3

## Working Wife, Widow, Mistress, and Voodoo Divorcée

MARIE LAVEAU KNEW ALL ABOUT OTHER PEOPLE'S BUSINESS,
BUT THEY DIDN'T KNOW MUCH ABOUT HER. SHE KEPT THINGS
LIKE HER MENS QUIET. BUT, DON'T WORRY, SHE HAD THEM.
—JENNIE COLLINS, WPA FEDERAL WRITERS' PROJECT

The candles on the high altar of St. Louis Cathedral burned with spellbound brilliance, as candles were said to do in the presence of Marie Laveau. Flowering vines flowed across the communion railings and around the ends of the pews where Marie's two half-sisters, also named Marie, had draped them in the custom of the day. A multicolored cross-section of the Creole community—women in rainbow *tignons*, men in formal French coats and cravats—gathered that August in front of the tall tapers of the Cathedral to stand witness to Marie's social achievements.

Marie's mother, a free woman of color named Marguerite Darcantel, glowed. Her daughter, like most brides of the period, probably wore a lacy gown the color of tropical flowers that bloomed at high summer. Seventeen-year-old Marie had achieved what many women of her class and color coveted but could never have, what her own mother had never known—a legal marriage. Marie's father, Charles Trudeau Laveaux, had not married Marie's mother. But he had taken their child, born out of wedlock, to a public notary and, in the presence of witnesses, swore that she was his "natural" daughter. Before he stood beside her at the altar of

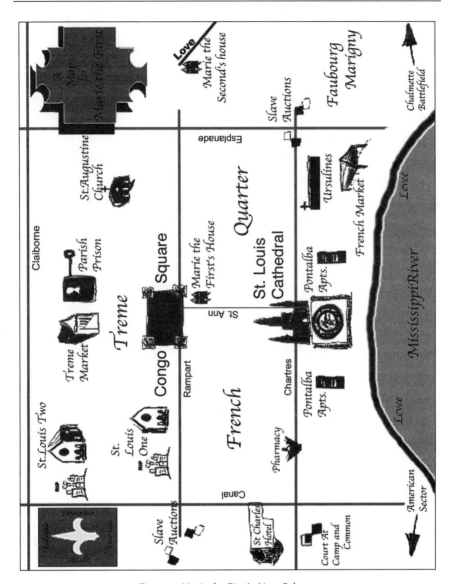

Figure 2. Marie the First's New Orleans

the cathedral, he acknowledged his paternity in writing, gave her the right to use the name Laveau, and deeded a piece of property on Love Street to her, a lot from his large holdings in the Faubourg Marigny.

Père Antoine had sharpened a quill pen in preparation for entering the events of August 4, 1819, into his sacramental record books—for on that day and in that sacred place, Marie Laveau married Jacques Paris, a free man of color from the island of St. Domingue-Haiti.

Young Marie Laveau had only a few chances to marry—and even fewer to marry well. For every eligible free man of color, there were three free women of color. Marie could not legally marry a slave or a white man; yet the civil and church authorities would have allowed—even encouraged— her to live as a mistress or concubine to a white man. New Orleans was notorious for its quasi-marital matches between beautiful women of color and white men who outnumbered white women three to one, a system of race-based relationships known as *plaçage* or "placement."

At the infamous Quadroon balls, elite women of color made semiformal contracts with white men who admired their daughters—another reason New Orleans earned a reputation for immorality and debauchery. In the dramas of *plaçage*—performances of racial and gender hierarchies— a white man agreed to support the young woman and any children they might have. Parents, particularly mothers, made the best deals possible for their daughters' futures. They hoped that the man would, if satisfied, support his mistress, and give her a house and an allowance in return for a visiting schedule. If all went well, he would provide suitable sums to their children to insure their education and community standing. Marguerite Darcantel, Marie Laveau's mother, did not have the social position to help her daughter find a "placement." Then again, her headstrong daughter may have shared the sentiments of other free woman of color who vowed to do what they had to do to escape life as a mistress.

*Plaçage* from the point of view of white women looked equally grim. They were powerless when male relatives upon whom they depended— husbands, fathers, brothers, sons, or grandfathers—picked women of color as mistresses. Although the arrangements of *plaçage* were as discrete as the closed shutters on the cottages in the "Quadroon Quarter," they were still visible. The children of these matches carried family names and the shapes of their noses everywhere they went. Everyone knew. French Quarter and Creole neighborhoods were small; a man's wife and his mistress lived down the street from one another, attended St. Louis Cathedral together, and shopped at the same markets. To make matters worse, women of color—the very word "Quadroon" carried the connotation of forbidden sex—had a reputation for exotic beauty with which white women could not compete.

Many free women of color managed to escape or resist the oppressions of *plaçage*. One of Marie's peers, Henriette Delille, born in 1812, was the child, grandchild, and great-grandchild of women of color who had contracted quasi-legal relationships with white men. Her older sister, Cecilia, entered an arranged, interracial match—but Henriette made other plans. She was good friends with rich, single, white women who spoke out against *plaçage* on the grounds that it violated the Catholic sacrament of marriage; she knew women of color who refused to attend the almost nightly Creole dances. Determined never to live in an immoral arrangement with a man who was not her husband, Henriette Delille took one of the few options left. She decided to become a nun.

But the Catholic Church would not accept into their ranks a woman of color born to an unmarried mother "living in sin." Henriette fought the establishment for decades for the right to fund a religious career with her inheritance and to initiate a religious order for women like herself. When they won their struggle at last, the nuns called themselves the Sisters of the Holy Family, a name that honors the Virgin Mary, her husband, and their baby son—marital legitimacy denied to women of color in *plaçage*. Henriette Delille may be the first Creole and the first woman of color in the United States whom the Vatican canonizes and makes into a saint. The nun was named for her grandmother, Henriette Labeau, sometimes spelled Laveau; although she and Marie Laveau had ancestors in common, miscegenation mixed with Voodoo was then, as now, a topic of whispers and shadows.

The two half-sisters of Marie the First found legal husbands. Père Antoine blessed the union of Marie Louise Darcantel to Louis Foucher, free man of color, in 1815. Marie's other half-sister, Marie Laveaux, the legitimate daughter of Charles Laveaux, handpicked a man named François Auguste, a native of St. Domingue-Haiti, to marry. In 1818 when she was fourteen years old, and to all appearances an adult woman of means, she signed her own marriage contract. Later, when she inherited money from her rich mother, she declared herself "divorced" and signed subsequent documents as Marie Laveaux Auguste "the bodily and financially separated wife of François Auguste."

The bride's father, Charles Laveaux, signed a marriage contract on her behalf on July 27, 1819. Laveaux was an astute businessman, so well-to-do and well-connected in the Creole community that his granddaughter Philomène later claimed he had been a rich white planter. The Love Street property he gave his daughter is like *tignons*—tied to both Marie Laveaus for decades. Marie brought the property from her father into the marriage, and her fiancé, Jacques Paris, contributed five hundred dollars in cash and his good character to the match.

But Jacques Paris, bridegroom and husband of Marie Laveau, never again appeared in official documents. The marriage may have lasted two, three, four years—estimates vary. Jacques dropped from sight sometime before 1824 or 1825. No one ever came forward to say they had seen or heard from him, and no death certificate, place of death, or cause of death has surfaced. Perhaps he returned to his home island of St. Domingue-Haiti. Maybe he was unfaithful and Marie sent him packing or he abused his young wife and she fixed him.

If Jacques Paris had died, Marie the First, her daughter Philomène, or someone else would have noted a date, a cause or a place of burial; Creoles in New Orleans relished the details of death and repeated them at every opportunity. The city directories of the decade deepen the mystery of Jacques Paris's disappearance. The 1822 issue mentions a certain "Paries, St. Yaque, cabinet-maker, 122 Dauphine," and includes an entry for "Parizien, Madame, widow, 65 Bayou off St. Claude." The following year the directory lists Madame Parizien again—but no St. Yaque Paries. In 1824, the directory lists neither in any spelling. Some undated, unsigned notes in the archives of the Federal Writers' Project suggest that Madame Parizien, widow, was really Marie Laveau, and that her address on Bayou Road was just down the street from her second husband's house. They hint that she disposed of a first husband to make room for the next one.

*Go see Marie Laveau,* people in New Orleans told each other. *She knows how to make a man fall in love with you, keep him faithful to you, bring him home when he strays or fix things so he leaves town forever.* In Catholic New Orleans women could kill their husbands and get away with murder more easily than they could separate from him—unless they knew how to get a Voodoo divorce. The richest white women of Marie's time, the Baroness Micaela Almonaster de Pontalba, born in 1795 into a great fortune and high social rank, was in an arranged marriage to a man who only wanted her money and son-bearing potential. Micaela's father-in-law grew to hate his willful, ambitious daughter-in-law; one day he shot her and left her for dead. She survived, disfigured, and still in need of a divorce or tasteful widowhood.

Marie Laveau the First fared better than the Baroness did. When Jacques Paris vanished, she achieved an even higher and more respected status than wife—she became a widow. For the remainder of her life, she carried her father's name and her "deceased" husband's name. On the marble front on her high tomb in St. Louis Cemetery One, she ordered the stone carver to engrave precisely what she wanted those who visit the site to know about her. In this tomb, she said, you will find:

> *Famille vve Paris*
> *neé Laveau*
>
> "The Family of the Widow Paris
> born Laveau"

∼

Marie Laveau the First did not need a husband to support her. She had property, social connections, and a career. One of the famous Creole fever nurses, she saved the lives of hundreds of people in the epidemics that struck the city of New Orleans with fierce summer randomness, claimed Dr. J. B. Bass, a practitioner of both Voudou and biomedicine in New York who had lived in New Orleans and worked with her.

"Did you ever see a person with the cholera?" he asked a reporter. "Well, you needn't want to for it is a most horrible sight. When it comes on you, you go just this way." Bass convincingly demonstrated a man shaking to death in an Arctic blizzard. "If that cramp and fit isn't broken in ten minutes you die. She made a charm of brimstone, tar and feathers, and when a person would be taken with a fit, she would lit it under their nose and it would immediately and perceptibly abate the cramps. She was very powerful in the yellow fever too, and in fact, was a mighty helpful woman in the community. She had a powerful knowledge of the human system, and knew what to do to keep off or cure any kind of sickness."

Marie Laveau's daughter Philomène said, "besides being very beautiful Marie also was very wise. She was skillful in the practice of medicine and was acquainted with the valuable healing qualities of indigenous herbs. She was very successful as a nurse, wonderful stories being told of her exploits at the sick bed. In yellow fever and cholera epidemics she was always called upon to nurse the sick, and always responded promptly. Her skill and knowledge earned her the friendship and approbation of those sufficiently cultivated, but the ignorant attributed her success to unnatural means and held her in constant dread."

Marguerite Darcantel, mother to the first queen and grandmother to the second, was—the *gumbo ya-ya* says—a fever nurse, hoodoo doctor, and Voodoo practitioner. People said she was a descendant of a Christian slave from the Kingdom of Kongo, a long line of Native American herbalists and healers, and several French and Spanish aristocrats. In a will dated October 22, 1817, Henry Darcantel, a prominent white man, rewarded a "Mulatta named Marguerite" for having taken exceptional care of him during his severe illness; he does not mention that their names make it probable she was also his daughter through *plaçage*.

New Orleans was a deadly place in Marie Laveau's time, and families like the Darcantels needed nurses. The city developed the highest mortality rates, the deadliest epidemics, and the worst public health system in the United States. The subtropical climate and below sea-level location of the port town were dreadful enough; but a chronic lack of leadership and appalling standards of sanitation made the situation worse. Between 1796, when city officials formally acknowledged the existence of yellow fever, and 1906, when people struck back at mosquitoes, thirteen severe and twenty-six milder epidemics of yellow fever struck. Between times fierce episodes of cholera, malaria, and an assortment of deadly diarrheal diseases hit the city. Prominent doctors, newspaper editors, and business leaders, however, convinced themselves that the city was a virtual health spa. In the "let them eat cake" school of public health, municipal authorities did not trouble themselves with the frequent epidemics.

The death rates for Creoles, especially free people of color, were consistently lower than those for the newly arrived Americans or European immigrants. The "seasoning" or acclimating effect of childhood cases of many diseases made the locals immune to most epidemic diseases—if they survived. In her youth, Marie Laveau came down with a mild case of yellow fever, mild in the sense that she did not die; through this, she acquired a lifetime immunity to Bronze John, the saffron scourge. She also received the best medical care in the city—her mother saw to that.

The *Louisiana Courier* on August 8, 1839, insisted that the summer's gossip about yellow fever was exaggerated. They admitted a few people had died—but there was no epidemic. "Still, we would advise all unacclimated people to leave the city, unless they possess a considerable share of moral courage, and can call around them should they fall sick, nurses who unite skill with experience in treating yellow fever. We are convinced that the recovery of the sick depends more on their attention and discrimination than on the skill of the physician."

Marguerite Darcantel and her associates in nursing had the opportunity to initiate fourteen-year-old Marie into the profession at the Battle of New Orleans in January 1815. "These far-famed nurses, the quadroon women of New Orleans, whose services are so consciously useful when New Orleans is visited by pestilence, freely gave their kind attention to the wounded British, and worked at their bedsides night and day." In addition to enemy soldiers, the women nursed forty men who survived both the battle and the amputation of their legs or arms, some as high as thighs and shoulder joints; twelve men died on the operating table. If Marie Laveau served as an apprentice during those dramatic days, as I presume, she learned how to give comforting, clean care. She brought fresh bedding and bedclothes; then aired and cleared the sick room. She was on hand for the necessary but nasty tasks; she emptied chamber pots, cleaned up after diarrhea or vomiting, and dressed open sores and wounds. For the patients, surviving high fever, amputation, or other sickbed traumas was equal parts good luck and good care. Sometimes Marie laid out bodies for burial.

Marie Laveau, Marguerite Darcantel, and the fever nurses of the period drew their medical worldviews and procedures from the major traditions that coexisted in Louisiana—Native American, European, and African. The women practiced an effective array of alternative, integrated, or holistic medicine. In addition to their bedside abilities, they had an extensive pharmacopoeia. Historic records mention ginseng, gum balsam, jalap, rhubarb, snakeroot, sarsaparilla, St. John's wort, sassafras, copal tree, maidenhair ferns, cottonwood roots, acacia leaves, elderberry bark, sage, Indian hemp, holly leaves, and hundreds more plants or parts of plants. The Laveaus purchased many materials from the Native American women who brought them to regular market spots in the French Quarter, Congo Square, and Bayou St. John.

Marguerite and Marie also bought nursing supplies at Louis Dufilho's apothecary shop at 514 Chartres, just upriver from St. Louis Cathedral. Monsieur Dufilho became America's first licensed pharmacist in 1816, and in 1823, he opened his own business. He and his family lived above the store, a classic French Quarter townhouse. A botanical garden in the walled courtyard supplied medicinal herbs for his pharmaceutical practice. Others he purchased in the markets or ordered from places like New York or Paris. Dufilho was a chemist. He sold paints, varnishes, glues, perfumes, and makeup, including lead-based rouges and lipsticks. Physicians, nurses, and other kinds of customers purchased patent medicine or the pharmacist's own handmade preparations. The pharmacy's lovely rosewood, brass-detailed cabinets held a wide assortment of materials for making the recipes, formulas, or prescriptions that Voodoo practitioners recommended. There were oils of cinnamon, cassia, bergamot, "Sanguinaria Aragon" or dragon's blood, antimony, coffee beans, verbena, lemon grass, cochineal, Guinea peppers, lodestones, cayenne pepper, iron filings, kerosene, elm bark tea, St. John's root, and many other classic ingredients.

The pharmacy's shelves openly stocked many of Voodoo's trademark remedies: Getaway Powder, Waste-away Tea, War Waters, Essence of Three Thieves, and Goddess of Evils. The mixtures in the pharmacy reveal their magical intentions—dragging powder, stay-away powder, confusion-to-my-enemies powder, whirlwind powders, and Hot-Foot powder—to name a few. The pharmacist, like the women of Voodoo, sold love, luck, and control over capricious fate under various names: Love Success, Lucky Devil, As You Please, Attraction, and the formula a song made famous— *Love Potion Number Nine*.

The citizens of New Orleans understood that Marie Laveau had magical powers. After all, she was a free woman of color, and, as one journalist noted, "the skill of their women in natural medicine is extraordinary. I tried to induce one to give me a recipe. She refused. It was her secret, she said, which she would impart only to her children. Is it any wonder many of these excellent nurses are suspected of being able to use their knowledge for deadly and secret purposes."

〜

Through the 1820s, the beautiful fever nurse and widow was, like the French Creole community of New Orleans, in full blossom.

And then Marie Laveau fell in love.

For the former French citizens of New Orleans, life in the 1820s was still a dazzling round of opera, theaters, balls, and meetings of social and pleasure clubs. Creoles of every color were proud of their educations, often completed in Paris, and of their composers, journalists, and writers. Creole intellectuals talked openly about the principles of a color-blind and radical racial democracy and argued fiercely for self-determination and inclusion as equals in the national growth. Visits of famous people like the Marquis de Lafayette, French general and hero of the American Revolution, were excuses for the parades, dances, and church celebrations Creoles loved so much, fresh reason to sample imported wines and invent new recipes for the lavish dining tables of the city.

The endless round of balls gave Marie Laveau ample opportunity to have danced with a handsome soldier, a veteran of the Battle of New Orleans. She and Christophe Glapion could have flirted at a church social—nuns and priests regularly provided cakes and wine for young people in the hope they would discuss religious topics. In the fluid social settings of the city, Marie and Christophe could have met at the wedding of mutual friends or run into each other at the French Market. They would have spoken about the outlandish manners of *les Américains* who were moving into their city, of General Andrew Jackson, hero of the Battle of New Orleans, and of the traveling circuses that set up their tents in Congo Square.

Philomène told the *Picayune*, "When Marie was twenty-five years old she was led to the altar by Jacques Paris, a carpenter. A year afterwards Mr. Paris disappeared, and no one knows to this day what became of him. After waiting a year for his return, she married Capt. Christophe Glapion. The latter was very prominent here, and served with distinction in the battalion of men of San Domingo, under D'Aquin, with Jackson in the war of 1815."

Yes, Marie the First wed Jacques Paris, but the bride was seventeen years old. Philomène seemed perpetually confused about her mother's age. True, the disappearance of Monsieur Paris remains a mystery—although he would not be the last family member to vanish. And, for all we know, Marie Laveau earned rather than adopted the honorary title of "Widow." No one and no document has ever contradicted her. But Philomène lied about her father's military service during the Battle of New Orleans—and she had excellent reasons to do so. Captain Christophe Glapion did not serve in the company of men from St. Domingue under Major Jean D'Aquin, and his daughter knew it. He did not stand with the honored and decorated "Sons of Freedom," the Battalion of Free Men of Color, on the parade ground in front of St. Louis Cathedral in January 1815, to celebrate American victory in the final battle of the War of 1812—although he had many friends and relatives in their ranks. Christophe's muster records and the small pension that he later received prove that he served in the Dragoons under a diminutive

Frenchman from St. Domingue named Henri St. Gême, an officer who wore tall plumes on his hat to make him appear taller. Major D'Aquin's soldiers were free men of color; the Dragoons were not.

Jean Louis Christophe Duminy de Glapion was white.

Christophe Glapion's family moved in the highest circles of French and Spanish colonial life—one of the "first families of Louisiana." Christophe's paternal grandfather was a French nobleman; the word *"de"* in a French family name indicates estates, aristocratic titles, or connections to the ruling classes. He and Christophe's father served as collector of royal fines in the Spanish administration. The family of Christophe's mother's was also well-placed. Christophe's sisters, several aunts, at least one grandmother, and a number of his female relatives attended the boarding school of the Ursuline nuns. Many were among the founding members of a religious sorority that connected white women to each other, to potential marriage partners, and to the Catholic Church. The names of these intermarried and interwoven families appear in every type of written record for that period; their race is always clear.

We know that the romance of Marie and Christophe faced two obstacles. First, the racial rules of the American administration and the laws against intermarriage in Louisiana were harsher than those under the French or Spanish colonial governments had been. And second, Marie was either a genuine widow like Christophe's own mother or passing for one. She had enjoyed a church wedding, a dowry, and the benefits marriage conferred. "Christophe," I imagine her saying, "why should I give up my safe, strategic position as a legal and proper wife and now respectable widow to live as a mistress to a white man? I've always hated *plaçage*. I support myself, own property, and have more freedom than white women do."

Christophe must have agonized about their difficult situation, sought advice from his military comrades, Creole peers, and relatives from both sides of *plaçage*. Then, as available documentary evidence reveals, he made a choice for love and performed his own miracle; he changed his social race. To live with and from all accounts to love Marie Laveau, the first queen of the Voodoos, Christophe Glapion decided to pass for "colored." Christophe understood the deprivations and perils of *plaçage*; his deceased father left two families, one on each side of the color bar; so perhaps the suitor, like the object of his affections, had also vowed to avoid the French marital-mistress system that caused so much pain to so many. His father's arrangements did, however, leave Christophe with a half-brother of color named Celestin Glapion, who became the model for his brother's actions and a bulwark for the couple as they planned the strategic hoax that daughter Philomène would testify to years later. As a person of color, Christophe could never marry a white woman and use his racial privileges to humiliate Marie or degrade her status to that of mistress. In becoming "biracial" and by giving up status for stigma, he proclaimed himself her equal partner in color and marital politics—a gift of love for any time or place.

Although Christophe could not legally marry Marie, as she had married Jacques Paris, nor give his legal standing to his children, his color change took him out of range of the problems of *plaçage* and most American racial laws. The benefits of his new social, albeit self-proclaimed, identity outweighed its disadvantages. Christophe gained access to the social and benevolent societies of Creoles of color and to their subterranean and backstairs networks of intelligence and mutual assistance. In the same manner that people of color moved in a seemingly casual manner into the ranks of white, Christophe passed into the local world of color; he did not need to register with the authorities or place a notice in the local newspapers. On occasion Christophe signed documents as a free man of color; he asked friends "to get my back"—in Creole vernacular a request for validation and protection. His color change allowed him to live with Marie; had authorities invoked the cohabitation laws against them, Captain Glapion and Queen Laveau knew hundreds of well-placed members of the Creole community who would swear in writing or before the altar of St. Louis Cathedral that both of them were free-born people of color. It is also impressive that their daughter Philomène, despite her quest for social acceptance, kept faith with her father's race of adoption decades beyond his death.

Race in New Orleans was not about physical appearance; it was about the artificial classifications people manipulated as best they could in times and situations not under their control. It does subsequent generations little good to ask whether the shape of Christophe's nose or the character of his hair gave him away—he was or could become whatever people thought him to be, like sexual orientation in our time, whatever he claimed for his true nature. They would make their images, their stereotypes, fit his looks. After all, no one agreed on the "true" color of Marie Laveau, only that she was uncommonly lovely.

Yet, in the company of Philomène, who wanted to be legitimate in the eyes of church and state, we can still fantasize that Marie and Christophe arranged a secret midnight wedding in St. Louis Cathedral. Père Antoine performed ceremonies of blessing for other couples in marital difficulties. To thwart the racial rules he loathed, he bent the canons of his church and his government when he could. Furthermore, he did not record everything in the parish record books. Whatever vows they may have taken, safe from the prying eyes of the law, Marie and Christophe kept them. Philomène was not wrong. They lived as husband and wife in full view of the Creole community, he as a free man of color, she as a Voodoo matchmaker and matchbreaker. They lie together in her tomb under the names of her father and her first husband.

~

By the summer of 1826 Marie was pregnant with a child Christophe was later able to acknowledge in notarized documents as his own. In the eyes of church and state, however, the healthy infant girl born on February 2, 1827, was illegitimate. Marie, like her spiritual namesake, Mary the mother of Jesus, was an unwed mother; and Christophe, either as a white man or a man of color not formally married to the baby's mother, could not give full legal standing to his own child. Hoping for a lightening of the laws, a way to barter justice or love against their racial fate, the couple waited eighteen months to present their child for the sacrament of baptism.

In the end, Père Antoine sharpened his quill pen once more, and on August 19, 1828, entered in his record book of births to people of color at

St. Louis Cathedral the names the couple had selected for their baby—
Marie for the Holy Mother, Heloise for Christophe's favorite sister, and
Eucharist, Holy Communion, light and movement in ritual shape, the
sacrament of grace that ran through the poetry of the *Catechisms* Marie
recited to her baby.

Legal and civil documents of the period sometimes use the names
Eucharist Glapion or Heloise Eucharist for the first Marie's first-born
child. Most of the time, however, to the enduring confusion of those who
wish to trace her, the child Père Antoine baptized as he had her mother
before her, the designated successor and princess of Voodoo, simply called
herself Marie Laveau.

# Chapter 4

## Marie Laveau Brings the New Orleans Saints to Town

YOU SPRINKLE HOLY WATER OVER THAT PICTURE OF YOUR SAINT AND HE
PROTECT YOUR PLACE OF BUSINESS. MOST EVERY HOME YOU GO IN, YOU SEE
SAINTS OVER THE DOOR. HALF THIS CITY IS RUN BY SAINT PICTURES.
—A CATHOLIC BUSINESSMAN

For three days in January, in the year 1829, all businesses in New Orleans closed their doors. The *Louisiana Courier* suspended publication and the legislature adjourned; flags on public buildings flew at half-mast. Creoles, Protestants, Freemasons, Voodoos, foreign dignitaries, soldiers, slaves, the governor, the full Supreme Court, the Senate and House of Representatives of Louisiana, and all manner of mourners—every age, class, color, and condition of servitude—filed past the mortal body of Père Antoine as it lay in state at the front of St. Louis Cathedral.

The Widow Paris, two months pregnant with her second daughter, no doubt joined the other women of color who, newspapers and eyewitnesses reported, had washed and dressed the priest's body for viewing. In the style of decorations they did for Advent or Holy Week, the women covered the requiem altar, the stepped platform on which his coffin rested, with black drapes and flowing white feathers. They lit a thousand candles—bank after bank of tall tapers filled the Cathedral with light. All written accounts of Antoine's funeral mention them.

49

Creoles blessed Antoine's memory; he visited prisons, lifted the souls of the dying to heaven, and fought against the racial laws that punished women of color and their children. His obituary singled out his work in helping fever victims, and his will divided his worldly possessions, less than five hundred dollars, equally among his godchildren—male or female, bond and free. Antoine was a saint, people cried, and they tried to collect souvenir relics from his body. They cut the coarse monk's robe that covered him into small pieces, praying for miracles of healing and justice from materials he had once touched. The mayor had to intervene.

Saints—"enchanted ones" or guardian spirits with superhuman powers—are made at moments like this and from people like Père Antoine. In the magical reality of nineteenth-century New Orleans, the man and the saint came to be merged. Marie Laveau the First had a special relationship to Père Antoine that gave her and many others in the city the same kind of affinity with the priest's patron saint—St. Anthony. In his home city of Padua, Italy, the original Antonio forced officials to pass the first bankruptcy protection law, which stated that if indebted people sold their possessions, they did not have to go to jail. Antonio was called "Wonder Worker" for the miracles he wrought. He was the patron of the poor and oppressed; when you made an offering in his name to poor people, the blessing came back to you. Many asked him to help them find lost articles.

The slave ships that arrived in Louisiana during the colonial period brought an African incarnation or manifestation of Anthony-Antoine-Antonio. In 1704 in the Kingdom of Kongo in central Africa, as a young Christian woman, Dona Beatriz, lay dying of a terrible fever, a man dressed in the hooded habit of a Capuchin monk appeared to her, and introduced himself, "I'm Antonio." He pulled her from the arms of death, then asked her to work with him to end the civil wars and restore the political fortunes of her country. Dona Beatriz, with Antonio by her side, became the leader of the Christian charismatic and antislavery movement in Kongo. Two years after his healing spirit appeared to Dona Beatriz, civil and church authorities in the disintegrating Kongolese Kingdom tried her for heresy and burned her as a witch.

Many of her supporters, imprisoned and sold into the slavery the saint hated, arrived in Louisiana with the embodied knowledge of spirit possession and resistance movements. They kept Dona Beatriz's vision of freedom alive; they brought with them a song or prayer called *Salve Antoniana* or "Hail Anthony." St. Anthony can help you, but only your intention matters. Marriage serves nothing. Baptism serves nothing. Prayer serves nothing. Good works serve nothing. "God wants the intention, it is the intention that God takes." St. Anthony is God's representative in the world, the door to Heaven. To each call, the response was: "Mercy, Mercy, St. Anthony, have mercy." When something bad happens in New Orleans, when ambulance sirens fill the air, when the legislature cuts a social service program for poor women, people on the streets say, "Mercy. Lord have mercy."

Marie the First passed on her special relationship with Père Antoine, St. Antonio of Padua, and, perhaps, through her mother, St. Antonio of Kongo—all joined in the Catholic "communion of saints" and the roster of folk saints in New Orleans—to her daughter, Marie Eucharist. Scrub the floors of your storehouse; then offer sweet smelling oils to St. Anthony, Marie the Second counseled a worried woman who had lost her business in the French Market and came to the priestess for help—"so that the spirits of contention and strife will leave and only good spirits of friendship and help will remain within your storehouse. In the front door you will put the picture of St. Anthony so that faith will enter, and on the back door you will put the picture of St. Anthony so that faith will not depart. Herein fail not, my daughter, to do faithfully each of these things so that prosperity will again smile on you."

Anthony had many incarnations; he came into people's lives through many channels. Père Antoine who arrived in Louisiana as the Spanish monk, Padre Antonio, merged with the Anglo, Italian, Portuguese or Kongolese figure into one folk saint—in New Orleans people call him Ant'ny.

St. Ant'ny, open dis do.' St. Ant'ny, please open dis do'
    An' dear St. Ant'ny who live in Jesus' love, Please open dis do'.
    St. Ant'ny, I consecrate myself to you—An' I use you as my patron saint.
    An' I ask you to keep my do' open. An' I ask you to send me customers,

An' I'll always use you, through our Lord givin' you the power
An' strength to send me customers, an' I give you lights on your altar.
St. Ant'ny, open dis do'. St. Ant'ny, please open dis do'.

St. Ant'ny, like Père Antoine, is compassionate and wears the color brown; but in New Orleans, St. Ant'ny also smokes big cigars and quotes Psalm Twenty-Seven in a tough voice: "When evildoers assail me to devour my flesh—my adversaries and foes—they shall stumble and fall."

The Catholic Church will never make Père Antoine an official saint. But their approval never mattered to Marie the First. As long as citizens in New Orleans blessed his name and carried out the deeds associated with it, Père Antoine lived. He opened the door for other saints who came to the city—called into service for the special assistance they offered the citizens. As one practitioner of Voodoo said, "You take care of the saint, and the saint takes care of you. We will meet some of them as we continue our journey home, to New Orleans. Those who care less for structure and more for freedom to create their own rituals will find Voudou à la New Orleans much to your liking. In this Crescent City, you will meet the very powerful and controversial Mother of the Saints, Mam'zelle Marie Laveau."

Marie Laveau and her daughter knew that God appoints saintly people like Père Antoine or worthy ancestors to be guardians and protectors of those still living. When those who need their help call on them and honor their name, they live again. "The Dead have achieved the next level of initiation, and we can benefit from their perspective," another contemporary priestess said. "Likewise, they benefit from our memory and the honor we pay them. If the doors between the living and the dead are closed, whatever is lurking on the other side becomes monstrous and frightening. If they are open, the atmosphere and qualities of both sides are free to exchange." Ancestors, saints, spirits, archetypes, even elemental forces like water and fire serve le Bon Dieu—the Good God, the creator.

Marie Laveau the First and the Second built altars for "benevolent conjuration," places of help for love, good luck, protection from the law, moneymaking, or husband holding. They put statues of saints on these shrines as the spirit of the occasion demanded them. For some purposes, they used St. Peter or St. John the Baptist. For others, only St. Michael or St. Rita would work. They often favored St. Raymond whom many Creoles called St. Maroon. A Maroon was an enslaved African who made a successful escape from one of the slavery-based societies in and around the Caribbean. Maroon communities sprang up in the swamps of colonial Louisiana as they did at the frontiers of all slave societies—so St. Maroon became the patron saint of runaway slaves.

St. Raymond-Maroon earned his good reputation by breaking bad laws—like those of slavery or prohibition. As a Catholic businessman said, "You go to the saint store and you axe for a St. Raymond saint. Now that saint is for you to put in a place like you are selling whiskey, or making whiskey, to keep the law from worrying you. You put that saint up over your front door where the man have to come in. St. Raymond keep the law away."

Saints and saint pictures do run half of New Orleans; the Laveau prayers that Zora Neale Hurston collected mention St. Anthony, St. Michael, St. Joseph, St. Matthew, St. Roch, the Virgin Mary, Mary Magdalene, and many others—all Catholic saints. The best-beloved saint in the city, however, does not belong to the Catholic Church or to the Laveaus. He may have had Voodoo and Creole parents at one time, but now the entire city claims him as their own. When I ask clerks in the grocery store, old ladies down the block, people who grew up in New Orleans, folks who moved here, blacks, whites, and tans, they have heard about St. Expedite.

It seems that a statue of a Roman foot soldier intended to be part of a crucifixion tableau became separated from its companions. When the missing piece turned up on the levee of the Mississippi in a box marked "*Expedite*," things began to happen quickly. Word spread of a recently arrived saint who could bring events to a rapid conclusion. In New Orleans speedy results are the true miracles.

St. Expedite-pronounced *Ex-pe-deet* or *Es-pi-dee*—wears the garb of a Roman soldier and crushes a raven beneath his foot. The bird manages to croak—"Cras! Cras!" *Tomorrow, tomorrow*—wait, procrastinate, do it later, mañana. Espidee, however, points firmly to a sundial inscribed "HODIE." *Today*. Do it now. One woman gave an example: "Once you is *gris-grised* always call on St. Expedite for help. I found salt on my steps one mornin', and right away I snapped my fingers and St. Expedite heard me. A woman across the street let out a scream and I found out later she had fallen off a ladder and broke her arm. She was the one what had tried to put a curse on me. You see how fast St. Expedite work?"

Catholic authorities preached fervently against such folk interpretations. Priests blamed Marie Laveau and her Voodoo associates for showing citizens of the city how to contact Catholic ancestors, spirits, and saints. Staff members of the WPA Federal Writers' Project agreed with them. "Everything has not always been legitimate and praiseworthy in his cult, and a type of devotion has sprung up, deviations from the path of righteousness. Dangerous manifestations have resulted in St. Expedite's adoption by voodoos and spiritualists in Louisiana."

Official, Rome-approved, reference books on Catholic saints do not mention St. Expedite. They do not realize that he lives in Our Lady of Guadalupe Church on Rampart Street in New Orleans, just down the street from Marie Laveau's house on St. Ann. The small, elegant sanctuary was originally named the Mortuary Chapel of St. Anthony. On October 21, 1827, Père Antoine dedicated it as a place from which to conduct funeral services for plague victims—a task that had to be completed very quickly. No one knows when the statue arrived at the little chapel, but for almost two hundred years people have been leaving little gifts at St. Expedite's feet—a slice of cake, new money, or a green plant. They beg him, please, just do it now.

Both Marie Laveau the First and the Second kept a statue of St. Peter on their altars; but people said they were asking for trouble. St. Peter as Papa Legba opens doors in Haitian Vodou and in other religions of the Diaspora. In Christian tradition, he carries the keys to the kingdom of Christ. In New Orleans Voodoo, however, St. Peter the Protector burns down people's houses if they do not promptly and appropriately recognize his power. An Episcopalian minister turned folklorist Harry Middleton Hyatt concluded, "St. Peter cursed, carried a sword and fought, and had been sent to jail. And that key of his has a double meaning—he opens the door for you, true; but he also locks the door on you. Worse, he is a pyromaniac!"

Another woman told the minister-folklore collector in the late 1930s, "St. Peter? He's good and he's bad. But you gotta handle St. Peter so rough. Yeah, you got to treat him dirty. If you drink, you gotta wet him with liquor." She offered him a beer. "If you curse and live a bad life, you gotta be cursing him. You gotta git up and pull your clothes up and pat yourself down there." To the astonishment of the unprepared interviewer, she did.

Another woman told him about St. Peter's sadistic tendencies. "If I wanted St. Peter to do something for me, I would take a pin and I will scratch my finger, or either my own self, and let it bleed, bleed, bleed, and I'll take a pin and write with my own blood and I'll take it to the cross-roads and I'll leave it there. You get you a broom and just wham him out, just call him all kinds of names. 'I asked you to do something and you didn't do it.' Just whup him up with that broom and he'll do it." Marie Laveau, First and Second, often wore blue sashes that marked a devotion to St. Peter. They kept him on their altars despite his bad reputation. They lit candles to him, and their houses never burned.

In New Orleans, a saint named Rita testified to the frequency of wife-battering and domestic violence, the hidden cruelties of culture. She would help any woman who wanted to leave an abusive man. But as long as he stayed in the house, Rita could not or would not assist.

If you a man got a wife, she'll separate you.
If you use St. Rita for anything, you gotta be a single person,
Cause she don't believe in husbands;
Cause she had a husband in her days, and he treated her mean.
But if you single—she help you.

The original Rita lived from 1381 to 1457. When she was twelve years old, her elderly parents married her against her will to a man who treated her with extreme cruelty. After two sons and eighteen years of unhappy marriage, Rita's husband was killed in a brawl. She petitioned to join a religious order—but the church authorities refused her three times on the grounds she was not a virgin. On the fourth try, they accepted her plea, and after her death, Rita became the saint of desperate causes—causes like finding tender husbands or reforming brutal ones. After both of the Laveaus died, people in New Orleans had no one except St. Rita to turn to for the "husband-magic" the priestesses had provided.

St. Rita never gave up the hope—the lasting belief—that women can change men, reform them, and make them treat their wives, girlfriends, and daughters better. In approved Catholic devotional pictures St. Rita is a wispy white woman who kneels in prayer as a ray of light enters her forehead. But if one asks the right people in New Orleans, they say that St. Rita is at work when you smell flowers that are nowhere in sight, when pink roses bloom in winter, and when the wounds of abuse spontaneously disappear.

Another New Orleans saint who protected people from abusive relationships was St. Michael the Enforcer. "Yeah he's another one he keep your enemy down, St. Michael, but you gotta always be rough. You jes' burn his light—it's a red light because he wears a red garment." St. Michael is the spirit to consult when you have an "unnatural headache," one that does not go away, one that does not feel like any headache you ever had. Someone is burning a candle against you. Their bad wishes and the lighted candles are curses sent to hurt you. Holy water and the help of St. Michael will remove the problem.

Michael was the kind of saint who gave the Voodoos a reputation for getting even. Statues show him with a dragon or evil spirit under his feet. He rids people of evil-wishers and evildoers, and provided power to the otherwise powerless. Henry Middleton Hyatt, the Episcopalian priest who interviewed more than thirty Hoodoo-Voodoo practitioners in New Orleans recorded a prayer to St. Michael from a man who wished to remain anonymous: "In the Name of the Father, Son, and Holy Ghost—let 'em drop dead. Let somebody blow their brains out—I don't care what happen to 'em." Yet St. Michael's power also worked to back up good intentions that required strength of character. To the lady who wanted to remain friends with former lovers and attract new ones, Marie the Second counseled, "On your left leg you will put the garter of St. Michael, made of the golden yellow and red. And in this garter there will be a bag make of pure chamois skin in the shape of a human heart."

Both mother and daughter used St. Roch in their spiritual practices. No one knows how or when he reached the city, but Marie the fever nurse called on him in sickbeds when a dying person lived an unsavory life and had little hope of a better one beyond the grave; and she invoked him in times of pestilence and plague as Europeans had done for centuries. Marie the Second went to the still-famous cemetery named for him, not to participate in the miraculous cures to which thousands of crutches and artificial limbs testify, but to fix hopeless legal cases. One man came to her about his brother, who had murdered a man. Marie told him to meet her at the St. Roch graveyard. "She fix up a little bag and put it on you, or else she would get in with the police, give him ten or fifteen dollars, tell him, 'Now you get to so-and-so.' And it wouldn't be nothing but mistrial, mistrial, mistrial." St. Roch did not wish anyone to die in prison as he had; so, in his mercy, he and Marie settled the matter—"the case never came up."

Marie Laveau the mother had an enduring and complementary spiritual relationship with various manifestations of St. Anthony-Antonio-Antoine. She worked with him in death as she had in life. But Marie the daughter danced in honor of a saint whom she could not have met while he was living, a spirit whose life stood in complete contrast to that of the princess of Voodoo. The glamorous French Quarter Creole had a deep but improbable spiritual relationship with a celibate dressed in animal skins, a desert dweller who did not drink, and a man who lost his only head to the whims of a woman wearing seven veils. St. John the Baptist was the patron saint of the Masonic Orders, and of the city's founder. Citizens of colonial New Orleans fired cannons and muskets at dawn, noon, and dusk on his birthday, June 24. Catholics went to church and prayed to him for the lasting health and well-being of both the governor and the little city herself. Marie Laveau the First and her daughters listened to the biblical stories of how John immersed his cousin Jesus in water and washed him clean. The Holy Spirit came upon them; to Voodoos and Christians alike, this is baptism, initiation, and spirit possession.

In Catholic legends John's feast day is June 24—but the evening before was sacred to the Voodoos. They had danced on June 23, the Eve of St. John, in honor of St. John the Baptist, since the early days of the colony; the St. Domingue-Haitian exiles added a new and deeper vigor to the celebrations of their adopted city. Many folk traditions in the world cherish the summer solstice, midsummer's longest nights. In France, Spain, and in the Alps, villagers light fires; they make teas from St. John's wort. In many parts of Africa, Chango, son of the Great Goddess, is honored at Midsummer. As Europe and Africa blended in the Diaspora, the Eve of St. John became part of the spiritual calendar of the Catholic Caribbean—associated with water, cleansing, and the apex of sunlight. The longest days of the year are a celestial event that belongs to all humans—to women, to men, to every color under the sun. But in Marie Laveau's city, "John" is geography, mythology, medicine, spirit, and song—more than a beheaded saint, an herb to alter consciousness, or a day in the church calendar.

In New Orleans—as nowhere else in the United States—John's day gained prominence just as slavery ended and Reconstruction began. Large numbers of newly freed blacks brought Hoodoo and southern conjure— the rural, Protestant versions of Voodoo—from the country to the city. African Americans had never celebrated St. John's Eve in the Catholic and Creole manner. They had their own John—Big John or High John the Conqueror. The gorgeous, trance-dancing Marie the Second used John in all his reincarnations to bridge the spiritual worlds from Creole Voodoo to Southern blacks and Hoodoo.

Everywhere she traveled in the South, Zora Neale Hurston heard stories about the man who brought the gift of two-headed conjure to his people. The word "high" may mean "on top of" or strong; it also refers to altered states of consciousness or getting high. Conqueror sounds like Conjurer; the name calls up, not just majesty, but mastery of magic. High John "had come from Africa. He came walking on the waves of sound. Then he took on flesh after he got here. . . . he came to be a man, and a mighty man at that. But he was not a natural man in the beginning." Hurston said that High John's job was done when emancipation and freedom came to his people after the Civil War. He retired with a secret smile into the soil of the South—his spirit became a healing plant. "The thousands upon thousands of humble people who still believe in him, that is, in the power of love and laughter to win by their subtle power, do John reverence by getting the root of the plant in which he has taken up his secret dwelling, and 'dressing' it with perfume, and keeping it on their person, or in their houses in a secret place."

In New Orleans, markets, botanicas, pharmacies, or stores stocking spiritual merchandise had offered the roots of St. John's wort for sale from the earliest days of the colony. In Europe, women harvested St. John's wort at midsummer and hung the roots up to dry; Native Americans and Africans knew the healing properties of the plant. Hundreds, perhaps thousands of Voodoo recipes prescribe the root for good luck and protection. Grate it and add to steel dust and graveyard dirt; keep the mixture in a bottle or place it in a *hand* or amulet bag to insure luck, success, and jobs. "Feed" it with oils, holy water, or incense.

"When I play dice," a gambling man confided to Marie the Second, "I go home with empty pockets. When I sit down with good men in the community to play cards, I draw only low cards. What, O Great Goddess of Chance—*luck be a lady tonight*—would I have to do to appease your anger, to gain your approving smile. To win, period." Marie counseled him to fill a chamois bag with the following holy articles: powdered John the Conqueror root, grains of paradise, powdered magnetic stone, eye of eagle, and tooth of shark. Before you enter a gambling house—Marie and the goddess warned—anoint the bag with Essence of Three Knaves and Two Kings.

Another man came to St. Ann Street for Marie Eucharist's help. His business had failed, his pockets were empty. His friends came no more, not even strangers would buy from him, he told Marie. She outlined what he must do to reach the God of Mammon. Clean your house well, the front steps in particular, she insisted. "For yourself you will take of the root of Big John the Conqueror and put in your purse," and every morning "put ten drops of the Essence of Three Jacks and a King on the root of John the Conqueror inside of your purse." At the end of the prayer Marie Laveau added a dose of two-headed character building. "My son, be sure that you treat your customers with due consideration and with honesty of purpose. Herein fail not as the Gods of Mammon will not continue to smile on you and give you gold and silver if you do not heed their advice. For the Gods of Mammon have two heads and can speak both good and evil at the same time. So Be It."

The John whom both Zora Neale Hurston and Marie the Second knew was a trickster, a wild card, a game of chance, a sophisticated magician, a con man, and a conjurer. Marie prescribed his remedies for her clients—not as tea or medicine, but as the physical incarnation of his power and the door that opened to his spirit. To European Americans, however, High John was simply another name for the devil, and anyone associated with him was a devil as well. "Marie Laveau? My god, yes, I knew that woman. She's got a devil in her," said a former slave who lived on Bayou St. John. "No, she don't kill nobody and she don't cure nobody, but she got a dozen devils in her. She dress in fine clothes. Them rich white womens give her plenty money. She got a hundred devils in her. That woman got a thousand devils in her. She a devil herself, and I've got a good rememberer."

Writer Robert Tallant in *Voodoo in New Orleans* repeated the devil gossip the WPA writers collected as though it were fact—"lips smeared with the blood of freshly slaughtered animals and fowls, they took their terrible oaths" to Lucifer, the Devil. But the European devil was not the embodiment or manifestation of African Americans' worst fears. White people had already bought and sold black people—body and soul. The devil whom Zora Neale Hurston encountered in her folklore odysseys through the South was a powerful trickster who competed with God. Sometimes he won—but when he lost, there was no bitterness in their contest. God could be defeated—so oppressed people themselves could trick, oppose, or challenge white masters who believed the devil was real.

The citizens of New Orleans had mundane or worldly troubles—problems they did not bother God with—but which they believed that people like Marie Laveau, both First and Second, St. Ant'ny, or High John the Conqueror could handle. They needed someone earthy and practical, someone who understood the quest to find and keep a good husband or to punish an unfaithful lover. They needed social and spiritual insurance that covered a place to live, a job, and a kind boss. They had "give us our daily bread" and "deliver us from evil" issues and turned to the saints could help. Saints are like friends; we don't share our troubles equally among them. Good friends expect reciprocity; when you ask for help, you must return the favor. Saints are also like therapists. They can deal with certain problems but not others, and they need to be paid. And, like humans, they are ambivalent and complex. Imperfect, they have likes, dislikes, and personality quirks like the rest of us. The saints of New Orleans will help with your problems—but as Marie the First and Second told clients—if you make them a promise, you must keep the faith.

∽

After Père Antoine's death, Marie Laveau the First moved beyond initiation and apprenticeship and into her own distinctive forms of spiritual and community leadership; newspapers began to refer to her as the "head of the Voudou sisterhoods" and "mother of the Voudou orders." Traditions like Voodoo are passed down through the females of a family line—from Marguerite, conjure woman, healer, and nurse, to her daughter, Marie Laveau the First, and on to Marie Eucharist, Marie the Second, also priestess or leader of the Voodoos. In women-led religions like New Orleans Voodoo, a priestess is a ritual leader who invites the spirits and saints into her body and her altar. She is a "root doctor and healer with knowledge of both the medicinal and the magical qualities of numerous herbs" and "a spiritual guide and teacher who accompanies and commemorates the major life passage of her extended family: birth, marriage, death of loved ones."

Marie—wife, mother, and priestess—maintained extensive social networks throughout New Orleans. Voodoo ceremonials and Catholic observances merged into one another and filled up her social calendar. She and Christophe had relatives throughout the French Quarter and the adjacent neighborhoods of Tremé and Marigny. They attended or sponsored rounds of weddings or parties in place of them, stood as godparents for dozens of baptisms, and welcomed the babies regardless of the circumstances of their birth. Between those celebrations they attended funerals for friends in their extended networks. Christophe Glapion had a half-brother named Celestin Glapion—Christophe's and Celestin's father had both a Creole wife and a Creole mistress, and a number of prominent African American citizens in New Orleans can trace their ancestry to this man's double marital arrangements. Celestin, a free man of color, a woodworker and master craftsman whose handmade *armoire* has a place of honor in the state museum next door to St. Louis Cathedral, helped Christophe mastermind the color change that living with Marie Laveau demanded. At various times, he and his fourteen children by two legal wives lived near the other Glapion family in town. Some of Celestin's many children had the same names as Christophe and Marie's children and grandchildren—thereby confusing researchers and genealogists for generations.

Marie's half-sister, Marie Laveaux Auguste, married young, bore seven children in quick order, and managed her considerable financial affairs with no interference from her father or husband. Christophe and Marie named their firstborn son for her husband, and the sisters served as godmother for each other's children. At various times, the two families lived only a few doors away from each other. But Marie Auguste was a wild child. She was in court regularly and once sued her father over property that she inherited from her mother. She spent money with abandon; at one point her husband notified the *Louisiana Courier* that he refused to pay debts his extravagant wife had accumulated. She moved to Paris, and in 1839 at age thirty-five, she died, but not before she ordered her body placed in an iron coffin and shipped back to New Orleans for burial—an unprecedented request in a hot climate. The deceased sister left a substantial inheritance of real estate and slaves, still in litigation years later. She also left a hopeless confusion in formal records and in folklore between herself and her more stable half-sister, Marie the First, who despaired for her sister's soul, befriended her suffering husband and neglected children, and worried that her own daughter, Marie the Second, would follow in the footsteps of her eccentric aunt.

Marie the First's rise to spiritual leadership in the Voodoo sisterhoods paralleled that of Sister Henriette Delille—the nun who refused to live with a man she could not marry. When Henriette and her friends tried to form their first interracial and lay religious sorority, church leaders refused to recognize them. The hopeful sisters petitioned the Church authorities again and again for the right to take vows of poverty, chastity, and obedience, for the privileges of celibacy, for a house where women could live together and be of service to all races. Henriette, the "servant of slaves," made strategic and complex alliances with other women across color lines. These women, for whom better records exist than they do for the Laveaus, immersed themselves in charitable and educational work among the city's poor and enslaved people. From the beginning of their ministries, the interracial Catholic sisterhoods ran afoul of both Catholic canon law and Louisiana secular law. In 1830 legislators forbade literate people to teach enslaved people to read and to write. Henriette and the other women she worked with substituted innovative teaching methods that complied with the letter of the law and still met the spirit of Catholic evangelism and religious instruction. They faced down rules, ridicule, and racial harassment. Marie Laveau—both First and Second—no doubt found it easier to lead the Voodoo sisterhoods.

In addition to continual family matters she attended to and her leadership roles in the woman-centered Voodoo community, Marie the First belonged to a number of social, aid, and benevolent societies. In the absence of effective city government, groups like the Masonic brotherhoods, the growing Voodoo orders, social and pleasure clubs, semisecret associations, burial societies, or various religious groups provided the majority of social services in New Orleans. Relief committees of the societies visited sick members. In cases of serious illness, someone stayed with the family and helped in the household until the person recovered or died. Some benevolent societies offered a pension for long-term disabilities and a safety net for times when few jobs were available. The central role of the societies was to care for sick people and orphaned children, and to see that members received a well-attended funeral and proper burial when they died.

"Marie is my slave. She is one year old, the daughter of Françoise, a free woman of color, and an unknown father," the Widow Paris told a clerk in the offices of the Catholic Archdiocese in the spring of 1838. "The baby died this morning, and her mother is not a member of a burial society, but I am." The clerk asked no questions; he made the entry as directed—the Widow Paris's slave child, Marie, is to be buried in vault number 247 in St. Louis Cemetery One. The Widow Paris did not own little Marie, but Françoise needed help to bury her child, and Marie the First knew how to negotiate with both officials at St. Louis Cathedral and the custodians of the cemetery. The Widow Paris also found a priest to say the burial prayers and lit her own candles for the passage of the child's soul.

Marie the First, Marie the Second, Philomène, and the men of the household belonged to a number of interlocking benevolent societies; all Creoles of their station did. Edward Ashley, a free man of color, blind from birth, and a spiritualist who held séances at his small house, told an interviewer from the Federal Writers' Project that the Widow Paris had belonged to the *Society of the Ladies with Tignons*. For formal occasions—the burial of their members in their communal tomb in St. Louis Cemetery Two was the most solemn—they dressed in black skirts, white waists, a blue silk scarf, and their distinctive Creole headgear. Another benevolent society—the *Ladies and their Sacred Friends*—paid tribute with food, candles, and holy water to the feast days of the saints who had made New Orleans their home, including Père Antoine and St. John the Baptist. At her death Marie the First was the last living member of a benevolent sisterhood that honored women and children; they called themselves—in loose translation and in honor of the high birth rates among Creoles—the *Society of Mother Hens and their Baby Hens*.

# Chapter 5

## Color Schemes and Protection Policies
## on St. Ann Street

THE STEPS OF HER HOUSE WAS RED WITH BRICK-DUST TO KEEP AWAY EVIL SPIRITS.
SHE POUNDED THE BRICK FINE, SPRINKLED IT ON THE STEPS AND SCRUBBED WITH IT.
EVERYBODY COPIED HER.—JAMES ST. ANN, WPA FEDERAL WRITERS' PROJECT

arie and Christophe made love in a hand-wrought walnut bed—
high and small as marital beds were in their time. A *Picayune*
reporter who interviewed her as she lay dying left us an account
of the distinctive furniture in her bedroom. Marie's first husband had been
a carpenter, and Christophe's half-brother, Celestin, was a master craftsman in a community full of artisans who made fine furniture from the
creamy yellow, rose-red, and rich brown woods of the forests and swamps that
surrounded New Orleans. But it is not who made the bed or what it was
made of that matters. It is what the *gumbo ya-ya* insists that Marie Laveau
the First, queen of the Voodoos, did there.

She gave birth to fifteen children in eight years in that bed—or so television programs, tourist propaganda, and Internet sites proclaim. I've often
heard this "fact" on tours through the French Quarter. One guide devised
a complicated formula for the alleged reproductive prowess of the queen
of the Voodoos: Marie the First bore several sets of triplets and a few sets
of twins in rapid succession—perhaps with the help of St. Expedite or
Our Lady of Prompt Succor.

Robert Tallant in his book, *Voodoo in New Orleans,* said this about Marie Laveau's children and husbands—and many quote him: "She was a pretty woman and men liked her. Just a few years after her separation from Paris one Louis Christophe Duminy de Glapion took up residence in her home and remained there until he died in 1835. Glapion, like Jacques Paris, was a quadroon from Santo Domingo and had fought in the Battle of New Orleans. Of this relationship little can be learned except that Marie bore him fifteen children in rapid succession and retained his affection until his death."

Christophe Glapion was not a free man of color from St. Domingue-Haiti. More to the point, he did not die in 1835—exhausted by an affectionate wife and the births of so many children. Tallant had only repeated what the *Picayune* obituary said about the Widow Paris in 1881: "Fifteen children were the result of their marriage. Only one of these is now alive."

For months I dug through libraries and archives, compared dusty documents, and sorted out names and dates; I stood in front of Marie Laveau's tomb as though the inscriptions carved there solved the mystery of bearing fifteen children in eight years and eased the pain of outliving fourteen of them, including her firstborn. At last I understood what French-speaking Philomène had probably said to the English-speaking reporter who interviewed her on the day of her mother's death.

"My mother had fifteen children and grandchildren."

Between 1827 and 1836 Marie the First gave birth to five children. In the two decades that followed, her surviving daughters, Marie the Second and Philomène, had ten children between them. Both sisters lived in the same house with their mother, father, and the babies they bore. Among the three women, there would have been miscarriages or stillborn babies. But such events are personal and do not appear in official records.

The expanding Laveau-Paris-Glapion household needed more room. But Marie and Christophe were not an average couple who could purchase a new home in an ordinary real estate transaction. By 1831, Louisiana lawmakers had instituted strict codes against interracial marriages and cohabitation schemes, closing every loophole they could find. They also prohibited

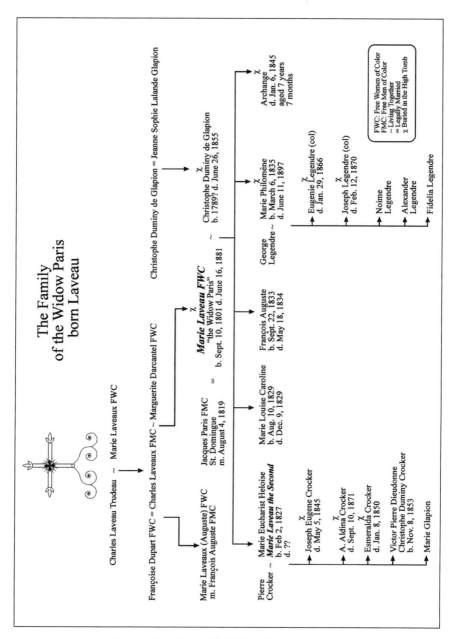

Figure 3. Genealogy of the Widow Paris born Laveau

a white man from acknowledging and settling property on his mixed-race children in his will.

So Christophe and Marie began to plot. In July 1832, Marie went to the office of L. T. Caire, a prominent public notary, a quasi-public official whose job it was to draft documents and preserve contracts between individuals. She asked him to write down and bear witness to her intentions: "I, Marie, a free woman of color, childless widow of Jacques Paris and resident of New Orleans wish to make a pure, simple, and irrevocable donation to my minor daughter, Eucharist Glapion, as a sign of love for her. This child, born since I was widowed, is the natural child of a relationship with Mr. Christophe Glapion who acknowledges her." Marie gave her first-born the property on Love Street, her dowry from her father. At a safe remove Christophe offered his five-year-old daughter as much legitimacy as a white man dared to under American laws.

Two months later, on September 21, 1832, Christophe Glapion walked to Stewart's Coffee House. Local French newspapers had carried notices of the public auction of a house from the estate of one Catherine Henry, a free woman of color, also known as "Pomet." Christophe sipped a cup of strong chicory coffee and bid $3,355 for a house on St. Ann Street between Rampart and Burgundy. Exactly at noon, the auctioneer nodded to him—Sold.

One week later the Widow Paris went to a different public notary and recorded her signature mark on a document that mortgaged the Love Street house she had donated to her daughter. Charles Laveaux, her father, loaned her the money and signed the mortgage; the amount is not given. That same day, Christophe Glapion—with money in hand—went alone to a third public notary and completed the purchase of the house on St. Ann.

Marie and Christophe's daughter, Philomène, wishing as always to "white-wash" the family's legacy, offered another version of how her family acquired the home on St. Ann. "Marie Laveau was born in the house where she died. Her mother lived and died there before her. The unassuming cottage has stood for a century and a half. The first French settlers built it of adobe, employing not a brick in its construction. When it was erected, it was considered the handsomest building in the neighborhood. Marie made the sight of it pleasant to the unfortunate. At anytime of night or day any one was welcome to food and lodging." "See," says Philomène in her quest for respectability, "People weren't coming to our house to buy Voodoo charms and spells to protect themselves." Yet not one word in any document backs up Philomène's wistful story of a woman-centered household on St. Ann; nor do the records support the *gumbo ya-ya's* magical legend of how Guinea peppers and prayers at the altar of the cathedral recalculated justice and rewarded Marie with a home.

Regardless of Voodoo magic or sleight-of-hand legal strategies, however, Marie and Christophe's household was still not safe from Anglo racial laws and punitive actions against people of color.

Five years after his wife had given her Love Street property to Marie Eucharist, Christophe Glapion went to another notary and sold the St. Ann Street house to Pierre Charles Marioux, a free man of color. The handwritten document of June 8, 1838, states, first, that a year and a half earlier, in a legal, civil ceremony, Marioux had married Marie Françoise Mahon, a free woman of color, and, second, that Christophe Glapion had sold the property to Marioux on one condition—he retained full rights to live there for the remainder of his life. Neither man mentioned a sale price or any logical connection between the two statements they signed.

Then the couple and their fellow conspirators waited fifteen months. On September 23, 1839, the Widow Paris met Marie Françoise Mahon, probably her niece, in front of the offices of yet another notary. There Marie Laveau accepted the property on St. Ann Street from her on behalf of her minor children, daughter Philomène and son Archange—another gift, a donation, pure, simple, and irrevocable. With no further explanation, the two women of color made their signature **X** marks. The document does not mention the name of any husbands—real or fictional.

Philomène was three years old, and Archange just a toddler; they could not be legitimate homeowners. The first document did not mention the two children; the second one did not mention Christophe Glapion. The only clear fact in these documents is two Creole women of color—Marie Françoise Mahon, who may or may not have been married to P. C. Marioux, and the Widow Paris, who acted as though she were both married and widowed—had exceptional legal powers denied to white women and wives in the rest of the South. Under Louisiana law, Marie Françoise had the power to give a house to Philomène and Archange that their father had "sold" to her putative husband, and Marie Laveau had the right to accept as the guardian of her minor children. The four Creoles had leveraged the law and their networks of family. As a result of the two transactions, Christophe received the use of the St. Ann Street house for the rest of his life. Philomène and her younger brother became co-owners, the property in their names, while their mother acquired nothing—or so it appears.

Marie Laveau and Christophe Glapion had circumvented a wide variety of Anglo-American laws—starting with the one that prevented persons living together in concubinage from giving each other "immovables" like real estate. Even movable property, slaves, for example, could not exceed one-tenth of the total value of the estate. It did not matter that the laws were randomly enforced; their punitive intention was clear. The couple's arrangement—or conspiracy—parallels the 1832 transaction that gave five-year-old Marie Eucharist the Love Street house. Marie and Christophe could not own property jointly; they could not pass it on to each other or to their children or protect it if conditions in the city worsened—as they did. Marie and Christophe were good fortune-tellers; they may also have followed the advice of the saints they consulted—"take out racial insurance on your household."

∽

Marie Laveau the Second's life looked very different from her mother's life. She was not an observant Catholic. The church was pushing women of color out of their sanctuaries, and there was no Père Antoine in her life. Her Voodoo ministry and spiritual mentors took her in directions her mother, Marie the First, had not chosen; and her love life was far more daring and indiscreet than was her parents'.

Marie Eucharist was an unwed teenage mother. Less than a decade separated the Widow Paris's last child, Archange, born in 1837, and Marie the Second's first child, born in 1843. The babies—Marie and Christophe's grandchildren—drew their first breaths in the high, small walnut bed on St. Ann Street; they grew up there with aunts, uncles, cousins, and many other relatives. The carving on the high tomb of the Widow Paris in St. Louis Cemetery One inscribes the names of two children—babies who were not born to Marie and Christophe. Marie the Second, Eucharist Glapion, was sixteen years old when Joseph Eugene Crocker was born, and twenty-three at Esmeralda Crocker's birth. Their father—whoever he was—was someone named Crocker.

The first man with that name whom I found in my search for Marie the Second's life was Bazile, the best looking, best-dressed man in New Orleans. Born in *plaçage*, educated in Paris, he had a degree in mathematics, was a fencing master, and was a builder of soaring, multidimensional staircases in antebellum mansions who fought the restrictions of color all his life. But Bazile Crocker—whose last name was sometimes spelled Croker, Croquer, or Croquiére—had a legal wife as well as a mistress. Both were women of color, and Creole society—however warm-hearted they were in such matters—allowed only two women per man. Bazile had a son named Joseph, shoemaker, a profession of some standing in the Creole community. The only evidence to link them was the name of Marie Eucharist's firstborn son, Joseph. But the Voodoo princess and the shoemaker did not wed one another.

Marie the Second hid her children and the identity of their father well. In a document notarized after her death, her last child, born when she was twenty-six, signed his full name—Victor Pierre Duminy Dieudonné de Glapion—linking the names, Pierre Crocker and Christophe Duminy de Glapion. In other legal documents, he signed himself Victor Pierre Crocker, sometimes Peter Crocker. Bazile Crocker's younger brother, Pierre, was a well-to-do stockbroker and equally prominent Creole of color. Pierre Crocker signed Christophe Glapion's death certificate; he was present at his deathbed and assisted the family as though he were a full member of the St. Ann Street household.

Pierre Crocker, however, already had a wife. Marie Eucharist Glapion had just turned two in February 1829, when Pierre, age twenty-six, married Rose Gignac. Pierre and Rose had eight living children over the next fifteen years, the last one born in July 1843. Joseph Eugene, the first child of Pierre Crocker and Marie the Second, was born in December of 1843. People in New Orleans—black, brown, or white—gossiped endlessly about Marie the Second, her beauty, glamour, and Voodoo affiliations. But not once did the *gumbo ya-ya* mention her married lover and their children. The only proof that Eucharist Glapion—Marie the Second—ever loved a man is their children's names carved in stone on the high tomb of her mother, the Widow Paris. Only circumstantial evidence of the flimsiest kind allows us to suppose that the gold jewelry Marie the Second flaunted was the outward sign of Pierre Crocker's affection for her.

In July 1850, the Widow Paris and Marie Eucharist the Second carried a year-old baby girl into St. Louis Cathedral. They assured the priest that the unmarried younger woman, Heloise Glapion (known to us as Marie the Second), wished to present her "natural child" for the rite of baptism. The older woman identified herself as Marie Laveau, the infant's godmother, and answered the priest's questions on behalf of the three of them. She called the baby Marie Glapion—the perfect name to conceal whom she might have been. The elder woman claimed that her daughter gave birth to this child in July 1849. The priest believed both of them, but the child belonged neither to Pierre Crocker nor to Marie the Second; something about the baptismal certificate was not true. Marie was pregnant with their third child, Esmeralda Crocker, in the summer of 1849, and could not have given birth to another baby then. But little Esmeralda died that winter; the civil records and the words carved in stone have convinced me of her loss. Given the family history of manipulating secular and sacred documents for private intentions, of girl babies named Marie, and of the priestesses' hunger for children, I think Marie the Second, with the help of her mother, adopted this child and falsified the necessary records. In common with many households in Louisiana and throughout the South, the Laveau women fostered, adopted, raised, mentored, or otherwise loved a variety of abandoned children or young relatives who needed their help. Their Creole benevolent and charitable societies made orphans within their networks a special concern, and the sacrament of baptism was more important to a child's spiritual salvation—certainly to Marie the First—than the incidental facts of her parentage or the lies necessary to secure such a blessing.

Marie the Second supported herself and her children in the classic mother-centered manner of New Orleans. The staff of the Federal Writers' Project believed the gossip that she earned her living as a hairdresser and used these networks in the community to further her Voodoo intentions. The brilliant social life of the 1840s and 1850s in New Orleans called for personal grooming services as earlier times had cried out for skilled nurses. Free women of color had a lock on the profession and demand was high in the Golden Age of the antebellum city. Hairdressing fits the hard edge, the love of excitement and glamour, that echoes through the accounts of Marie the Second. People called her flamboyant, shrewd, and hell-bent. No one ever mentioned piety or religious devotion when they described her. She was the kind of woman they suspected would have had an affair with a married man and helped others in the same predicament. "Marie called herself a hairdresser, and that's how she got in the good graces of the fine people," one woman insisted. "Marie Laveau gained entree to some of the best homes in town, pretending friendly interest, but often working mischief, as in practically every home where servants were employed, she had workers to do her bidding," concluded the WPA Writers' Project.

A French-speaking free woman of color, a hairdresser named Eliza Potter, came to New Orleans early in the 1850s. Like Marie the Second, she was an intimate attendant in hotel rooms and private homes, and listened to, whether she wanted to or not, her clients' most intimate confidences. "Nowhere do hearts betray themselves more unguardedly than in the private boudoir, where the hair-dresser's mission makes her a daily attendant," she said in her memoir from which I paraphrase the following conversation to offer separate insight into Marie the Second's career.

"Can you keep a secret?" asked Madame Preval halfway through her combing.

"You look like a knowing woman, an independent one, and I need advice."

"I can keep a secret better if I never know it," answered the woman with secrets of her own to guard.

"I found a letter in my husband's pocket yesterday—the woman wrote him that she had left a key for him with the hotel porter. They're meeting this afternoon. I'll do anything to make him love me."

"I think you need to consult a fortune-teller," replied the hairdresser as she gathered her scissors and combs.

That afternoon the hair stylist kept an appointment with another Creole woman in a suite at the St. Charles Hotel. "I'm so nervous and my hair is a mess," she moaned. "His wife doesn't appreciate him the way I do. What can I do to make him love me?" A knock on the door interrupted the conversation. The hairdresser opened the door.

"Bonjour, Monsieur Preval," she said.

"I think you need to consult a fortune-teller," she whispered to the young lady as she collected her perfumes and brushes.

Nothing—not epidemics, suicides, hurricanes, or Louisiana politics—cast gloom over the social rounds of society matrons who followed the brilliant social season in New Orleans and paid their hairdressers for intimate services. Eliza Potter's memoir is filled with overheard conversations; sometimes the people she served were not aware that she spoke French. Often they simply paid no attention to a woman of color who happened to be in the same room, just as they failed to recognize themselves in the hundreds of satirical verses of the *Calinda* that the Laveaus and their friends sang in Congo Square. "You just can't get decent help anymore," one aging woman complained. "I don't know what the world is coming to; my maid just steals whatever she fancies—you know how people like that are." The *Calinda* replies to these accusations:

> I am a Creole maid, more beautiful than my mistress.
> I have stolen pretty things from Madame's armoire.
> Danse Calinda, Danse Calinda. Boudoum, Boudoum.

Everyone who sang the song knew that the beautiful young maidservant had taken a few silk scarves that made her mistress look sallow—and that she had borrowed Madame's husband as well.

Creole hairdresser Eliza Potter heard the same stories of social sorrows that Marie the Second's Voodoo formulas and prayers sought to ease. Upper-class women begged both women for help. They had husbands who strayed, friends who gossiped without cause, and neighbors who slandered them. The beauticians heard more gossip than they wanted to. There were couples who passed as married but were not. Clients or their husbands passed bad checks. Those in arranged marriages made alternative sexual arrangements and lived out forbidden desires. Marie and Eliza dressed the hair of women whose families made expensive displays during the season and for the rest of the year depended on their slaves to support them. Some families invested all their money and lost it, gambled away their plantations, or otherwise fell from economic grace. Husbands hit wives whom they suspected were unfaithful. The *Calinda* had verses about many of them:

> A little man no bigger than a rat, the rascal beats his wife and says,
> Madame, this will teach you, don't steal my fruit when I'm not here.
> Danse Calinda, Danse Calinda. Boudoum, Boudoum.

"My family want me to marry Monsieur Hymel. He persists, brings me gifts, calls on me. Help me—I don't want to marry him," the client begged her hairdresser. "What can I do?" The WPA writers had the answer: pay the beautician-turned-priestess money, and she will handle your problems. They said that Marie earned a fortune in fortune-telling and matchmaking. "She also made the most of her profession, using it advantageously to assist lovers, for recompense, of course." Marie carried letters from a married woman to her married sweetheart; she whispered love messages "in the pink ears beneath the elaborate tresses she deftly piled into the modish coiffure of the time." Her career as priestess of Voudou began with combs and scissors—"for it was now that she began to learn things that would be to her profit later."

∼

The *gumbo ya-ya* often claims that both Marie Laveau the First and Second were skilled businesswomen who supported their families by selling herbs, charms, and *gris-gris* materials for lovers and gamblers. But none of the street vendors, market women, or Voodoo practitioners—despite rumors—became rich that way; and hairdressers with children work hard for the money they earn at any time in history. Christophe Glapion, and later his widow, received a state pension for services rendered during the Battle of New Orleans. Glapion's name was attached to a number of special mortgages for free women of color or white women. These documents suggest that Christophe was literate and had some working capital, good contacts in the business community, and a habit of helping women—none of which earned him more than it took to raise a fast-growing family.

The community of color that Christophe Glapion passed into probably had better resources than his own white family did. The estates Christophe's father and grandfather once owned had dwindled by the time his mother, Jeanne Sophie Lalande Ferriere Glapion, died at her home on Bayou Road in January 1835. The court appointed Christophe executor of his mother's estate and ordered an inventory of her property. The Widow Glapion left some furniture, tables, cabinets, silver dishes, and two slaves—Peter Paul, African, fifty years old, valued at four hundred dollars; and Adele, Mulatto, Creole, age seventy five, "knowing a little of everything," and valued at six hundred dollars. The seven heirs paid off the genteel debts of the long-widowed woman and parceled out the antiques—Christophe and Marie took the handmade cypress *armoires* for their large family because the St. Ann house had no closets. Nothing in the death and property settlement of Christophe's mother's suggests family discord about his marital arrangements—or much money.

The Laveau-Paris-Glapion household on St. Ann Street was full of children, visitors, and relatives. Their neighbors told the interviewers from the Federal Writers' Project about the constant traffic and welcoming atmosphere. Through their mother and grandmother, Marguerite Darcantel, both of the Maries maintained cooperative networks, exchanges of food and services, with many Native American women. "Marie Laveau used to trade her business with the Indians for herbs. They come from the country by the river and the gulf—often with papooses on their backs. They sold their fruits and vegetables in the market, and they used to sell their baskets, herbs and other things in the French Market and the Indian Market near Broad Street. Those Indian women would sleep on the ground in Marie Laveau's yard with their babies in baskets and all the wares they come here to sell. In exchange for that hospitality, they would leave bags of gumbo filè, sassafras roots, big baskets of vegetables, and baskets of all sizes for every use."

Thanks to Marie and Christophe's undercover maneuvers, the St. Ann Street household became a sanctuary, a workplace for the adults, a playground for the children, and an asylum for those who sought help. The stories about their hospitality, however, took on a different tone when journalists wrote about them. Even scholarly journals of history published the white community's value judgments as fact; John Kendall, a local magazine writer in the early twentieth century who is still quoted as an expert on the Laveau household, wrote in the *Louisiana Historical Quarterly*, "After dark, you might see carriages roll up to Marie's door, and veiled ladies, elegantly attired, descend and hurry in to buy what the old witch had for sale. An arrant fraud, no doubt, but money poured into her lap down to the last day of her evil life."

The first spiritual imperative of New Orleans Voodoo, the core value of both Marie's ministries, is sealed in one word—*protection.* Marie and Christophe protected each other and their household on St. Ann Street to the ultimate limits of their psychic and legal abilities. The partners practiced the values of hospitality; they welcomed babies, family members in trouble, and guests as they came; they fed all comers well. Then, as their children and grandchildren were born, as their daughter's career broadened the family's social networks, and as the racial climate of Louisiana grew ever more troubled, the couple turned their attention to the greatest obligation of the Voodoo spirits and saints, to one of the consuming passions of their lives.

# Chapter 6

## Freedom à la Mode, à la Marie

THE VOUDOUS BECAME A POWERFUL SECRET ORDER, A SPIRITUAL SECT,
A SYSTEM OF FREE MASONRY. THE VOUDOUS WERE EVERYWHERE,
IN EVERY HOUSEHOLD.—*PICAYUNE*, JUNE 22, 1890

By sunrise the French Market was in its usual uproar. In the high-pitched squeal of unoiled wheels, still drowsy mules had pulled carts up to the curbstones at three in the morning and unloaded their goods—eggplants and alligators, beefsteaks and eggs. At the end of the vegetable market, sellers hung dead chickens head down from the roof; live ones in their coops screeched against the same fate. Thin mangy dogs scavenged for scraps among the limp cabbage leaves rotting on the muddy floors of the market. The smells of monstrous cheeses and the curses of twenty languages filled the air. Merchants yelled out the bargains of the morning, commanding housewives to stop and buy at their booths. The Widow Paris sat on one of the four-legged stools at a marbletop table lined with white cups and saucers and paid five cents for a cup of café au lait.

Making her way through the boisterous crowds, her split-reed Indian basket on her arm, she selected fresh produce, green peppers, green onions, garlic, a bottle of wine, and some sugar to make pralines for her little ones. Native American women gave her pecans in return for her hospitality. At the butcher's stall she selected long lengths of handmade *andouille* sausage and asked if he had saved any beef hearts for her. She stopped to chat with the baker's wife and topped off her basket with a long loaf of crusty

French bread. On Mondays she cooked red beans and rice while she did the family laundry; on Fridays she made oyster stew or seafood gumbo—Catholics did not eat meat that day—and prepared for the Voodoo gatherings that evening. With each purchase, she reached into the pocket of her dress and paid in French *francs*, Spanish *piasters*, and American nickels or dimes.

Errands she needed to do in the Faubourg Marigny would have taken her through the intersection of Chartres Street, just downriver from the convent of the Ursuline nuns, and Esplanade Avenue, a boulevard of mansions and trees. She had to pass a number of raised, well-built Creole cottages with green-black shutters on the doors and floor-to-ceiling windows. The houses sat on the front of long fenced lots, typically sixty by a hundred feet in size with kitchens, privies, and two-story slave quarters in the back. Nothing about the houses, charming examples of Creole architecture, looked peculiar. But Marie knew, as did all the citizens of New Orleans, that many of the quiet cottages were another kind of market. The people in those houses bought and sold human merchandise—or were themselves bought and sold.

The slave-trade houses were quiet and decorous—no rattling chains, no cries or beatings to disturb the neighbors, and none of the clamor associated with slave auctions in other cities. Private settlements and word-of-mouth bargains sealed the exchanges between buyers and sellers in the tasteful cottages along Esplanade Avenue. The sellers or slave traders were people of social standing in New Orleans; there was no stigma on businesses with names like Slatter, Wilson, Bruin, Lamarque, Hart, Neville, Foster, Vignie, and White. Paintings and engravings from the period show buyers dressed in formal attire—top hats, frock coats, watch chains, ties and bright men's scarves. Wives sent their husbands to negotiate the purchase; widows delegated the task to male relatives.

Meanwhile, fifty to a hundred people spent their nights in small cells within the fence, exercised in the courtyards and ate in the common room of the compound through the day. Sometimes they bathed, shaved, put on the clothes provided them, and made an appearance in the showrooms that fronted on the street. Enslaved men and women stood on the sidewalks or on the galleries—the "men wore good quality blue cloth, with vests, white shirts, well shined shoes, and high beaver hats. Women were adorned in multi-colored calico dresses with bright silk bandanas." During one noontime sale, a young Creole girl about sixteen years old threw herself at the feet of a man who had failed to conclude a price for her he liked. "The girl—who for seven years had been suffering bad treatment at the hands of her master begged him to buy her, promising that he would have no reason to ever regret it." Finally the man consented and paid 2,000 *francs* to the merchant. But wives of city councilmen and others who passed objected to slaves who served as their own bargaining agents, to the strong questioning gaze of men and tears of women standing on the sidewalk; the council passed an ordinance in 1852 to prevent the public display of the traders' wares.

There is no indication that the Widow Paris ever entered one of the cottages or stopped to read the advertisements for the sales and auctions of slaves that papered bars, coffee shops, and public buildings. She rarely had to pass the second cluster of slave-sale houses around Baronne and Gravier Streets at the opposite end of the French Quarter next to the cock-fighting pits, barber shops, boot sellers, and leather-tanning factories of the city's central business district. Marie Laveau, Christophe Glapion, their daughter, Marie Eucharist, and their Creole friends were not in the market for English-speaking slaves. They did, however, twist and break the law to help friends within their networks; they were in the position to help enslaved men and women who spoke French and those with Creole connections. Each time the Widow Paris walked past the cottages at Chartres and Esplanade, she may have started a conversation in French, and listened for a response.

Marie the Second worked as a hairdresser in the best hotels in town. The St. Charles on the other side of Canal Street and the St. Louis in the French Quarter held tasteful slave auctions in their carpeted lobbies, and Eliza Potter stumbled across one at the St. Charles not far from the cluster of slave-sale houses in that part of town. She and her client had become involved in a heated conversation about *plaçage*. Upset, Eliza rushed into the lobby just as a muted cry rose from below. "I stopped and looked down in the rotunda, and there was a slave-market. . . . Several were put up and sold off to the highest bidder; some seemed satisfied with their lot, and others, apparently, grieved to death. I have seen people as white as white could be and as black as black could get, put up and sold in this elegant hotel. . . . In spite of my feelings, some lodestone or electricity always drew me to the rotunda, where I daily saw people, both young and old, bought and sold."

The rumors about Marie the Second, a hairdresser who used her profession as a source of urban intelligence in the service of Voodoo magic, probably had far more to do with race and slavery than with getting rich or getting even. She was privy to gossip about who had died, how their estates were to be divided and sold, and who was coming up for sale. She could pass that information on to her French- and English-speaking acquaintances in a position to help. The *gumbo ya-ya* claims that Christophe Glapion ran an underground railroad to send enslaved people to freedom, and that both of the Marie Laveaus used Voodoo magic to help slaves escape. Dr. Bass, practitioner of Voodoo medicine in New York who worked with Marie the First in New Orleans, told a reporter, "Before the war, she made a pile of money by selling charms to runaway slaves to prevent them from being captured." The constant traffic, day and night, at the house on St. Ann Street was only a cover for the Voodoo queen's illegal and immoral activities—or so it was said. The white community suspected that people of color like Marie Laveau were helping slaves in creative ways. They knew that sympathetic whites in their own social circles supported such ventures.

In newspaper interviews, a prominent white doctor spoke with authority about "negro fetishism"—which he defined as magic to help slaves escape or otherwise improve their lives at the expense of their owners. He offered medical evidence for and advice about the "mystical connection between the negro and the serpent." "Snake-worshipers" and Voodoo followers caused many problems in New Orleans, particularly with the slave population, he wrote. In the 1930s and 1940s, the staff of the WPA Federal Writers' Project dutifully cited his expert testimony.

In the three decades before the Civil War, New Orleans was the leading slave market in the United States—the reason that the phrase, "sold down the river," signifies the ultimate betrayal. Slavery was the text and texture of urban life. The slave-trading season, like the theater season, ran from September to May, and tourists visited the slave-sale houses just as they walked through the French Market or attended the splendid opera house. The municipal management of New Orleans in the antebellum period was so fragmented that some slaves walked to another section of town and calmly took up life as free people. The Creole community of color provided refuge to runaways who spoke French, those with free relatives, and those who could pass. New Orleans was a metropolitan magnet; some people bought slaves, some sold them. Many others, however, escaped from their bondage.

Although statistics about successful escapees—like the numbers and names of those who passed for white—will never be available, many succeeded. Free people of color like Marie Laveau had many strategies to help runaways. They claimed them as their own slaves, hired them, and sometimes married them. Escaped men worked in mills, cotton-presses, cigar factories, on the railroad and in private homes. Women found jobs as cooks, gardeners, midwives, maids, and prostitutes. Many sold fruits, vegetables, flowers, cakes, candy, drinks, or other goods in the French Market and on the street where they formed powerful networks of gossip, information, and support.

It is little wonder that whites began to blame Marie Laveau and the Voodoos for bad relations between slaves and masters. When danger peaked and power was most limited, magic played its greatest role. As a prominent scholar of black culture and consciousness wrote, "The whites were neither omnipotent or omniscient; there were things they did not know, forces they did not control, areas in which slaves could act with more knowledge and authority than their masters, ways in which the powers of the whites could be muted if not thwarted entirely." Voodoo was a way to shift power relationships.

At the beginning of my search for Marie Laveau, I found hundreds of formulas that appear to treat the problems of bad husbands and unfaithful lovers—but the techniques make just as much sense in the light of slavery. Zora Neale Hurston wrote down a recipe called "To Send Away." Take some dirt from the footprint of the person and parch it. Take nine dirt-dauber nests, parch and grind them, add ground red pepper, and tie them up in a clean white cloth. "Carry to river at twelve noon. When you get about forty feet from river, run fast and wheel suddenly at brink and hurl dirt over left shoulder and don't look back. Say, 'Go and go quick, in the name of the Lord.'" Another formula, called "To Run a Person," prescribed writing the person's name on seven slips of paper. "Take a toad when the moon is wasting. Roll those names up in a small ball and give to the toad. Take the toad in a box over into another town. The person will leave and never return."

In the time-honored morality of magic, any part of a person—a name, hair, semen, photograph, or a footstep—carries his or her essence. A skilled practitioner takes those remains and places an intention on it through practical actions and prayers. Since the power is in the intention, the formula works equally well on precious friends and deadly enemies. The technique is neutral—what works to eliminate an unpleasant person will also work to help a beloved enslaved person escape bondage. "They git cayenne pepper, graveyard dirt and put the dirt from off they step— and they done roll it in a paper and shove it in that chicken in the backside, and turn that chicken loose. See, like chicken fly and run, go over the fence, and you can't ketch 'em. But you gotta do wit' a black frizzly chicken. That's the way the person will wander away at night and you'll never know when they left. You never hear from them from this day to that." The formulas vary; the intention is to cause the subject to disappear and never return. "Get some of that fast-foot powder—*hot foot powder* they calls it— put it in them shoes."

The *gumbo ya-ya* claims and Robert Tallant in *Voodoo in New Orleans* repeated the gossip that late at night people saw Marie the Second on a secluded road on the outskirts of the city. She carried a plate of food—roast chicken, mashed potatoes, and green peas, sometimes red beans and rice or gumbo— and placed it with coins and something to drink under a tree. It was better that those in charge believed she was engaged in "primitive ritual and fetish worship" than in defying their runaway slave laws.

～

Christophe Glapion did not notice the scent of magnolias heavy on the May air; he was preoccupied as he walked to the notary's office that morning to meet Charles Darcantel—a prominent white man and his wife's uncle on her mother's side. Notaries were the most respected and well-trained professionals in Louisiana; their job was to act as impartial outsiders and to draft, witness, and preserve contracts drawn up among private individuals. Christophe was no less distracted when he walked out of the official's office and into a sudden rainstorm with Alexandrine—a slave girl he had just purchased from a Creole couple for one thousand Spanish *piasters*. Alexandrine, also known as "Ninine," was about seventeen years of age.

The color situation in New Orleans had tightened after 1831 when Nat Turner led the most successful, sustained slave revolt in United States history. Federal authorities executed Nat Turner, but not before he confessed his mystical origins. Turner, who was born with special markings on his head and chest, said that the Holy Spirit had sent him a sign and told him of miracles that would come to pass. Turner's sacred worldview offered a place in which magic, spirit visitations, and slave rebellions came together, and his insurrection set off waves of white reaction. The new laws prohibited education for slaves and tightened the penalties for "illegal assembly"—slaves, free people of color, and whites gathered in one place. No one could free or emancipate bondspeople without the consent of the parish governing boards. Slaves could not purchase their freedom with their own funds as they had in the past. Whites were once again forbidden to free slaves through wills or other documents.

Marie and Christophe, living together as man and wife in defiance of the cohabitation laws and manipulating public documents to make their house on St. Ann safe, began to break the new pro-slavery laws as well. They enlisted Charles Darcantel to witness Christophe's purchase of

Alexandrine and to sign the long transaction, handwritten in French and specifying a currency that by 1838, when they started a long series of such transactions, had been out of use for thirty-five years. With full knowledge of the fraud his friend was about to commit, and regardless of his own feelings about slavery, Charles watched as Christophe Glapion signed his name—Jean Jacques Christophe Paris.

Christophe Glapion, Marie Laveau's second husband, had bought a slave woman under the name of Jacques Paris, her first. He inserted Jean, his baptismal name, and Christophe, his first name, and inscribed a flowing signature—"*Paris*"—in his own handwriting at the end of the document. Although most people in the French and Spanish periods had a variety of names, they rarely used those of a wife's long-disappeared husband.

"Jean Jacques Christophe Paris" had purchased Alexandrine with one constraint—*la condition d'affranchissement stipulée*—"the condition of freedom is fixed," what is also called in the archival records, *Statu libre*, a pledge of freedom. Ten days later, "Monsieur Paris" sold Alexandrine to a Monsieur Dumartrait with more stringent conditions attached. Christophe Glapion, a.k.a. Jacques Paris, gave up all rights to her—except the guarantee of her liberty. The document obligated Alexandrine to pay back the thousand *piasters* that bought her freedom to Monsieur Dumartrait, who agreed to emancipate her when the debt was paid. Furthermore, the document guaranteed that all of Alexandrine's future children would be born free and live free. Should something happen to Monsieur Dumartrait, any heirs he had were obligated by law to meet all the preexisting conditions, and to insure that none of Alexandrine's children—regardless of any unexpected events— would ever be enslaved. This was not an ordinary slave sale; their story falls between the handwritten lines.

Dumartrait was a white man in love with an enslaved woman of color. French authorities had always understood how a man and a maid might make a sexual bargain with a little help from family and friends. Under French law an owner could free or manumit a slave (*manumission* literally means "to send away by or from one's hand"). Spanish colonial authorities went a step beyond and allowed women of color to buy their freedom and their children's for a fixed sum agreed to by an owner or through a court ruling—a process called "self-purchase." Women of color had the right to initiate their own manumission proceedings. Even if their owners refused to cooperate, bonded women had the right to petition the city council for a "certificate of liberty." So Dumartrait contacted his old friend Christophe Glapion for help, and the two of them conspired to free Alexandrine, to protect her, and to insure freedom for all children the couple might have with a marriage contract on the French and Spanish model of *plaçage*.

Christophe understood the difficulties of making a love match across racial lines and protecting the children who followed. White Creoles—with Christophe Glapion posing as a free man of color who could never appear to contradict his successor—had found a way to outwit Yankee laws that had limited self-purchase, emancipations, and manumissions for people of color. For Alexandrine and the future of her unborn children, an arrangement that resembled *plaçage* was an improvement over slavery. The price she had to pay back was low—between 1830 to 1850 young women like her often sold for seven to ten thousand American dollars; furthermore, there is no evidence that money changed hands. A thousand *piasters* would make a proper gift from a man to a woman he loved, but to whom he could not give a last name. Once released from slavery, Alexandrine joined the growing ranks of free people, the company of many strategic women of color like her, where she had the chance to buy other relatives out of their bondage.

Three months after Christophe Glapion had purchased and then freed Alexandrine, the Widow Paris made her signature X mark on a complicated document and purchased Irma—an enslaved woman about twenty years old. This transaction in August 1838 was also a "*Statu libre*," completed on the condition of Irma's freedom; it cost Marie Laveau 750 Spanish *piasters*. A white woman, Mrs. Constance Peyroux, sold, gave, or otherwise transferred Irma to her husband, Pierre Oscar Peyroux, also white. Then Monsieur P. O. Peyroux turned around and, in the same transaction, sold Irma to the Widow Paris. The conditions of their deal were strict; Irma had a daughter, Coralie, twenty-one months old and a son Armand, about

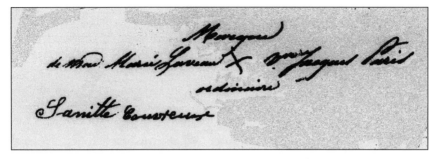

Figure 4. Marie Laveau's signature mark
(Notarial Archives Research Center, New Orleans)

a year old. But the children were not part of the sale—Coralie and
Armand were free. They had been baptized and were to remain with their
mother. Furthermore, the sale gave Irma the right to purchase the freedom
of any other children she might have. The document expressly prohibited
the Widow Paris from selling or mortgaging Irma, separating her from her
children, or taking any action whatsoever that compromised Irma's liberty.

A year and a half later, Marie Laveau returned to the same notary and
certified that no other liens or legal actions existed against her, the owner
of Irma. She insured that no one could sue her and seize Irma or her children as payments for debts. Should the Widow Paris die suddenly, Irma's
protection from court action and Louisiana's punitive inheritance laws was
secure. The Widow Paris sealed the outcome of her intentions about freedom for Irma forever; she paid a public notary to write them down and
asked her family member, Charles Darcantel, to witness the transaction.
Then they all signed in ink—Marie put an X, her solemn signature mark.

In 1843, Christophe Glapion purchased a woman named Juliette a.k.a.
Nounoute, about eighteen years old, for 210 *piasters*—on the strict condition of liberty when she reached her twenty-fifth birthday. Four years later
Marie Laveau went to a different notary and reconfirmed the original agreement. The document noted that Juliette was baptized in St. Louis Cathedral
under the name Clemence; it discussed at some length the calculation of
her birthday for purposes of her liberty. Juliette was then about twenty-
two years old; she would reach her twenty-fifth birthday in 1850.

On April 27, 1848, however, Madame Marie Laveau sold Juliette to Sanité Couvreur, a free woman of color for three hundred *piasters*—still on the strict condition of her liberty. The books in the Office of Conveyance confirm the transactions. Nothing in the documents tells us why the stipulation of her freedom was so strictly set for her twentieth-fifth birthday or what happened to Juliette in the meantime. Even in its confusion and complexity, however, the case of Juliette confirms that Marie Laveau and Christophe Glapion never signed the same documents, and that they had extensive dealings and contacts throughout the Creole community. The only constant in the long series of transactions was *"Statu libre"*—freedom for women of color and their children.

That same April, Christophe Glapion bought Peter, a black man about thirty years old, and a year and a half later sold him for 450 *piasters*. The motivation behind this transaction, if any, is not revealed in the document. Although he signed his real name, not that of his wife's ex-husband, Jacques Paris, Marie Laveau's husband once again lied to the notaries. Christophe Glapion swore in writing, and in front of witnesses who knew better, that he was *"Célibataire"*—a bachelor. With this strategic falsehood, he laid deeper layers of protection over the St. Ann Street household, over his children and grandchildren, and his increasingly controversial wife.

～

In the Creole geography of New Orleans, slave-sale markets clustered on the downriver side of the French Quarter and in the new American section of town across Canal Street. But within the parallel racial worlds of the city, people of color forged new forms of freedom in two unparalleled places— St. Augustine's Catholic Church and Congo Square, both in Tremé.

Racial discrimination in Catholic circles had grown since the days of Père Antoine, and to spare white sensitivities, people of color like Marie the First were supposed to stand or kneel at the rear of the city's churches. Many congregations cut enslaved people off from Catholic worship and communal life. But Sister Henriette Delille and her Creole friends of all social classes envisioned a place where every person in the community—regardless of social heritage or condition of servitude—could worship together. In the 1830s, she and three other free women of color gained control of a part of the estate of Claude Tremé, a white Creole, who had subdivided his holdings and sold off large tracts to free blacks for nursing homes, schools, and places of meeting for the hundreds of social and benevolent societies they formed.

Free people of color raised the money and provided the skilled and unskilled labor for the construction of the church. When a powerful group of white Catholics conspired to take over the sanctuary for themselves, to exclude slaves from worship, and to force Creoles of color to the back of the sanctuary, free people purchased all the pews themselves, and reserved those at the front of the church for their enslaved brothers and sisters. St. Augustine's Catholic Church opened in 1842—the congregation's creed became "all those who know the gifts of God are welcome at His table."

Marie the First, like older Creoles, continued to worship at St. Louis Cathedral; the priests there had made their peace with her. Her daughters Philomène and Marie the Second attended St. Augustine's just across the street from the St. Ann Street house; priests from that church baptized their children. The Creole church in the heart of Tremé, the largest community of free people of color in the United States, was only a few blocks from St. Louis Cemetery One and from Congo Square.

Congo Square was the crossroads, the pivot for people of color, and the epicenter of their mystical geography. It was Camelot, Mount Olympus, Jerusalem, or Mecca—the intersection of jazz, modern American dance, Creole resistance, African American esthetics, and New Orleans Voodoo. From the mid-1700s to the mid-1800s, it was market, dance arena, community center, and spirit theater to the growing community of color, bond or free. No other place in America where black people gathered is as well documented. No other spot is more directly associated with the soul of American dance and the roots of jazz.

Only a few songs that Marie Laveau the First sang in Congo Square on Sunday afternoons or at Voodoo rituals in private places have survived.

Common people and local color writers alike believed that her trademark song, the *Counja* or "Conjure Song," would never be completed—each time people sang the Voodoo hymn they improvised and new verses emerged. No one wrote down the tune, yet the words that have survived suggest the beat, the rhythm, and the openings to spirit visitations that Marie so often performed. Each time the chorus and audience yelled the word *Counja*, the drums gave one loud beat and the dancers clapped their hands; many held gourd rattles filled with pebbles or homemade tambourines. Women formed a circle, hands, feet, the whole body moved in time with the drum—"swaying, swinging, writhing, thigh beating, breast patting, and chanting."

> Counja. Counja. Counja is a-coming now.
> Hide your head, it's coming now.
> Close your eyes so you won't see it.
> Boom, boom, it's a-comin' now.
> Counja. Counja. Counja is a-comin' now.

"Counja was the Evil Spirit sometimes referred to as the Zombi," the WPA writers reported. "There is not much meaning attached to it." White writers and observers in both the nineteenth and twentieth centuries failed to see the relationship of conjure to freedom—if only the liberty of one's soul through music and dance. They could not see themselves parodied in the *Calinda*; nor could they envision the spiritual power of the *Counja*. Therefore they could not imagine the subversive energy of the *Bamboula*, which both Maries sang in Congo Square, and which seemed to offer only innocent verses about having a good time. The satirical *Calinda* said of the popular song:

> White with a little black, I dance the Bamboula,
> You shall never see any grander Ga-la-la.
> Danse Calinda, Danse Calinda. Boudoum, Boudoum.

Like the *Counja* and the *Calinda*, the *Bamboula* had a can't-stop-dancing beat, but one of the few verses that journalists collected from those who attended the dances in Congo Square speaks without imagination or reference about people who eat baked potatoes.

When the potato will be cooked, we shall eat it, we shall eat it.
Even if it is in the soup, even if it is in the ashes,
Even if it is in syrup, we shall eat it, we shall eat it.

The song is a riddle that makes no sense in food-loving New Orleans—unless the words were a code for something other than cuisine, an encrypted message that the slave-owning class could not comprehend. In light of the pro-slavery obsessions of the press and white public and the abolitionist passions of free people of color in that period, in the face of Marie and Christophe's plots and perjuries, I hear it this way:

When freedom comes we shall devour it.
Sweet or spicy, burnt or blazing—
We shall devour freedom when it comes.

There is evidence that the song to the Great Serpent Spirit that Marie the First sang in Congo Square also encoded messages about freedom. Eyewitnesses spoke in awed tones of the serpent centerpiece of Marie Laveau's dances of spirit possession. In his book, *Voodoo in New Orleans*, Robert Tallant said that "a great caldron would be set to boiling over a fire in the center of the clearing in which the ceremonies were being held and into it would be tossed offerings brought by members of the sect: chickens, frogs, cats, snails, and always a snake. The queen would begin a chant: '*He is coming, the Great Zombi, he is coming to make gris-gris!*'" Then the practitioners danced, pausing only to eat, drink, tear off pieces of live chickens with their teeth, and draw blood from each other, "clawing and biting and falling to the ground in embraces of frenzied lust." He concluded that "they were *possessed*. They had the *power*. What they called power was not all faked, nor was it caused by alcohol. Make no mistake about that." He suggested that the Great Zombi, an evil spirit, caused "the transference of emotional electricity from one to the other, until the entire group was a seething mass of magnetic shocks."

Yet "Zombi" was once a beautiful word, a benevolent concept, the spirit to call upon at the hour of one's death. African Christians in the Kingdom of Kongo called their supreme deity—*Zambi a Mpungu*. In that long-ago time and place from which so many people of color in Louisiana had come, "Zombi" was the name given to God.

In St. Domingue-Haiti, a "zombi" is a person raised from the dead. Soulless, the former person is only an empty physical shell who must work on plantations for eternity. If we suspend discussion of whether or not this is possible or how Haitians may have achieved such results, we are left with chilling metaphors about slavery. The zombi legends—some of which came to New Orleans with the St. Domingue-Haitian émigrés—meant that not even death could free a slave.

Marie Laveau the First kept snakes in her house before her altar and danced in possession trance in Congo Square and elsewhere with a spirit she herself named *le Grand Zombi*—this is one of the few historical facts we know about her. Did she mean the supreme God of Africa's embodied memories, the spirit of freedom—or a slave beyond the grave, bondage beyond eternity?

Marie's signature marks on the notarized documents that freed women of color and their children, that protected her house and her family, answers the question for me; she did what she had to do, what she knew how to do, to fulfill Voodoo's obligation, to earn Voodoo's greatest gift. When the Great Serpent Spirit sang to Marie Laveau in Congo Square and insinuated himself into shapes that only conjure and poetry can, she submitted to the drums, and her songs echoed his voice—*There is life after slavery. There is freedom before death.*

# Chapter 7

## Life in the Cities of the Dead

I'VE SEEN THE PEOPLE TAKE SOME OF THE DIRT FROM THE GRAVE HOME TO

SPRINKLE AROUND THEIR HOUSE. THAT'S ALL VOODOO STUFF,

YOU KNOW.—*GUMBO YA-YA: FOLK TALES OF LOUISIANA*

The weather on January 6, 1845, was more like summer than winter. In warm showers and high humidity, the family on St. Ann Street hurried about the duties that death had forced upon them. A neighbor fastened white crepe on the front door—the sign a child had died. Someone summoned a priest. Friends stopped the clocks in the house at the hour death came and covered the mirrors with dark cloth. Fresh-brewed chicory coffee filled the large urns the family kept on hand for such occasions. A member of the benevolent and burial society tacked hand-lettered signs on the Death Notice Board at St. Louis Cathedral and at St. Augustine's Church, on posts, sheds, or fences, and another contacted the custodian of St. Louis Cemetery One, requesting him to open the tomb of the Widow Paris for its first tenant. The women prayed as they washed, perfumed, and dressed the lifeless body of Archange, little archangel, seven years and seven months old, Marie and Christophe's last son.

Marie the First and her two daughters, Marie Eucharist and Philomène, donned the mourning clothes Creole women wore for the death of a relative, no matter how distant. With large extended families and high death rates, some women remained in mourning most of their adult lives. Even young girls wore black dresses, a simpler version of widows' thick, trailing veils. Creole women made wreaths and mourning jewelry from the hair of the deceased and decorated their homes as if to celebrate death's visits. Honoring the dead of New Orleans demanded proper clothes and elaborate performances of grief.

Sometime between 1834 and 1845, the Widow Paris prepared in a frank New Orleans manner, both Creole and Voodoo, for the deaths to come. She and her husband purchased land from the Catholic Archdiocese, perhaps with the rest of the money Christophe's mother left him, and negotiated with a tomb builder to construct a crypt for them, another home for their family, this one in the oldest and most famous cemetery in New Orleans. The tomb builder carved Marie Laveau's social identity and station at the top; he signed his own name at the bottom. The paperwork, more secular than sacred, has long since vanished.

The forty-four cemeteries of New Orleans lend themselves to mystery, ghost stories, and occult tourism. Local citizens call them the "cities of the dead." First-time visitors receive a surreal shock—ancient ruins, marble monuments, and tall crypts celebrate death and refuse to sterilize, deny, or make it merely a medical fact. Against the skyline, angels, crosses, and statues of grieving mothers make the auras of decomposition exquisite. Mile after mile of tombs resemble houses, small mansions, or places of worship—neighborhoods where another branch of the family lives. Many are architectural masterpieces, worthy to be the final resting place of kings and queens. Death-bound real estate was sometimes the most valuable property the inhabitants of the city owned, all that is left of them.

The founding fathers of New Orleans picked an unsound site for their new town, a swamp with poor drainage and a high water table wedged between a mighty river and an unstable lake. Below them, as far as the imagination reaches, there is only the mud that residents called *gumbo*. When the first townspeople dug graves, heavy rains floated corpses to the surface, and caskets popped up with loud sucking sounds. Gases from the decomposition of bodies blew off heavy marble slabs. Cemeteries were places less of rest than of restless tectonic activity.

The Creole citizens of New Orleans came to be infatuated with tales of open graves, gruesome deaths, and skeletons or ghosts who led independent lives along the avenues of the cities of the dead. They stopped digging holes for burials below the fluid surface and began to erect tombs above the ground. Burial and benevolent societies based on ethnicity or other shared social histories built massive communal tombs for their members; they guaranteed the living a place of death with their own kind. New Orleanians also built high, wide walls around and within the cemeteries and partitioned them into stacked rows of crypts—layer upon layer, hundreds of single tombs they called "oven vaults" because they resembled bakers' ovens. A sealed casket in the southern summer is subjected to hundreds of degrees of heat, so decomposition was rapid. New generations of tenants rented the oven vaults like apartments rather than owned them. After a year, when the previous inhabitant no longer needed as much room, new renters slipped in feet first.

Marie and Christophe built a third kind, a "high tomb" of whitewashed plaster over soft red bricks. Their pitched-roof dwelling has three closure tablets or marble-fronted openings, a border, corner design, and a carved cross. When someone in the family died, the custodian of the cemetery removed the marble plaque mortared or screwed on the face of the tomb, and broke through the brick or stucco layer. He removed and burned whatever casket pieces were left from prior burials. Other remains were pushed to the back and fell down into the cavity on the floor of the tomb.

One rule applied to every type of tomb: a casket must remain walled up for a year and a day before the crypt was reopened—minimum time for an adult body to decompose. If this sounds too short a period, bear in mind the subtropical climate, the flimsy nature of caskets, and the circulation of air still possible in the aboveground tombs. Moreover, Catholics in the nineteenth-century city did not embalm or cremate; they seldom used undertakers or filed death certificates. The inscriptions on the fronts of tombs do not always match the documents or the occupants. Many people lie buried with no epitaph or records to mark their passing. Many tomb markers have been weathered or spirited away. Carved in stone may well mean written in water.

Creoles paid regular social visits to the cities of the dead; some came every day, most once a week or once a month. They sat on the benches that lined the shell paths; sweet olive trees scented the air and masked the smells. Homage to ancestors and their dear departed peaked on November 1, the Feast of All Saints or the Day of the Dead. The day before—October 31 is All Hallows' Eve or Halloween—men, women, and children carried buckets of whitewash, scrub brushes, lye soap, paint, and gardening tools to the cemeteries. The cities of the dead stayed open until late in the evening so families could clean up and decorate before the morning. Candles filled the cemeteries with light. Then, in the early morning hours of the first day of November, families like those in the Laveau-Paris-Glapion household made the rounds of the cemeteries and greeted their loved ones.

Outside the cemetery walls, on Halloween and All Saints' Day, the market women sold pralines, peanuts, rice cakes, sausages, bread, and treats for children, such as skeletons on a stick, miniature coffins, or skull-shaped candy. Nuns raised money at the cemeteries' gates for orphans whose tin pans or cowbells attracted the public's attention. Relatives arranged offerings at their family tombs—gumbo, coffee, sweet potato pie, or canned goods. They draped rosaries and placed decorated crosses or holy statues on the tombs. They placed flowers, tissue paper or silk, seasonal ones in bloom. Today, their descendants bring potted plants and plastic flowers.

Creole mourners like the Marie Laveaus owed their observances at the Feast of All Saints on November 1 and All Souls' Day the following day to Africa and to France. In Mediterranean countries and in their New World colonies, Catholic families gathered and recited the rosary at the graves of their dead. Creoles in New Orleans, like Christians everywhere, placed resurrection and reunion beyond the grave at the center of their creeds. In West Africa, a person aspired not to be resurrected but to spend eternal life as an honored ancestor. Throughout the Diaspora, Africans brought rich religions of ancestor worship to Louisiana; a wealth of rituals and memorials honored the spirits of the dead—ancestors who remained part of the lineages of the living. Their survivors sought spiritual favors from them and made plans to join their ranks. In central Africa, Christians in the Kingdom of Kongo placed lighted candles in a circle around the graves of their loved ones and said the rosary on the first day of November. They erected altars in public squares and made offerings of chickens, pigs, rice, cloth, and tobacco in front of them. Then they formed a great candlelit procession that fanned out to the cemeteries—each family going to the place where its own ancestors were buried. Like many Africans, they wore the color white, which symbolized the Other World, that of spirits and ancestors. "Black was the color of the living"—the color of This World. Small wonder that the Feast of All Saints became the highest and holiest day of New Orleans Voodoo.

In 1845, the year of Archange's death, public dances had resumed in Congo Square just before St. John's Eve, the Voodoo's midsummer celebration on June 23. It is unlikely, however, that either of the Laveau women was there to celebrate. Both were in full mourning for the death of a son and a brother in January. Marie the Second was pregnant with and then nursing an infant that year, a little girl whom she named Aldina. And in May 1845, her first-born son died.

Five months after they buried Archange, just as the sweet olive trees blossomed in the cemetery, the members of the Laveau-Paris-Glapion household—accompanied this time by members of the Crocker family—made another sad procession to St. Louis One. Joseph Eugene Crocker, just a toddler, the son of Marie Eucharist and Pierre Crocker, was the second person buried in his grandmother's high tomb. His burial violated the "one year and a day" rule. But the boys' bodies were small and the household prominent and persuasive enough that the custodian of the cemetery waived the rule.

The family hired a stonecutter to engrave the children's names on the middle of the three marble-covered bays. Then, in an act of grief and commemoration unusual for landowners in the city of the dead, they commissioned a second plaque and placed it on the ground in front of the tomb. The grieving family left the boys' favorite desserts on their stone at the Feast of All Saints that year. Today the constant wear of tourists traipsing across the marker has made it difficult to read. In translation from French, it says: "Archange Glapion died in January, 1845, age seven years, seven months. Joseph Eugene C. died in May 1845, age fourteen months."

Marie and Christophe lost their infant daughter, Marie Louise Caroline, born in the late summer of 1829, baptized on her mother's birthday in

September, before Christmas that same year. Then in 1834 their first-born son, François Auguste, named for the émigré from St. Domingue-Haiti who married Marie the First's wilder half-sister, Marie Laveaux Auguste, died just short of his first birthday. The Widow Paris and her husband, Christophe Glapion, raised two children out of five to adulthood—Marie Eucharist and Philomène. In January of 1850, five years after Archange's and Joseph's deaths, Marie the Second buried her infant daughter, Esmeralda. From age sixteen to age twenty-six, Marie the Second bore at least four children and buried two of them. Her sister Philomène buried two infants out of the five she carried to term. The household on St. Ann sent half of its children to live in the cities of the dead. They were not alone.

In New Orleans, one out of every two children died before their first birthday. The 50 percent infant mortality rate was one of highest in the world, and these figures fail to count miscarriages or stillbirths; only the women themselves kept those grim statistics. The loss of children is the primal embodied suffering, the most intimate and ultimate link of women to the spirits. Women's religions across the planet evolve from the intense interplay of maternal life and child loss. Some women are barren or their pregnancies do not take hold in their bodies. Many babies are born too poorly tied to life to remain. Some children run away, are taken into other's custody, are sold into slavery or pass for white; there are many ways to lose one's children.

It is not that women "escape" into religion when their children die or are otherwise lost to them. It is that the crucible of grief forges a new awareness, an altered state of consciousness about life. Parents, especially mothers, want contact with their dead children; trances, prayers, or spirit possessions comfort them. Some women become mediums or begin other kinds of spiritual ministries. Pregnancy is like spirit possession—an intimate, incarnated, and encompassing connection with a creature not oneself. Spirits, babies, or men inhabit, enter, or use women's bodies for a time. Spirit possession, like pregnancy, is an act of courage—"the willingness to interact with one's deities face to face . . . From the point of view of the audience, the possessed individual *is* the deity. Deities are seen to be physically present on earth, and seen to look like—to wear the bodies of—women." The visits of spirits, like an easy pregnancy, a safe delivery, and a healthy baby who outlived its parents, were gifts that offset other tragedies and traumas.

New Orleans Voodoo, as the Laveaus practiced it, is one of many women's religions on the planet. It belongs with the American Shakers, Christian Science, the nineteenth-century Spiritualism Movement, and the twentieth-century Feminist Spirituality Movement—to name a few. In Latin America and the Caribbean, women-centered religions sprang up wherever the African Diaspora crossed paths with the pageantry of the Catholic Church. Women's religions are not set apart from the world's larger and better-known religions; they are an organic parallel, a female counterpart, a way to acknowledge women's experiences and losses.

A Laveau prayer from Zora Neale Hurston's collection speaks to these burdens. "Oh my daughter, I have painfully heard your prayer and I say unto you . . . the love of the Mother is eternal, while the love of the lover is passing and the love of the friend is changing and quickly forgotten. Be you of good cheer and stout heart, for the help of the Man God is with you and the help of all the good spirits and the great angels is for you. And they shall see that you fail not in your undertaking. So Be It."

In addition to the staggering child mortality rate, the frequent epidemics that gripped the city helped populate the cities of the dead with new residents. Between 1837 and 1843, four epidemics swept away 1,500 to 2,000 persons each; another epidemic in 1847 killed 2,700. Then the summer of 1853 turned New Orleans into a hospital and an open grave. Forty thousand people fell ill from yellow fever—forty percent of the summer population of the city. One out of ten died. The "saffron scourge" or Bronze John, as some called it, carried off entire families and city blocks. The largest, deadliest epidemic in America's history was the last installment in the Widow Paris's career as a public health and fever nurse. The *Louisiana Courier* told the truth in 1839—get out of town for the summer or hire a skilled fever nurse like her.

Sanitary measures in New Orleans were primitive at best. When the gutters flowed at all, they filled with human excrement. No one removed trash or the dead bodies of dogs from the streets. The already spongy ground was pitted with holes where stagnant water accumulated in the summer rains and made warm homes for mosquito eggs. City fathers blamed "bad air"; they were equally suspicious of outsiders, immigrants, and the Voodoos. Physicians falsified death certificates, and newspapers conspired to hide the facts of the looming plague until people fell down and died on busy French Quarter streets.

The only people in New Orleans who coupled common sense with competence were the fever nurses of Marie the First's generation and a group of privileged, young white men who called themselves the Howard Association. Like the Red Cross, the Howards gave food, medicine, money, and assistance in civic disasters. The men grounded their home-based medical care and neighborhood public health campaigns on the experienced nurses and nursemaids of color who had raised them and attended their families through multiple illnesses and deaths.

As the yellow fever epidemic grew in the summer of 1853, the Howards made these women of color the backbone of community healing and help. Philomène said of her mother, "A committee of gentlemen, appointed at a mass meeting held at Globe Hall, waited on Marie and requested her on behalf of the people to minister to the fever stricken. She went out and fought the pestilence where it was thickest and many alive today own their salvation to her devotion." A national news magazine reported that the entire population of New Orleans "stood to their duties, to the call of affection, of friendship, of humanity. *The delicate forms of females, spirit like, flitted in every direction.* Where in history can you find a more noble display of courage, fortitude, humanity, and true nobility of soul?"

Parson Clapp—that was his true name—had stayed in New Orleans through the worst summers, buried his own daughters by himself, and wrote a journal of the plague times in the city. A good friend summoned the Protestant minister at the height of the epidemic.

"Yellow Jack will never take me with him," he bragged.

But three days later, Parson Clapp's friend vomited black blood in such sickening quantities that death was inevitable. The man could not draw breath, and his legs and arms were cold in the summer heat; his doctor gave up hope of recovery.

Then a woman—"an old French nurse in the room, who had spent her days in taking care of the sick, and was familiar with the Creole mode of treating the yellow fever"—spoke to the two men. "If you will allow me, I think I can cure this gentleman."

"She called for *ptisans* [herbal teas], spirits, warm water, and various other remedies. We commenced rubbing his body all over, and using every possible means to excite perspiration. In less than two hours, he began to grow warm; the vomit ceased. He is still living, and enjoys good health."

August in New Orleans is an unspeakable month even with air-conditioning. But in 1853 the mayor ordered cannons fired at sunrise and sunset to scare away the pestilence. Barrels of tar burned at street corners. Green bottle-flies swarmed on swollen corpses—a banquet of death in the cities of the dead. Newcomers who did not understand local customs tried to bury their dead below the ground; heavy rains floated the corpses of friends and family members to the surface. The coffin wagons, too full to carry more bodies, dumped their loads into plague pits near the gates of cemeteries. By the second week of August, burials averaged two hundred corpses per day, especially in the cemeteries to which the poor were taken. The city ran out of coffins. Even the grave diggers became ill. Only the mosquitoes prospered.

And still it poured. The *Picayune* said on August 8, "It has rained, rained, rained, day after day, and day after day for so long that our memory hardly runneth to the contrary." That same day, the *Delta* noted how shallow the graves had become—a foot and half to two feet deep with only a few inches of dirt on top. Both newspapers were clear—nurses and grave diggers were the most critical people in the city.

∼

At the peak of the epidemic and her mother's community health-care duties, Marie the Second was at home on St. Ann Street in the last trimester of her last pregnancy. As the epidemic waned and the death toll dwindled, she gave birth to Victor Pierre Christophe Duminy Dieudonné de Glapion, also known as Victor Pierre "Peter" Crocker. Later that winter, when the city had returned to its glittering round of balls and amusements, Marie the Second summoned a priest to baptize her newborn son. Her younger sister, Philomène, age eighteen, stood as godmother to her nephew. With Archange, Joseph, and so many other children held in memory, Marie the Second added a blessing and a word of gratitude to her son's name. *Dieudonné* means the gift of God.

〜

Through the spring of 1855, Christophe Glapion lay in the high walnut bed, sick and weak. From the few hints left in legal documents we can form a simple portrait of his dying days. His wife and daughters cooked for him— stewed chicken with rice and bread pudding topped with a special rum sauce were favorites of Creole cooks. Pierre Crocker dropped by every day to visit his old friend, see his children, Victor Pierre and Aldina, and perhaps plan a time when he and Marie Eucharist could slip away from her practice and sickbed duties. Pierre Cazenave, an undertaker and the richest Creole of color in New Orleans, had some joint business dealings with Christophe; when he came to St. Ann he could have brought *calas*, steamed rice cakes purchased from one of the market women on Rampart Street. Christophe's sisters and his brothers-in-law were concerned; they and other Creoles in their social circles dropped by to see him. In the New Orleans manner family members and friends brought food and left cash—the amounts did not matter, but the circle of reciprocity did, and Christophe and Marie's generosities were well-known.

On June 26, 1855, Christophe Duminy de Glapion, sixty-six years old, died at home. A brief announcement in the *Times* the next day invited friends and acquaintances to St. Ann Street at five o'clock for funeral services and a twilight walk to St. Louis Cemetery One.

But Christophe's protective plots on behalf of his family did not stop with his death. At some point before the end, he and Pierre Crocker made a plan. Judging from the documents still available, Christophe asked his son-in-law and friend to take care of the paperwork, keeping the name *Marie Laveau* out of all written records. Make certain that no one concocted any Voodoo scandals against them and that the laws about people of color that the state legislature had recently passed did not hurt the family on St. Ann, Christophe must have begged. On June 29, Pierre Crocker went to the Office of the Recorder of Births and Deaths to carry out the first stage of their agreement. In New Orleans, a person who witnessed a death swore an oath that it took place as stated, that the deceased was who he claimed to be, and that no one had broken any laws. Crocker signed such a statement for his father-in-law—swore in writing that he himself had attended the deceased through his final days and hours, swore that Glapion was not married, and that he lived on St. Ann Street. Then Pierre Crocker, a free man of color, looked the Recorder in the eyes and swore that Christophe Glapion died a free man of color.

At the bottom of the certificate, the Recorder of Births and Deaths, who accepted Pierre's testimony on everything else, had no sympathy for Christophe's racial miracle. He left handwritten instructions to his clerk: FILE IN THE WHITE PERSONS FOLIO.

Christophe Glapion, listed as a bachelor and restored to his original race, left no will. The St. Ann house was in Philomène's name; the Love Street property in Marie Eucharist's. Yet within days of Christophe's burial, three men—the undertaker, another Creole businessman, and his brother-in-law—petitioned a judge to appoint one of them as executor of Christophe's nonexistent estate. They agreed there was no money, then made extravagant claims about their specific ties to the deceased and the rights owed them on the poor man's account. Their insistence may have distracted the judge from asking questions; he appointed the white businessman—Monsieur Pierre Biron, Esquire—as executor.

Biron, one of the visitors at Christophe's bedside, was also part of the plot. The final accounting that he submitted to the court later that summer said that the deceased man left only $294.60 after the funeral expenses and a few legal debts were paid. And, by the way, he added, "There is some old wearing apparel unencumbered in this matter and belonging to the deceased which are in possession of an old woman who always attended on the deceased during his sickness." Selling these old clothes, Biron claimed, would be more trouble than they were worth—only "about $71." Pay off the deceased man's nurse with them, he concluded.

If we trust the written and notarized legal documents, Christophe Glapion, a white bachelor, left less than three hundred dollars and some used clothing when he died. An old woman, his black servant, nursed him during his final illness and took the clothes as payment for her services. Other money matters and potential problems emerged in the period after Christophe's death; extensive, complicated paperwork reveals suits and countersuits about business matters he had not had the opportunity to complete. Yet nothing in the documents noted that Christophe's wife and oldest daughter were at the peak of their careers as master manipulators of the justice system. Not a word was said about the army of saints who handled legal matters for citizens who paid them proper spiritual respect. At each turn of the wheels of justice, however, the verdicts of the courts favored the St. Ann Street household and brought some cash settlements to the women Christophe schemed to protect.

The Creole way of death lent itself to Voodoo accusations. In nineteenth-century New Orleans most people died at home. Their family made burial arrangements; someone put a notice in the paper or went before a notary and swore that the deceased died in a natural manner. No wonder people believed that the Voodoos knew how to kill people or make them disappear—with no legal consequences. A person could get away with murder as easily as he or she concealed illegal love or signed false statements in sworn public documents.

Despite persistent rumors that the couple had amassed significant wealth, the archives contain no such evidence. Christophe Glapion's military pension and whatever business dealings he had ended with his death in 1855; we see the life of Christophe Glapion chiefly through his wife and daughters. In one of Marie Laveau's prayers, a man has come to the priestess with the age-old question even the best of fathers ask—what can I do to earn my children's respect, to win their love? The Good Mother speaks: "You will write your children a loving letter and sprinkle some of this *Essence of Do As You Please* onto the letter and all over the four corners of the letter, and send it to them so that it will get into their hands as they open it. For no matter what they may do or say against you, still it is your duty to love and protect them even unto the last day of your life. So Be It."

〜

Marie Laveau, the Widow Paris, age fifty-four at her husband's death, conducted her life as, but never called herself, the "Widow Glapion." Marie the Second was twenty-eight years old when her father died, thirty years old when Pierre Crocker—still married to Rose—died two years later at age fifty-four. His will indicated that he departed the world with far more assets than his father-in-law had but revealed no gifts to his mistress or to their children. Pierre lies in St. Louis Cemetery Two, and no other man, lover, or husband, has ever been linked romantically to the last Voodoo queen. Through the 1850s, in the period that brackets Christophe Glapion's and Pierre Crocker's deaths, Marie the Second, single mother and head of household, lived on Love Street. Despite her strong, even flamboyant personality, Marie the Second craved privacy, a limited commodity in the crowded household on St. Ann. She had managed to conceal her private life—her married lover and their children—from public view in her own time and, later, from journalists and researchers, and she tried to hide her professional activities the same way, albeit with less success.

Philomène was twenty when her father died. To those of us who wish to understand her apart from her infamous mother and older sister, she left only one clue about the texture and goals of her own life. Each time she talked to reporters, she called herself "Madame Legendre."

George Legendre was a clerk for the Union Bank; he listed St. Ann as his home address and himself as head of household and husband of Philomène beginning in 1855, the year Christophe died. An assortment of his brothers and cousins moved into the Laveau-Glapion household and lived there until after the Civil War. Many families took in boarders to make ends meet during and after the grueling wartime occupation when housing was scarce. Young males—then as now—moved in with relatives until they were established and could afford housing on their own. George and his male relatives paid rent and contributed in other ways.

Philomène gave birth to five babies to whom she gave the Legendre name. She buried two infants in her parents' high tomb in St. Louis Cemetery One—Eugenie Legendre in January 1866, one month old, and Joseph Legendre in February 1870, also one month old. No inscription to these children, if it ever existed, remains visible. Marie Philomène Glapion called herself Madame Legendre in the city directories and to *Picayune* reporters. Neighbors called her Madame Legendre. Her death certificate says that she was a Legendre. But the carved epitaph for Philomène on her mother's high tomb in St. Louis Cemetery One tells a different story. It says in French, and I translate: "Marie Philome Glapion died on the eleventh of June, 1897, age 62 years. She was a good mother, a good friend, and missed by all who knew her. Those who pass pray for her."

Some people see "Marie" and "Glapion" and assume that the Voodoo queen herself died in 1897; but this is the marker Philomène's children placed for their mother—the truth of their birth hidden in plain sight. Philomène Glapion and George Legendre were never husband and wife. George was white. Philomène had inherited the family curse; she loved a man she could never marry. The situation must have been difficult for George too; Eliza Potter, the Creole hairdresser, might have been speaking of Philomène and George Legendre—or of Marie and Christophe: "I knew a gentleman who was cashier to one of the largest banks in New Orleans who married a colored woman. He got a physician to transfer some of her blood into his veins and then went to the court and swore he had colored blood in him."

Neighbors who knew the Laveau-Glapion family on St. Ann often mentioned Philomène Legendre to the Federal Writers' Project. "Mrs. Legendre, I remember her well," said one. "She was Marie Laveau's daughter, Blair Legendre's mother. His father was a white man." Someone else claimed that some members of the Laveau-Paris-Glapion household did what many of their own loved ones had done: "Yeah, her daughters was good-looking girls. I think one of them passed for white." Another neighbor knew Marie the Second well, "I saw her every day. I was young but nobody could ever forget her once they saw her." She had also followed the fortunes of Philomène Legendre's grown children. "The family is friendly and nice but they disown any kin to Marie. They pass for white and will have nothing to do with colored people. They want to keep their secret.*" Someone in the Federal Writers' Project added the asterisk—their professional investment in protecting white people's racial secrets: "*These people have definitely crossed the color line; it might be well to omit names in this part but they are included to emphasize the fact that Marie Laveau's descendants are now passing for white."

The grandchildren of the Widow Paris and Christophe Glapion— Philomène's and George's children—passed for white as many people of color in New Orleans have. New Orleanians with one or more African ancestors still recite the litany of lost community members, kinfolk, and neighbors, sometimes entire families, whom they know moved into the white world; they say it is more difficult to visit them there than it is to contact relatives and friends in the cities of the dead. Passing mirrors the terrible losses of slavery times when loved ones escaped or were sold down the river, never to be seen again. There are many ways to bury a person forever in a city of the passed.

# Chapter 8

## At the Altar of Love and Luck

"WAS MARIE THE SECOND AS GREAT AS PEOPLE SAID SHE WAS?" ZORA ASKED.

"BETTER." LUKE SIGHED. "EVEN QUEEN VICTORIA ASK HER FOR

HELP AND SEND HER A CASHMERE SHAWL."

On Monday evenings, Marie the Second sneaked back into Congo Square. On one side a live oak stood, the queen of New Orleans' trees, a tree whose leaves remained green despite harsh summers and balmy winters. The branches of the ancient tree swooped to the ground. Children walked up them high into its heart, and two grown men could stand inside its hollow core at the same time. On the ground in front of the tree Marie spread a white tablecloth. She lit a candle in each corner, and placed statues in the middle—St. Peter the Protector and St. Maroon, the patron saint of runaways and others who break bad laws.

Marie's friends brought food—a goat they had slaughtered and cooked, fried chicken, red beans and rice, jambalaya, gumbo, candy for the children, bright and expensive fruit like apples or oranges, and good things to drink. They sang, danced, and ate, and then danced some more. The authorities never tried to stop them. When the dancers finished, they put the leftovers in the hollow of the tree and placed money beside the plates, coins in the amount of fifteen cents, either three nickels or a dime and a nickel. *Faith-Hope-Charity; Father, Son, and Holy Ghost,* they chanted as they left.

The next morning children came to Congo Square to search for candy and nickels. An old black man, who as a child had spied on Marie when she danced and who looked for treats beneath the Wishing Tree, said,

"There was a big hollow tree in the square where everybody that believed in Marie Laveau would come and put money—fifteen cents—and liquor and jambalaya. We used to sneak there and take the money and drink the liquor. We left the jambalaya." Others who needed a square meal—no questions asked—took the food. One man who attended Marie's Monday evenings in Congo Square said, "Whenever there was food placed in the tree somebody would always take it. Nobody ever put anything in there that would harm anyone. It was their way of paying for the square and a way to help somebody who needed help."

White citizens of New Orleans spread many rumors about the hollow tree and the dancing of the Voodoos in Congo Square; their accusing accounts persisted in the decades and century beyond the priestesses' deaths. Newspaper reporters who had never attended the gatherings repeated the gossip, assuming that Marie's malice and lurid magic, not her brand of Creole benevolence, were at work in the old plaza. "No more dramatic spot could have been chosen by these wizards and witches for their nocturnal rites. The square itself is odorous of romance, of duels, and abductions and of undiscovered deaths. A stone's throw away are the hoary walls of Parish Prison. Behind it the holy walls of the venerable French Cathedral."

Years ago, the *Times-Democrat* said in 1891, "when the voodoos were a power among the ignorant and superstitious denizens of the slums contiguous to Congo Square" they entered at night and "when the moon shines through the rain" prepared the "haunted voudoo tree for their fetish dances":

> In its hollow were deposited the feet of toads, the heads of chickens, the preserved toes of dead Negroes, and a great steaming tin bowl of stew compounded of various disgusting and unsavory articles. The individual to be charmed was stood in the hollow tree, the voudoo queen sat down in front of him, her oldest hag beat upon a tankard, and the rest of the crew joined hands and danced with the most horrible contortions of face and body around the enchanted tree. The person to be charmed placed beneath the bowl of stew the money which he owed the witches for their enchantment.

Yes, said an eighty-year-old black woman, I was at the Voodoo potluck parties they had in Congo Square on Monday nights, "and the dancers were like savages, like you see in pictures and read about. They used to put tablecloths on the ground and had great bowls of gumbo and chickens and cake and wine and nickels all around." I knew Marie the Second—nice white ladies used to go to her dances, and they consulted and confided in that woman. I knew her, the woman repeated, but I never respected her.

Young Marie had never intended to join her mother's spiritual craft, never aspired to be a priestess of Voodoo. She liked parties; she loved the attention men paid to her striking good looks. She danced the *Bamboula* and the *Calinda* in Congo Square on Sunday afternoons—the sheer joy of rhythm and movement was her Creole birthright—but nothing shifted in her soul. Yet each time she ran into Jim Alexander, a Voodoo practitioner and respected two-headed doctor of Hoodoo, he confronted her; he told her that she radiated power. He offered to initiate her, to be her mentor, to take her through the door to the spirits. She turned him down time after time, because, as Luke Turner told Zora Neale Hurston, "Marie, she would rather dance and make love." One night, however, "a great rattlesnake"—Luke's own phrase—entered her bedroom and spoke to her.

Just as pregnancy and death transform social relationships, initiations or "openings," as the Voodoo of New Orleans called them, recast one's spiritual alignments. After the visit of the serpent, Marie the Second went to Dr. Jim Alexander and asked him to reveal the sacred space of spirits and saints to her. He shepherded her through initiation and an apprenticeship with the spirits who had chosen her for their own until she could serve them herself. St. John the Baptist, High John the Conqueror, Lightning, Thunder, and the great Rattlesnake remained at her side until the hour of their deaths, physical or spiritual. After her own initiations at the hands of Dr. Jim, she unlocked the passage for Luke Turner, her grand-nephew.

Open the door to the spirit world of New Orleans to me the way Marie did for you, Zora begged. But Luke refused. The city has passed strict laws against fortune-tellers, he claimed. The police are arresting us and forcing us to move to Algiers—an exile for city-dwellers across the Mississippi River. When she pestered him again, he named an impossible price. Finally, she found the key that unlocked his stubborn refusals. Enlighten my ignorance, she pleaded—what was Marie Laveau like?

Luke spoke quietly as though Zora were not present, as though his memories alone had called Marie back to life. "Turner again made that gesture with his hands that meant the end. Then he sat in dazed silence. After a long period of waiting I rose to go. 'The Spirit say you come back tomorrow,' he breathed as I passed his knees. . . . The next day he began to prepare me for my initiation ceremony, for rest assured that no one may approach the Altar without the crown, and none may wear the crown of power without preparation. *It must be earned.*"

For nine days Zora performed ritual cleansing. "This prepared period is akin to that of all mystics. Clean living, even to clean thoughts. A sort of going to the wilderness in the spirit. The details do not matter." The young anthropologist meditated; she assembled snakeskins and new underwear. Then for three days she lay on the skins in front of Luke Turner's altar, fasting and silent—"while my spirit went wherever spirits must go that seek answers . . . for sixty-nine hours I lay there. I had five psychic experiences and awoke at last with no feeling of hunger, only one of exaltation." When she rose from three days and nights of deep trance, Luke and five other men stood before an altar they had constructed and talked with the spirits there that night, relaying instructions to the newly born initiate. Come to us, the spirits spoke through the men.

| | |
|---|---|
| Zora: | "How must I come?" |
| Luke: | "You must come to the spirit across running water." |
| Brothers: | "She has crossed the dangerous stream in search of the spirit. What is she called?" |
| Luke: | "I see her with the lightning and with thunder. She shall be called the Rain-Bringer. Do you hear me, Spirit. Will you take her. She is worthy." |

When the spirit had consented to Zora's admission, Luke Turner and the brothers painted a red and yellow lighting bolt down her back from right shoulder to left hip. They drew a pair of eyes on her cheeks and a sun on her forehead. This part of the initiation ritual, like so much in the life of Marie the Second, was about water and the flow of spirits, babies, and history through a woman's body.

When the men had dressed and veiled Zora, they cut the little finger of her right hand and caught the gushing blood in a cup. They added wine and their own blood; each drank from the cup. The ritual drama turned into a ritual feast. Zora, who had not eaten for days, sat at a splendid altar. In the center rested one large candle stenciled with her name, thirty-six yellow candles, a bottle of holy water, and six bouquets of flowers—two yellow, two red, and two white. Around the edges of the table rested five cakes iced in different colors, St. Joseph's bread with honey, breads in the shape of serpents, fried okra, and spinach pies.

The last part of Zora's initiation took place at midnight near Lake Pontchartrain on St. Joseph's night, March 19, 1929. Luke, Zora, and the brothers made a broom, and placed four lighted candles in the corners of a clearing. As Luke Turner sang, Zora wrote her petition to the spirits on nine sheets of white paper. A man led a dazed sheep into the clearing. In places where animal sacrifices are sacred, animals are fed, cleaned, cared for, and killed in compassion and respect. Those who end their lives thank them and send their souls to a good place. Then the community cooks and eats the meat in the feast that follows. Little is wasted—organs like hearts or livers may be used for healing rituals, skins may be made into drumheads such as those played in Congo Square. Those who follow these ancient customs say that the life force and blood of animals allow spirits to reveal themselves, to carry messages to other spheres, and blessings to return.

Turner's chants grew louder and more urgent; the men stroked the animal. "A knife flashed and the sheep dropped to its knees, then fell prone with its mouth open in a weak cry. My petition was thrust into its throat that he might cry to the Great One. The broom was seized and dipped in the blood from the slit throat and the ground swept vigorously—back and forth, back and forth—the length of the dying sheep. The sweeping went on as long as the blood gushed. Earth, the mother of the Great One and us all, had been appeased."

When they buried the sheep and the petitions, Luke Turner and Zora Neale Hurston lit a white candle on the sheep's grave and returned to the city. Afterward, Zora wrote about her initiation into the spiritual lineage of

Marie Laveau the Second; her academic colleagues filed it under "Negro superstitions."

Marie the Second became, by the standards of later times, a counselor, therapist, and social worker. Born well into the American national period, she spoke English as a second language. She was as good a Catholic as the church of her time permitted a woman of color and an unwed mother in love with a married man to be. The reluctant princess became the bridge between her mother's French Creole brand of Voodoo and the Hoodoo that southern blacks brought to New Orleans. Just as the St. Domingue refugees and exiles brought an infusion of French Creole spiritualism into the city after 1809, African Americans from the rural South brought their Hoodoo imagination and poetic dialects into the city before the Civil War. Southern Hoodoo and Creole Voodoo merged like two great rivers and flowed through the city; their union may have been Marie the Second's transcendent gift to New Orleans and the reason why scholars cannot easily sort out the fluctuations between the waves.

∿

Every Friday evening, Marie the Second presided over Voodoo services at St. Ann Street. The sisterhoods never had a church or sanctuary in which initiates and spiritual seekers could meet. But numerous New Orleanians, Creole and Anglo, rich and poor, attended services in Marie's yard or at her altars. As they entered her house with small offerings for the night's ritual, they took off their shoes. Before she escorted them to her altar, she scrutinized each one. She "never allowed you to enter her house with anything crossed. Once I went to her house with a man who had two pins crossed inside his coat. As soon as he entered, Marie Laveau said, 'Uncross those pins before I can do anything for you.'"

The altars of Marie the Second at the St. Ann Street house spilled over with the furnishings of her spiritual life. There were statues of St. Anthony, St. John the Baptist, St. Peter, St. Michael, and others as the liturgical calendar or the occasion demanded—a balance of spiritual forces and intentions.

Incense, rosaries, feathers, silk sashes, and ashes from the rituals performed in honor of Spirit stood on cloths in white or bright colors beside "power points" or articles that concentrate magical powers—mirrors, gold bells, a gourd rattle, a piece of brick from the cemetery, carved pieces of wood, an unusual stone, or objects with no apparent meaning. To honor the Dead, she placed white candles, a glass of water, shoes, toys and clothing her dead children had touched, or mourning jewelry made from the hair of the deceased. Marie remembered the Ancestors with a favorite food or wine, perfume, flowers, candy, and objects they had once loved or that carried the essence and memory of them.

Altars have a life and a language of their own. They speak of abundance and pay homage to the richness of sacred space. Through them people who do not often read books or write down their prayers build a visible conversation with the spirits. If Marie the Second or a client with whom she worked received an official letter from City Hall about taxes, for example, she placed it on the altar to help them solve their problems. *Gris-gris* ingredients for making *hands*—amulets or medicine bags—were on or close to the altar, materials such as salt, brown sugar, iron filings, arrow root, spices, or pieces of High John the Conqueror root. She had bowls of sweet basil, camphor leaves, cinnamon, cloves, mustard, birdseed, and bottles of Red Drink, a favorite New Orleans soda. There were always painted jars, a jewel-color flask filled with water from the ocean, a half pint of gin, and bundles wrapped in red flannel. People whom Marie the Second helped brought her gifts for her altar—plaster statues, blessed water, a sharp knife, or Mardi Gras favors. The altar lived and breathed in the light of its candles, although one woman mumbled, Marie "used to have so many candles burning in her house, that I don't know why it didn't catch on fire."

The Friday evening gatherings began with rapping or thumping to call the spirits, then the invocation to the storms that were Marie the Second's spiritual signature. "Before the meeting, Marie Laveau would thump her feet." She told one man, "don't be scared, he is not going to hurt you, but when he comes it will be with lightning and thunder." Her reassurance did not comfort him. "And I saw the lightning go through the room. I was so scared."

Sometimes the rituals spilled into the fenced back yard. One man peeked over the fence and saw "a white sheet was spread out on the ground, and lighted candles was stuck up all around the edge of it. All the dancers, men and women, was naked. The first thing they did was to dance around the sheet wit' bottles of whiskey and rum in their hands, sprinkling the sheet with liquor and throwing it on each other. Then they would begin crossin' hands from one side to the other, and all the time singin' them Creole songs. Marie Laveau used to stand in the middle, and she was the only one wit' clothes on. She would tell the dancers what to do and holler all kinds of funny things. Sometimes she'd take a mouthful of whiskey and blow it in somebody's face."

Naked or not, Marie the Second usually wore a blue dress with a full skirt, a *tignon* with seven points, gold hoop earrings, and big gold bracelets. Another man who attended the Friday evenings said, "Marie would call the men to dance with her from time to time. I have seen those men turn the women over like a top. The men had large handkerchiefs that they could put around the women's waist and would they shake. The meeting lasted from seven to nine and they would have things to eat and drink." At the end of the Friday evening services, Marie the Second gave those present a Voodoo bene-diction and blessing. Everyone extended his or her left hand. Marie rubbed some liquid into their palms, "and when you left you surely had the belief."

∿

Between the Congo Square dances on Monday and the evening services on Friday, Marie the Second accepted appointments with clients at her altar on St. Ann Street. One woman in town had heard that Marie the Second "fixed" bosses, husbands who strayed, and landlords. On the day before her belongings were to be thrown onto the filthy sidewalk, she knocked at the priestess's door. "I have been ill and cannot work. I cannot face my landlord," the visitor confided to the priestess-counselor. Marie the Second escorted her into the room with the altar she used for personal work. Then Marie placed the coins the woman brought on the richly decorated altar along with gifts of flowers, cigarettes or cigars, food, candy, and wine or other liquors the spirits liked. She lit candles and began her prayers to the Good Mother. As she presented the sufferings of her client, she asked for guidance. Her identity or ego, her selfhood, slipped away, and the two—the divine feminine and the earthly priestess—merged into one. Merger is another form of spirit possession, perhaps less dramatic in its manifestations, but equally rich in wisdom. At that moment, Marie was not in her ordinary-reality single head; she was double-headed. She was "not a woman when she answer the one who ask. No. She is a god, yes. Whatever she say, it will come so."

The Good Mother spoke to the woman through the voice or medium of Marie the Second: "Lay your burden at the feet of the God of Peace and Plenty." Tell your landlord about your sickness and your troubles until the God of Pity and Compassion dwells in his breast. Rub your sleeves and blouse with yellow duck and snake root and with Bend-Over Oil. Pray to the God of Pity, "I bind myself and truly promise that each night for nine nights, as the stars rise in the heavens, I will burn a white candle of peace to your memory and for thanks at the goodness received from your hands." When you burn the white candle, the spirit told Marie's client, put the name of your landlord under your own name on a strip of the most expensive paper you can find. Place it so the wax of the candle will flow on it and watch until hot wax consumes the paper. "O, my daughter, go in peace and abide in plenty. So Be It."

Another time a man came to Marie Laveau with his problem—he received no respect from his lodge brothers. They gossiped behind his back and ignored him at their meetings. The Good Mother told him to make a *hand*, a circle of pure chamois skin filled with Ruler's Root. She told him to carry cigars on which he has dripped two drops of pure oil of roses. Give them away to those who support you and wish you well, she counseled. Then the spirit offered Voodoo advice: "And, my son, be sure to bear with those who wish you ill and speak not too badly of them, but tell the whole truth and the naked truth." Offer a glad hand, a ready smile, and "treat others with good cheer and honest purpose that you may be loved and honored in your day and be remembered even after the cold grave has closed in on you. So Be It."

Another woman visited Marie the Second, her neighborhood therapist. Filled with anger, doubt, strife, and bitter regret, she feared she had been "crossed." Her family did not visit her; strangers refused to greet her. She was lonely, miserable, and jealous of her boyfriend. The Good Mother told her that her dirty house—not her body or her soul—was at cross purposes. Clean it up; scrub the front steps and sprinkle holy water, the essence of St. Michael, and oils of Our Lady in the four corners. Rub Three Kings and a Jack Lotion on her clothes. Put Root of Attraction into her right pocket. Then burn nine green candles in front of a picture of St. Expedite every night for nine nights in a row. Smile at friends, sympathize with strangers, and seek good spirits to live in your home.

A woman wanted to be able to make friends and keep them, but everything seemed to work against her. "Oh, good mother, the evil spirit seems to completely envelop me. I have no attraction, no sympathy from my kind. My lady friends look on me with indifference. I invite them and they say yes, but they do not come. They pass me by in the market place and bow to me sometimes, but more often they look me not in the face. They stop to speak to others, but when I approach there is no more to speak about and everything becomes quiet."

My daughter, you are *dis-spirited*. You have lost the magnetism that lures people to you. First, you must value your friends as you wish them to value you. Next you must take a round chamois bag—round so there will be no beginning and no end to your friendship—and put magic silver sand and powdered violet root in it. Powder yourself with pure white, sweet-smelling powder; it has the power to attract friendship. Scrub your house in lavender; bathe in verbena, Florida water, and handfuls of salt. When these tasks are completed, ask St. Anthony to intercede for you at the throne of God. Put his picture up in your house and invite people to come; he will warm their hearts towards you. Do all this faithfully. Go in peace.

Marie the Second's practice centered on social skills more than mysticism. A man came to her; he too felt "crossed." Everything went wrong. His boss did not like him and assigned him the worst jobs. Back home, his neighbors argued with him. "I am disgusted as all my ambitions and all my hard labor goes for nothing. I am disgusted with trying and have no reason to try and better my condition." The Good Mother was sympathetic—to a point. She insisted that the God of Prosperity smiles only on those who treat him well and honor his altar. She ordered him to wear Wonder of the World root tied with a good linen thread around his neck and to write the name of his boss with the blood of a white dove. Put on good clothes and sweet-smelling oil.

Then the Good Mother gave him a pep talk about his work habits. Stay away from bad spirits because they cause bad thoughts. Listen to the voice of good spirits; they bring peace and good fortune. "And at all times remember well that the good workman is worthy of his hire and that the bad workman is not fit even to lie down with the pigs and the cattle. So do your duty well and faithfully so that you will be looked up to and respected by the ones whom you labor with and those whom you serve. For this way only is the true way and the wide and free road to prosperity. So Be It."

Each petitioner was different, each solution tailored to the distress at hand from the materials at hand. The problems people in New Orleans brought to Marie Laveau sound like those of advice columns, television talk shows, or horoscopes. It was not the physical body of the person that hurt and needed healing; souls, personalities, houses, jobs, and social relationships suffered. She preached the magical morality of Voodoo: a pot of gumbo does not appear on the dining room table because it is "meant to be." Nothing—absolutely nothing—happens "naturally." Fate, coincidence, serendipity, and synchronicity do not exist. Good luck and bad luck are not whims of the spirit world—everything that happens comes from the strong intentions and actions of the petitioner or priestess and the pity or compassion of the spirits.

In the two decades before the Civil War, Voodoo thoughts and actions permeated the consciousness of New Orleans. Everyone—judges, newspaper reporters, and folks on the street—understood the Voodoo vocabulary of cause and effect. Everyone knew where to find the "paraphernalia of conjure"—items that are still for sale in spiritual pharmacies throughout America. The Voodoos in Marie Laveau's time were more realistic about death and sex than Catholics or Protestants were. For their frankness, however, they received a bad reputation; people said the priestesses caused marital conflicts, ran houses of prostitution, or used love and separation magic in a promiscuous manner. "I'll tell you one thing she do," said an old man who remembered Marie the Second as a meddler in affairs of the heart. "She make people fall in love, live together, marry, then she separate them. That's what she do."

Marie took nine lumps of sugar, nine of starch, and nine of steel dust. She wet them with cologne. She put a teaspoon of the mixture on a piece of material and tied it with colored ribbons. She made the ingredients fit the intention—brown sugar for people of color, fine French perfume for women, Jockey Club for men, and ribbons in the colors of desire. "Make nine bags and call out his name over each one," she instructed her clients. "Put them under a rug, behind the armoire, under a step or over a door. He will love you and give you everything. Distance makes no difference. Your mind is talking to his mind and nothing beats that." Creole gossipers in New Orleans laugh when they tell me how to keep a man true. They always swear that someone they know did it and it worked. Measure his "member" with a piece of silk string. Tie nine knots in the string. Curse "outside women" while you tie each knot, and say, "You and so-and-so will fail in the bed." Wear the string around your waist. He will never have sex with another woman except you. The Laveau formulas work because—as the Good Mother promised—"Love is at the bottom of all things and rules the world." In the event that a person wishes the opposite to happen, they use something to make a person disappear—it is still possible to buy "Losement" or "Hot-Foot" powders in the spiritual pharmacies of New Orleans.

Perhaps a woman found the man of her dreams and insured his fidelity—but she needed a brief break. She lit Sneak-Away Candles. "He be lying in bed asleep. She'll light a green candle and a pink candle together with his name wrote on there. Well, before that candle burns out, she gonna be back home. And when he do wake up, she gonna be in bed with him, although she done been everywhere she wants and he won't know a thing about it. Those candles work on a man's brains."

Marie the Second, in common with her mother and other women of Voodoo, acted as a matchmaker and matchbreaker. "One of the daughters of a rich family wanted to marry a man that her mother and father didn't like, so they went to Marie Laveau. If she would do something to make the girl change her mind, they would pay her well. Marie told them to leave it to her. She took four pigeons, got them drunk, wrote four letters, put them in their mouths, then she turned them to go in the air and I am telling you—that girl never married that boy!"

Beyond love and luck, Marie the Second knew the formulas and rituals to recast the course of legal proceedings. Within her circles, when people ran into troubles with the law, they came both to her and to her mother for help. "A poor woman came crying and told Marie that her son was in jail and she wanted to get him out but she had no money. Marie told her to go home and not worry. In an hour Marie Laveau went to the woman's house with the son and never asked a penny for her work."

Lala Hopkins, a well-known practitioner whom Marie the Second had initiated into Voodoo, said that her mentor had taught her "courthouse work." She bought "a beef tongue, split the end, put the names of the witnesses in it and sew it up and put it on ice. That freeze their tongues. She rolls wine apples on the floor. The judge discharge the case and they roll out of the jail. When Marie Laveau want to have a prisoner released, she got the district attorney's name, and the judge and jurymen." With an icepick she made a hole in a block of ice—which was harder to find than beef tongues. She wrote their names with powdered sugar to sweeten the judge and placed nine candles around the ice. Then "Marie lays down on her back and strikes the floor three times asking deliverance of the prisoner."

Marie the Second worked just as hard for people who were guilty of lock-them-up-and-toss-away-the-key crimes. A woman came to her who felt persecuted. Her enemies said that she caused disturbances. From the looks of her petition, the woman had been caught in armed breaking-and-entering.

She told Marie, "Now the learned judge and the high sheriff and the men of the law have threatened to put me in the dungeon where there is no light and the vermin crawl over you and eat out your heart. Where only gloom will be my companion; where I will never see the face of the sun."

The Good Mother replied, soothe the anger of the sheriff and law with essential oils and herbs tied in a paper. Hang up a picture of the Sacred Heart of Jesus and wear a piece of cloth or a shawl with the Lamb of God on it. Burn nine candles every day for nine days—burn a piece of paper with your enemy's name on it. On the day before the trial, burn incense—the same incense the great King Solomon used. Your lawyer will have "wisdom in his words so that they will be believed by the judges and high sheriffs and you shall at once be set free. Just to avoid further trouble, nail a magnetized horse shoe above your door to repel law suits and attract good fortune."

Hundreds of stories from dozens of sources speak of a generic Marie Laveau who used Catholic connections and Voodoo magic to influence the legal system and to protect members of the community from its grasp. Marie the First had supernatural power over the laws of city and state, people said, and Marie the Second inherited her mother's uncanny abilities. Both of the priestesses knew how to influence someone about to testify in a court case; they could make a person disappear for the duration of the trial, make him testify in a favorable direction, or keep judges and jurors from believing a word he said.

Mother and daughter knew influential people in town; they had powerful saints on their legal team. The folklore about the two makes it clear that, guilty or innocent, paying customer or not, many New Orleanians benefited from the women's skills at intervention—both spiritual and political. "When the judge and sheriff saw her, they submitted to anything. She would say, 'This is my friend. I want him out!' That was enough. She took Guinea peppers—those lil' red peppers like you call bird-eye peppers which she used for all kinds of tricks, hoodoo, and *gris-gris*—and put two or three under the judge's bench."

The Widow Paris also had her own unique ministry of justice, private missions of mercy at Parish Prison, a spiritual speciality she did not share with her daughter. Still under the influence of Père Antoine, the Widow Paris began at some point in her career to leverage Voodoo justice and mercy on behalf of men who were not just in ordinary trouble with the law but were facing their last hours on death row. One day, for example, at the pleas of his family, she walked up to the heavy wrought iron gates of the three-story stone jail in Tremé to reclaim a prisoner who was without any doubt guilty of the capital crimes for which he had been charged. When the guards and trustees objected, she shoved a picture of St. Peter the Protector at them. "They ran leaving the gates open," her neighbor reported about the incident. Marie walked out of the prison with her criminal client in tow, and "the prisoner's case was never called."

# Chapter 9

## Madame Laveau's Prayers, Poisons, and Political Pull

IN THE NAME OF THE FATHER, SON, AND HOLY GHOST, LET THAT POLICEMAN

WALK ON, KEEP THAT POLICEMAN WALKING ON, KEEP HIM GOING ON.

—SPELL FROM HARRY MIDDLETON HYATT,

HOODOO-CONJURATION-WITCHCRAFT-ROOTWORK

The July morning set for the double execution dawned blue and gold. Thousands of people had thronged the streets outside Parish Prison to wait for the noontime hangings. Judges, doctors, reporters, and civic leaders filed onto the wooden benches in the cobbled courtyard below the windows of death row. Marie Laveau, the Widow Paris, stood in front of the gallows.

The condemned white men—Jean Adams and Anthony Delille—were guilty of the gruesome murder of a slave girl named Mary. Clad in white shirts, pants, and caps, with their arms pinioned tightly with a rope across their backs, they stumbled into the sunlight.

The hangmen blindfolded the prisoners and adjusted the ropes around their necks. Delille, a Frenchman to the end of his life, used his last words to curse America and all its citizens while Adams silently braced his shoulders. Marie Laveau the First said nothing.

At that moment, the sky above the prison turned the color of iron. Lightning circled the crowd. Babies began to cry and women fainted.

A prominent white lawyer inside the prison was convinced that God's fury had descended on them. "The chimes of the Cathedral bells were just announcing the hour of twelve," he said, "when a sheet of lighting—a sheet so blinding, so dazzling, so stunning as to partake of the unnatural—illuminated the scene and rent the skies in twain. Nothing so weirdly, so terrifically grand, so indicative of the power of an offended Deity had ever before been heard." Someone in the crowd whispered—it's just like the crucifixion.

A reporter from the *Picayune*, drenched in the downpour that followed, said, "Although the rain came down as if the floodgates of heaven were opened to deluge this world again, the multitude in the street still stood their ground." So did Marie Laveau.

The storm failed, however, to drown the noise of the wooden trapdoors as they opened. In the flashes of lightning, those who came to witness a double execution saw two nooses swinging in the wind—empty. On the stone pavement twelve feet below, Adams and Delille crawled painfully on their hands and knees; the ropes that bound them had fallen away. The crowd surged forward. Police had to restrain them with clubs. Then the sky cleared as suddenly as it had darkened, and for decades after, journalists and lawyers thought they understood what had happened at noon that day. Robert Tallant, author of *Voodoo in New Orleans*, said, "A tall woman in a tignon moved away from those spectators who had remained, impervious to the whispers, 'There goes Marie Laveau.' Thousands of Orleanians were convinced that she had caused the storm and that she had tried, almost successfully, to save the lives of the two men. And because of this case the Louisiana Legislature met and forever outlawed public executions."

Another witness that day, a white man, called Marie "an arrogant and consummate imposter," and said, "this horrid execution shocked the conscience of the community. Public hanging became henceforth a thing of the past." Louisiana was the first state in the union to outlaw executions as spectator sport or carnival parades. The Widow Paris cheated the gallows, not of death, but of humiliation and shame—or so people say. But she also failed to save Adams and Delille or summon the power to spare their suffering. Neither the crowd's pity nor the storm's fury deterred prison officials, who bandaged and bled the two men, lifted them onto the flawed gallows, and hanged them again.

Sometime in the 1830s or 1840s, the queen of the Voodoos began to visit men on death row in Parish Prison. "Marie Laveau devoted herself entirely to her self-imposed duties as unofficial spiritual adviser to the criminals in the condemned cells at the Parish Prison," one journalist wrote. "This phase of her activity was wholly Catholic, into which she permitted no trace of Voodooism to creep." The Widow Paris carried hot bowls of gumbo and platters of fried fish to a condemned man and prepared "an altar in his cell before which she prayed with him—a box about three feet square, surmounted by three smaller boxes rising in a pyramid to an apex, on which the Voodoo queen always placed a small figure of the Virgin Mary."

Her daughter Philomène, in common with the reporters, found no trace of Voodoo in the prison ministry of the Widow Paris. My mother works only within the Catholic traditions of Père Antoine, she insisted to a *Picayune* reporter in 1886. "Although Marie Laveau had taken none of the vows of a religious order, her heart prompted her to visit the Parish Prison whenever its walls held any unfortunates condemned to death." According to both her daughter and the *gumbo ya*-ya, the Widow Paris cooked the men's last meal; she knelt to pray with them through their final night. She was confessor, comforter, and—at the end—witness to their deaths.

Sometimes she found ways to free them either from the gallows or from prison itself. "Whenever a prisoner excited her pity," Philomène said, "Marie would labor incessantly to obtain his pardon, or at least a commutation of sentence, and she generally succeeded." Marie Laveau's name was often coupled with such miraculous rescues. John Bazar, for example, "was convicted and sentenced to hang on May 27, 1870. On the morning of that day he prayed with Marie Laveau in the prison chapel, which she had decorated, and was then led to the gallows. His arms had been bound, the noose and black hood adjusted, and the Sheriff had started to raise his hand to signal the executioner, when a messenger galloped into the courtyard with a reprieve from Governor H. C. Warmouth."

Marie Laveau picked, if not the saddest, certainly the smelliest place in New Orleans to do her work. Like the Tower of London, the Tombs of New York, or the Bastille of Paris, Parish Prison was an urban legend. The jail, finished in 1834 and located on the site of an old soap factory, cast its shadow across Congo Square. Tremé, Orleans, and St. Ann streets bounded it on three sides; the fourth side is named Marais—French for "swamp." Built to hold four hundred, it was overcrowded with underfed, unwashed inmates; serious offenders mingled with those awaiting trial for minor offences.

At the iron door to the death row cells, a table held prayer books, a crucifix, and religious statuary. Above the door someone painted a death's-head and crossbones and wrote the word "Condemned" below the drawing. The cells were so wretched that prison officials allowed the Widow Paris to bring art supplies in the food baskets she carried. A Creole painter who murdered his mistress whitewashed the walls of his cell and covered them "with most curious drawings in charcoal or black chalk." The vivid scenes depicted his temptations, his evil deeds, his death, and finally, his vision of forgiveness and resurrection. On another occasion Marie helped James Mullen decorate his coffin with fringe, metallic crosses, and satin cutouts. Each night he slept inside it, pillowing his head on the lace christening dress of the daughter he had murdered.

Early on a May morning in 1871, the Widow Paris's grandchildren helped her carry supplies to Parish Prison. They constructed a stepped box, the base about three feet square, and covered it in white muslin deeply fringed with silver lace. On the top she placed a statue of the Virgin in a long veil embroidered with filigree flowers and surrounded her with pink and white camellias. A reporter from the *Picayune* saw the altar they built in the cell of two men condemned to hang. Here is proof, he wrote, that the Widow Paris has been rehabilitated: the "good Christian woman, erroneously described by a portion of the press as a 'Voudou priestess,' is in reality a devout and acceptable member of the Catholic communion."

White men—reporters, lawyers, and guards—watched Marie as she counseled men on death row. They despised her; then admitted that she had the power to fix prison sentences, to arrange pardons for men condemned to the gallows, and to inspire one of the few liberal or compassionate laws the Louisiana legislature passed in her century. It may be no coincidence that another woman—a descendant of Louisiana Creoles and a Catholic nun—started a similar ministry to prisoners on death row at the infamous Angola penitentiary a century later. In her book, *Dead Man Walking*, Sister Helen Prejean describes the tentative correspondence she began with Patrick Sonnier, sentenced to die for the murder of a young couple in Lover's Lane. She visited him in his cell, took him small comforts, and prayed with him. As the date of his execution neared, she offered to watch with him through his last moments if his legal appeals failed.

"If you die, I want to be with you," she said.

Patrick refused, "No. I don't want you to see it. It's terrible to see. I don't want to put you through that. It would scar you for life."

Sister Helen responded, "I can't bear the thought that you would die without seeing one loving face. Just look at me." The sight of your execution will not break me, for there is love and support in my life, Sister Helen reassured the condemned man. "God will give me the grace."

Other layers of stories, however, about Marie Laveau's work at Parish Prison circulate through New Orleans—tales that take her ministry of mercy to men in cells for the condemned beyond the boundaries of Catholic consciousness or conscience. Tour guides in the French Quarter—for good reason—relish the popular and oft-repeated tale of how the Widow Paris "cooked up" and countered the death sentence of a man condemned to hang.

Antoine Cambre came from an old New Orleans family and worked as a watchman in a ballroom, a job tied to the police force and filled with opportunities for lucrative but illegal activities. Poorly educated, he hated the foreigners who poured into his city. He drank and gambled well beyond the relaxed standards of the French Quarter. Late one night he shot and killed a German lamplighter; the judge sentenced him to hang. Cambre was terrified to die on the gallows. His friends flocked to his prison cell and urged poison on him. Suicide is preferable to the humiliation of hanging, they begged. But Antoine could not kill himself, even to spare his family, and so he waited for the governor's intervention.

On the day before his scheduled execution, prison officials found Antoine Cambre dead in his cell. A lawyer and frequent visitor to Parish Prison later wrote, "It was generally rumored at that time, that he had succumbed to an attack of malarial fever, but the autopsy revealed the existence of poison in the stomach and intestines." The Widow Paris, a friend of Antoine Cambre and his family, he continued, "had ready access at all times to Cambre's cell, and would cheer him for hours with her sprightly talk. As the time for his execution was fast approaching—it was on the eve, I believe—Marie approached him."

"My young one, before you die, if you have to die tomorrow, tell me what you would like to eat. I'll make you a good dinner." Cambre mournfully shook his head.

"Then I'll make you a filé gumbo such as you have never eaten in your whole life," said the temptress.

The sophisticated lawyer who had heard this story from a prison official he trusted assumed the worst. Marie Laveau gave Cambre the spiritual and culinary gift he could not ask for—"I'll make you a gumbo such as you've never eaten"—and it killed him.

A Creole newspaper, the *Bee*, however, told a different story, one that was not widely circulated in the city, one the WPA writers did not hear and tour guides have never shared with tourists. At Cambre's death, the prison physician who had attended him the week before he died summoned the warden, an appointed official and a captain in the police force. Together they convened the city coroner, a deputy coroner, an ex-coroner, four prominent citizens, and a number of newspapers reporters for a hurried inquest. Cambre died in early August, the season for lethal fevers; and the prominent members of the panel listened to the doctor's description of Cambre's symptoms, the course of his illness, and his responses to the medications prescribed. The panel took the doctor's word and stated for the record that the condemned man died of a pernicious or intermittent fever resembling malaria. There had never been an autopsy.

The doctor described Cambre's last moments and the third person in the cell that day, his friend and spiritual counselor, the Widow Paris.

"At breakfast time he got up and walked across the cell to take a glass of water. At half past twelve o'clock he arose and walked across the cell, drank a glass of water and laid down again, when he was seized with a burning fever. A colored woman, who was much attached to Cambre and frequently visited him in prison, remained with him until he had breathed his last."

These two distinct accounts of Marie Laveau's role in Cambre's death are strangely reconciled in a long-buried tale of the death of another prisoner. Six weeks before Antoine Cambre's death, his cellmate, Eugene Pepe, alias Eugene Adams, had died of poison in such agony that his shrieks could be heard in the street outside the prison. Pepe-Adams—a former policeman and good friend of the Widow Paris, his spiritual counselor—had been sentenced to hang for the stabbing murder of one man and the shooting of another. The poison was not, the newspaper made clear, a merciful release from the horror of the gallows, but a successful plot to silence him and to prevent him from testifying in court. "There has been a rumor on the street that Adams had threatened to make a confession" about a recent murder that implicated prominent citizens in town. Although the warden assured reporters that he knew nothing about such a rumor, he ordered no inquest nor made any inquiries into how Pepe-Adams got the poison that killed him. The quick and casual verdict was suicide.

Stories like this circulated in the community and may testify to the secret powers and strategic motivations of Marie Laveau, her daughter, and the practitioners whom they trained. Zora Neale Hurston worked with a priest in New Orleans who killed a man without resorting to poison— "*Don't fool yourself. People can do things to you. I done seen things happen,*" she said. In ritual vengeance for a betrayal, the priest, Anatol Pierre, prayed, sent his intentions to the spirits, burned nine black candles, and slept in a coffin for ninety days. "And the man died."

∼

New Orleans was one of the most dangerous places in America—"the dueling capital of the South, a major headquarters for career criminals, site of some of the most intense ethnic strife in the country"; and one policeman claimed that "nothing would ever put an end to murders, manslaughters, and deadly assaults." Although the crime rate was high, the police caught few murderers, the courts sentenced even fewer of them, and of those, the governor pardoned most. Given the crime rate, public executions were rare. The state attorney general complained that the New Orleans police force was useless, witnesses were afraid to testify, no one wanted to serve on juries, the courts failed to keep paperwork, and only one in five crimes were ever solved—complaints that are still voiced. The city's violence and chaos helped the Laveaus leverage the legal system on behalf of clients. "Marie was in with all of the lawyers, policemen, judges, and big city officials," summed up one citizen.

The police department, one of the largest employers in the city, acted more like a private army for the mayor. Policemen and politicians often appointed themselves and their relatives, in-laws, and best friends to serve as lawyers, magistrates, or judges—a loosely organized brotherhood to which Marie the First and the Second had ready access. Nathan Hobley, a Voodoo practitioner who had worked with both priestesses, said, "Marie was smart, the cleverest person I ever knew. People in trouble consulted her. She went to court for them and never was known to lose a case. She had a good lawyer.*" The interviewer from the WPA Federal Writers' Project added an asterisk and a note of warning at the end of her transcription of the interview: "*Hobley then mentioned Lucien Adams and Judge Moise of Section B. To Be Censored."

Lucien Adams, whom historians call a "notorious thug" and whom the WPA project protected because of his color, always appeared in public in a snow-white linen suit. "Judge Adams," as he liked to call himself, "stopped by Marie Laveau's house every morning on his way to his office. He lived over on Rampart street. He surely was a fine man and fine looking too. He always dressed in white, look like a fresh suit every morning." Adams was also a violent man who used strong-arm tactics to break up meetings of abolitionists or to fix elections; he was a political mercenary who intimidated and beat up citizens; in one case, he was accused of a murder of a key person only a few days before a contested election. The kind of "enforcer"

who made St. Michael look good, Adams regularly stopped in for breakfast at the Paris-Laveau household.

In addition to Judge Lucien Adams, a policeman named Thomas Adams
revolved in the Laveaus' social or spiritual orbit. "Adams? Well, Marie
Laveau made him Chief of Police," a neighbor, Mary Washington, reported
to the WPA interviewers. "He was an ordinary policeman. He started doing
business with Marie Laveau and in a little while he was sergeant. He was
next transferred to captain and finally made chief. That's why the policemen didn't mess with Marie Laveau." Citizens and historians alike held
Thomas Adams, a businessman, member of state legislature, and chief of
police at intervals from 1858 until 1866, in high regard. He sometimes ate
breakfast with the family on St. Ann.

The Widow Paris needed every legal connection and all the political or
secret networks she could muster during the dangerous decade leading up to
the Civil War. By 1850, New Orleans was the wealthiest city in the United
States, cotton capital of the world. It had the second greatest port and the
third largest population in America. The brilliant theater and opera season
drew thousands of travelers who came south for the easy winters. They raved
about the plays, dances, symphonies, and round after round of elegant parties.
Private dinners in the Quarter rivaled the meals and service in the finest restaurants of the world. Brokers, bankers, and businessmen flourished beneath the
three pillars of prosperity: cotton gins, sugar refining, and steamboats. Visitors
used words like exotic, glittering, and bewitching. Some called it "the Golden
Age" or the "Flush Fifties." Others retorted it was the "Feverish Fifties."

A volatile, mercurial quality filled the air. Immigrants from Europe
poured into New Orleans. Irish and Italians moved into distinct neighborhoods, founded Catholic churches, and brought their own folk saints and
savory recipes. Whatever the immigrants' backgrounds, whatever the color
of their politics, white politicians counted the newcomers as white. Thus
the white population rose on waves of immigration as the population of
free people of color dwindled. In a city of roughly a hundred and sixteen
thousand residents, one out of every fifteen people was enslaved; one out
of ten was a free person of color.

Although the 1850s glittered for many, below its sparkling surface, the undertow dragged Creoles deeper. Free people of color lost the freedoms they had won in colonial times and retained into the early American period. Those who foresaw the coming catastrophe, single men with job skills, and families with relatives in the north migrated. Some moved to Paris or other parts of Europe; others went to Liberia, Haiti, or Mexico. The community lost its best writers, musicians, intellectuals, and leaders—sensitive, educated, and articulate people who might have provided the focus of protest or action.

For the Widow Paris and her daughter, Marie, the decade of decadence and despair—more the age of lead than of gold—began in June of 1850 with a midsummer's night party in honor of St. John the Baptist. The police raided a gathering of women at a private home and arrested Betsey Toledano and sixteen other women, free and enslaved, black, brown, and white. "Some of the females were entirely nude and others had but a single garment on," the *True Delta* observed. "All were directed to dress." Once clothed, the seventeen women were taken to jail where the court charged them with the crimes of illegal assembly and interracial revelry. The reporter called Ms. Toledano "a fat negress," "an obese negress," "a fortune-teller," a "practitioner of witchcraft," the "Pythoness of the Temple," and a notorious madam or operator of a house of prostitution. The women at the gathering addressed Betsey as the "Dauphine." Police hauled away a cartload of banners, flags, wands, snakes, jewelry, musical instruments, candles, and statues from the June raid, the first of many that summer.

The Widow Paris was angry. How dare the police confiscate those women's ritual equipment and ceremonial regalia; how dare they treat *Sainte Marie* in such a sacrilegious manner. A week after the raid, she did something she had never done. She crossed Canal Street, entered the American Sector of New Orleans, marched into the office of the civil recorder or magistrate at Camp and Commons Streets, and swore out a criminal warrant against a city official. She demanded that the court return to her a statue the police had seized. She set the value of the object at $50, but a *Picayune* reporter countered, "We saw the thing called a 'statue'—it is a bad looking rag baby, worth about four dimes." For the first time in print, the press identified and labeled Marie Laveau, alias the Widow Paris, free woman of color, as the "head of the Voudou women."

A week later the police raided the "fair daughters of Voudou dressed in fig leaf pinafores" during their celebrations at the beaches of Lake Pontchartrain. The women fought back. An unnamed woman from the "mysterious order of Voudous" filed charges. She and her friends cited unconstitutional and illegal interruptions of religious ceremonies. They insisted that they had broken no laws, yet officials illegally fined them; extortion was the word they used. And last, they charged, the police had assaulted, battered, and mistreated them. On the morning of the trial a great crowd gathered outside the court to hear what they thought was a civil suit against the police for damages, extortion, false arrest, and religious persecution. The judge dismissed the case when no witnesses to the charges of unlawful assembly appeared.

The raids continued. Wherever neighbors heard singing or held grudges against each other, they reported mixed-race Voodoo rituals to the police. Hundreds of people collected around the courts in the American sector of town for the hearings. Anonymous women—black, white, and brown—paid their fines and faced down the harassment, then returned to fathers, husbands, masters, or mistresses. At the end of July, the police arrested Betsey Toledano again; the *Crescent* called her "a stout and intelligent free colored woman, high priestess and chief spokeswoman."

At her hearing, Betsey Toledano spoke in English, forcefully and without apologies. Voodoo was not an accusation or a crime; it was a heritage from her grandmother who came from Africa and educated her granddaughter in the precepts and symbols of this religion. Yes, Toledano admitted, she held frequent meetings of women at her house to sing innocent folk songs and discuss certain feminine mysteries. The stones and goblets the police seized were to protect the house against lightning; that was an African custom. Betsey showed the court her necklace, a gift from the grandmother. Made of lovely, rare seashells, it gave her power over rain; she could bring down a shower whenever she pleased. Betsey gloried in being a priestess of a society so venerable and beneficial as the order of Voodoos. She reminded the court that, although she was willing to entertain reasonable questions, her faith and her honor as a Voodoo placed a seal on her lips about other matters.

Amidst the intense raids of July and August, a special hearing was set to consider the disposition of the statue that the Widow Paris had sued to recover—the press dubbed it the "Virgin of Voudou." Its fate, not the workings of justice, compelled the city's attention. At lunchtime outside the city court, a "compact crowd of sturdy Anglo-Saxons, marching in close column, occupied the southern banquette [sidewalk]. The opposite banquette was equally crowded with Africa's daughters of every age, of every shape, and of every shade of color, from a bright yellow hue to sooty." The "dusky damsels" were headed to court to retrieve "the chief relic of reverence and veneration, a quaintly carved wooden figure, resembling something between a Centaur and an Egyptian mummy." Dozens, perhaps hundreds, of women of color desired the statue; white men wanted to see them fight over it.

When the court doors opened that morning, "a young Quadroon was the first to present to the police officer the ransom of $8.50 for the Voudou Virgin. He accepted the offer, and she grasped the mysterious relic. She had not well left the presence of the police office, when another, and another, and still another of the colored sisterhood came, presented the stipulated sum—aye, its double, and claimed the Voudou Virgin." Dozens of women petitioned the court to return the statue to them—name your price, they begged; the police regretted they had not set the amount higher. The *gumbo ya-ya* says the "young Quadroon" was twenty-three-year-old Marie the Second, and that Marie the First, age forty-nine, knew the right people. One week later, the Widow Paris went back to court in person, filled out the requisite documents, and withdrew her legal suit.

The raids on women's interracial gatherings in the summer of 1850 circled the household on St. Ann Street. Like creeping floodwaters in the low-lying city, they came right up to the front steps. Marie the Second continued to hold her dances, rituals, and potluck dinners every Friday evening—but she was in danger and began to fortify her protection policies with the saints and spirits, and to look for safer places to dance and host Voodoo gatherings. It was already dark, though still hot outside, when she heard them coming. At the third heavy knock, she opened the door. When the first policeman tried to grab her arm—Luke Turner's pride in his Aunt Marie glowed in the story he told anthropologist Zora Neale Hurston—"she stretch out her left hand and he turn round and round. Then two come together—she put them to running and barking like dogs. Four come and she put them to beating each other with night sticks. The whole station force come. They knock on her door. She did work on her altar and they all went to sleep on her steps."

Newspaper reporters treated the Widow Paris with grudging respect; to them she was a full member of the gallows fellowship, head of "the Voudou orders," and someone with political connections. They were not able to find and interview Marie the Second—or even to imagine her existence; still they feared the kind of power that put police to sleep on the doorstep.

⟨~⟩

But the Laveau prayers, magical protections, altars to saints, and a retinue of lawyers, judges, and policemen were not enough to hold bad luck and hard times at bay. Throughout the decade that followed the arrests and hearings in the summer of 1850, New Orleans' newspapers belabored the Voodoos. They inflamed enslaved people's passion for freedom and fostered intimate connections among the wrong kind of people, the press claimed. Above all, the Voodoo women kept slaves from their rightful duties to their masters. "There can be no doubt of the vast injury they do to the slave population. Carried on in secret, they bring the slaves into contact with disorderly free negroes and mischievous whites. The police should have their attention continually alive to the importance of breaking up such unlawful practices," insisted the *Picayune*.

In 1852 the Louisiana legislature decreed that anyone who freed an enslaved person had to send them out of the United States—permanently. Three years later, they passed a law to keep free people of color from outside the state from entering Louisiana. The state legislature prohibited free people of color from forming any new religious, benevolent, charitable, scientific, or literary societies. The following year, a New Orleans city council ordinance banned drums, horns, and trumpets in the city. They outlawed all forms of freedom of speech, freedom of religion, and freedom of assembly for free people of color. The new law said that "a great and constantly growing evil now exists in the City of New Orleans in contravention of the law and the well-being of the institutions of the South, and to the safety of the institution of slavery."

The press became more and more strident. In the *Picayune*, September 17, 1855, editors bemoaned the "uppity tendencies" and insolence of free people of color. The newspaper complained that free blacks acted as through they were "a Grand Order" and hinted that they were a dangerous and subversive group even when they did not violate the laws of "illegal assembly." News writers lumped Creoles of color in the same category as Negroes, blacks, and slaves and waited for the arrests or harassments that peaked each year around November 1, the Feast of All Saints, and June 23, the Eve of St. John's Day.

The Louisiana legislature passed its shortest and harshest law in 1857: all manumissions and emancipations of any kind for any enslaved person for any reason whatsoever were forbidden. Then a new state law in March of 1859—the final stroke of white paranoia and fantasy—ordered all persons of African descent to choose their own masters and resign themselves to a life of slavery. Although authorities could not enforce laws that required free people of color to adopt voluntary servitude, they reminded the women of the Laveau-Glapion household who held the power.

A short article appeared in the *Picayune* in July 1859. "Knowing ones" said that Marie Eucharist Laveau, a "negro," ran a disorderly house in the Love Street neighborhood—"a regular Voudou concern, where witches and sorceresses met and went through fantastic pranks." When a neighbor complained that "all sorts of hideous noises proceeded at night, like fighting and the worst kind of revelry," the authorities issued a warrant for her arrest.

In the face of repression, in the bleakest hours before the Civil War, the Laveaus and the Creole community turned—as they had throughout their history—to the good works of their benevolent societies and to personal contact with the spirits. Creoles of all colors held séances to contact the spirits of the deceased. They invited sympathetic Anglos. Women who had lost children and wanted to contact and comfort them, and be comforted, attended their meetings. Men spoke to well-known figures in French history, philosophers, Catholic reformers, leaders of the Enlightenment, and, as always, to Père Antoine. The spirits they contacted spoke to them of the ideals of brotherhood betrayed, the burdens of their quest for social justice, and the suffering that surrounded them. Those who attended the séances begged the spirits they contacted, put an end to slavery, give us back the Creole life we love.

By the end of the glittering decade of the 1850s, New Orleans had lost its economic soul to railroads and to war. The city fell to Union troops in the spring of 1862—the first southern city to be occupied in the Civil War and the first to be "reconstructed" along the new racial lines that northern policymakers planned to impose on the South. Creoles of all colors in New Orleans, families like the Laveaus and the Glapions, did not take sides in the war, brother against brother or sister against sister. Instead, they prayed for victory for themselves—any victory by any army that would restore their former position of cultural and political dominance in the city.

The Widow Paris, who began her career nursing wounded soldiers, friend and foe, at the Battle of New Orleans in 1815, tended men of color from the Louisiana Native Guards. Members of the benevolent societies to which she belonged searched for scarce food in the occupied city and gave it to families of soldiers. When federal authorities built a special gallows near the levee at Esplanade Avenue to hang William Mumford, a handsome gambler, for the crime of tearing up a Union flag and wearing a piece as a boutonniere, Creoles were outraged. Although Mumford expected to be reprieved, Yankee justice did not answer to Creole conjure of the kind the Widow Paris had practiced at Parish Prison. His death on June 7, 1862, was the first public execution since the Adams-Delille hangings a decade earlier, and the last until the lynchings of the Jim Crow era of segregation and racial terrorism.

The Widow Paris, both her daughters, and her granddaughter, Aldina, would surely have walked in full mourning clothes to St. Rose de Lima Church on July 29, 1863, for the funeral services of Captain André Cailloux, a Union officer born a slave. Thousands of people of color, bond and free, joined his funeral procession in defiance of the orders of both the Catholic archbishop and the military authorities. Benevolent societies in distinctive costume marched in long ranks, one after the other, to honor their Afro-Creole hero. Cailloux belonged to the Louisiana Native Guards, a militia of people of color, slave and free, French-speaking Catholics and English-speaking Protestants, who fought with distinction and bravery—for both the Confederacy and the Union. Counterintuitive as this fact seems, people of color had, since the earliest days of the colony, offered their services to whatever de facto government was in power in Louisiana, always in defense of the city they loved and always with the hope of improving their social and political status as Creoles.

For Philomène, the war years meant babies, not Creole politics. Between the death of her father in 1855 and the peak of Reconstruction in 1870 she gave birth to five little ones, and buried two in her mother's high tomb. In common with all young mothers in the occupied city, she had difficulty finding cloth to make diapers and new clothes for her growing children. Medicines, soap, fresh foods, rice, sugar, salt, and coffee were scarce and expensive. The housewives' *gumbo ya-ya* talked of black market bargains in the underground economy and of casualty lists—friends and relatives of the St. Ann household were fighting and dying on both sides of the conflict. The Union soldiers who paced the streets and markets must have made young women like Philomène nervous.

Marie the Second spent the war as a rebel—though not a Confederate. Despite the lack of direct evidence for her activities during the war years, she was the type to have joined with other beautiful women of the city who lifted their skirts and exposed their shapely legs and bottoms to Union officers as they walked through the Quarter. Many high-spirited women in New Orleans tossed the contents of their chamber pots from the balconies of their apartments or spit on the hated invaders. Like the Spanish governor with his provocative *tignon* policy, the occupation leaders tried to control the unruly women of New Orleans with a decree: the infamous "Woman Order" proclaimed that any woman who insulted an officer of the United States Army would be considered a prostitute. When General Benjamin Butler, the "devil of Dixie" who wrote the order, sailed away, the so-called "women of the streets" waved white handkerchiefs and called down a curse upon him that did the Voodoo orders proud: "May you return to that miserable Yankee hole that gave you birth; when your wretched wife appears in her stolen finery, may all eyes turn and all fingers point; and may the spirits of the brave Creole men you executed haunt you forever."

The harassments, raids, and legal restrictions of the 1850s had forced the Voodoo women to search for safer and more distant places at which to hold their meetings. The racial legislation of Louisiana and the Union occupation both brought danger and terrible deprivations to New Orleans. So when the Civil War ended, Marie the Second decided to celebrate. To hell with Reconstruction; let's drink to a new Creole dawn and dance till the sun comes up. At the peak of midsummer, she caught the Smoky Mary railroad and rode it to its final stop on the beaches of Lake Pontchartrain. There she threw passionate parties and provided a banquet of New Orleans food, drinks, and music for the citizens of a war-weary city. Black, white, tan, and brown, Confederate gray and Union blue, reporters and tourists, the sober and the drunk, believers and disbelievers came to her lakefront celebrations. So did St. John the Baptist, the most improbable saint in New Orleans, and High John the Conqueror—conjurer, trickster, devil.

# Chapter 10

## How John, the Devil, and Mam'zelle Marie Hoodooed the Media

THEN MARIE LAVEAU COMES OUT WITH A THIN, THIN GOWN ON—ALMOST NUDE.

SHE WOULD START DANCING SO SLOW-LIKE. MAN, I'M TELLING YOU,

SHE COULD BEND HER BODY INTO ALL KINDS OF KNOTS.

—WILLIAM MOORE, WPA FEDERAL WRITERS' PROJECT

Marie Laveau the Second, reigning queen of the Voodoos, stood in the prow of a shallow barge. In her purple dress, rope belt, gold jewelry, and tall white *tignon*, she looked as perfect as the weather above the firelit beaches of Lake Pontchartrain that midsummer's night. Hundreds of people lined the shore, waiting for her. As she stepped from the boat, they clapped and hailed her with the words and rhythms of the conjure song everyone knew belonged to her: *Mam'zelle Marie, fe chauffez. Mam'zelle Marie, chauffez ça,* which I have translated on the advice of speakers and scholars of Louisiana Creole as, "Ms. Marie, make it hot, turn up the heat, feel the power."

She sang to them in response: *C'est m'a, coupé ça, c'est m'a, coupé ça,* which I interpret as "It is there, it is real. Cut it, kill it, finish it."

Marie spread a large white cloth on the beach. On one side she set a cross; on the opposite side she placed flowers, three candles, and a picture of St. Peter the Protector. In the middle she stood a portrait of St. John the Baptist whose birthday the Voodoos celebrated each summer on June 23. "They celebrated on St. John's Day because they wanted to be like him," a

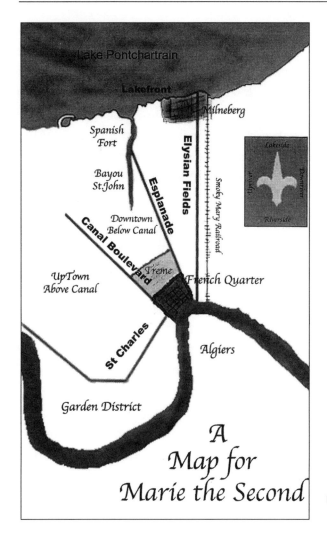

Figure 5. Marie the Second's
New Orleans.

member of her choir that night said. "You see, he was a great man and always
did what was right." As the drumbeat built, she and the other members of
her circle added their gifts and offerings to John. Then everyone gathered
in circles around the priestess and knelt in the sand. Marie rapped on the
ground three times; the spectators shouted with her—*Un-Deux-Trois,*
"One-Two-Three."

Marie ordered a fire built on the lakefront beach. Some men brought a
large pot and filled it with water from a barrel. An old man prayed in

French as he added salt. A young girl sang and shook in peppers. Someone opened a box and pulled out what a *Times* reporter who saw this ceremony in 1872 believed was a fat snake. The power of suggestion is strong given the association of the Laveaus with serpents—but the long, slippery object could equally have been homemade *andouille* or *boudin* sausage for which Louisiana is famous. They then cut the "snake" into three pieces. Marie, the old man, and the girl each took a piece and put it into the boiling vat. The drumming and singing continued as Queen Marie called for "a cat," cut the animal's throat, and threw it whole into the pot—the reporter put the quote marks around "cat" as if there were some doubt. Then she lifted up a live black rooster, its feet tied to its head, and plunged it into the boiling water.

Amid songs and yells, Queen Marie ordered the ritual participants to undress. The reporter paid closer attention to this phase of the ritual. Men of his period believed that a woman was "undressed" who did not have on all the required layers of clothing or was dressed in casual clothes in front of people from a different race or gender. So their phrase "entirely nude" must be taken lightly; it often meant that only the last see-through layer of clothing remained.

Everyone grasped hands and circled the pot. Marie took a shot bag of multicolored powders from the pocket of her dress and poured the mixture into the pot. She sang another song; the crowd knew it too and joined in the chorus: *C'est l'amour, oui Mam'zelle, c'est l'amour.* "This is love, yes girl, this is love." In the light of the fire against the cloudless night, Marie danced, and no one who saw her ever forgot. At midnight, she paused and shifted the tempo of the celebration. "It's time to enter the water," she proclaimed, and signaled everyone to follow her into the warm shallow waters of Lake Pontchartrain—jump, splash, swim, bathe, play. Wet clothes clinging to the bodies of dancers and revelers offered journalists yet another view of "entirely nude." Marie's friends had set up large tables covered with white tablecloths and were serving fried and baked chickens, jambalaya, gumbo, red beans and rice, light sugared cakes, and heavy sweet spirits, rum, champagne, and fancy liquors. Dance, eat, drink—Marie told them—this night will last a year.

When Marie glimpsed the sun rising over the eastern edge of the lake, she ordered a man to sound the conch-shell horn. Everyone held hands in a circle and Marie spoke to them about St. John, about the work he did. She asked them to kneel where they stood, pray, and receive his blessings. At her signal, "four nude black women with white handkerchiefs on their heads" quenched the fire, sprinkled blessed water over the ashes, and collected them in empty wine bottles to take home. "Here is day," the queen of Voodoo said, "we must welcome it with song." *Mam'zelle Marie, chauffez ça*—the crowd sang, not in triumphal greeting, but in gratitude for food, drink, jolly company, and perfect weather. The bugle shell sounded its final notes.

People in New Orleans argued with each other and with the interviewers from the WPA Writers' Project about Marie's intentions. Were the celebrations at the lakefront sexy, drunken debauches or deep spiritual moments? A white woman who lived for seventy-one years near Lake Pontchartrain insisted, "On St. John's Eve this whole section was looking like a scene in hell with the fires of their torches and their burning pots and bonfires. The police would come out sometimes, but she—that Laveau woman—would hoodoo them and they would take off their clothes. Can you imagine all them people, white and colored, dancing around like devils, and all of them naked as jaybirds?"

Marie the Second's signature dance on St. John's Eve had a number of names—the Congo Dance, the Creole Dance, the shimmy-tail dance, or the *Fe Chauffez*-"fay-show-fay." "You won't believe it, but them Fe Chauffez dancers balanced lighted candles on their heads the whole time they danced and the candle flames never went out. They was a sight!" Unlike most journalists in the city, the Voodoo spirits seemed to know when and where to find Marie the Second at midsummer. Many spectators and participants witnessed their arrival to the beat of the drums and the chanting voices. "The dancers would stomp their feet and move their bodies. One foot would move to the left and then one to the right and then they would shake. They shake down and then shake up. The tom-toms went loud when they shook. They bodies would look like a burning top. The women and men was half-naked. White and colored. Beautiful mulatto women would fall on the floor shaking and hollering louder than the tom toms. Even white women would do funny things."

William Morris kept insisting, "Man, I mean to tell you, Marie Laveau was a beautiful woman. She danced so long and so fast until she either went into a trance or was completely exhausted and fell to the ground. They had to bring her to with water."

Everyone in New Orleans—journalists, tourists, politicians, and spirits—assumed that they were invited to Marie's midsummer gatherings. "White ladies what had money" paid Marie Laveau ten dollars each to come to the Fe Chauffez dances. "You'd see 'em come, all dressed up and wearin' thick veils, but when they sent their carriages away, they'd take off their shoes and stockings and all their clothes 'cept their chemises. You can't see nothing like that nowadays, no." Marie could not have attended every event on the lakefront on St. John's Eve. The press claimed that thousands of people lined the beach from Milneburg, past the mouth of Bayou St. John, and on to West End. The dozens of gatherings foreshadowed similar events in New Orleans like the Jazz and Heritage Festival—famous for great music, food, good times, and comfortable clothing in the company of multiracial strangers. "She had meetings everywhere. Marie Laveau could do anything—not afraid of nothing. On St. John's Eve, she invite everybody to her meetin'—the big judges, lawyers, the police and all the firemens. They wouldn't arrest her—they was too afraid. Along the lake from Milneburg to Spanish Fort, in Congo Square, and private meetings at her home, there was more white than colored."

Luke Turner had helped his Aunt Marie set up the celebrations. In his account of those nights a group of friends— "those around her altar"— built an outdoor sanctuary near Lake Pontchartrain, and arranged for food, drinks, drummers, and publicity. Marie withdrew to prepare for the ritual and gain power from the spirits of Snake, Sun, and Water. "Nobody see Marie Laveau for nine days before the feast. But when the great crowd of people at the feast call upon her, she would rise out of the waters of the lake with a great communion candle burning upon her head and another in each one of her hands. She walked upon the waters to the shore. As a little boy I saw her myself. When the feast was over, she went back into the lake, and nobody saw her for nine days again."

A man who remembered attending dances in 1874 and 1875 said, "That stuff must be in the old newspapers cause Marie Laveau had all the newspapermen, policemen, and high officials at her picnic. There was plenty of food. I don't know where Marie Laveau got all that money from but she did spend a lot of money on that St. John Eve stuff. Man, but that St. John Eve was just like Mardi Gras for the people. The sky was always blue. Funny thing, Marie Laveau never had no trouble with the rain."

～

Although slavery and the threat of slave uprisings had passed at the end of the Civil War in 1865, authorities retained their nervous habits. They tracked large crowds of black people, established curfews, and gradually pushed the Voodoos out of old neighborhoods next to the French Quarter, out of large rear yards and alleys, and out of businesses abandoned or shut for the night. They kept Congo Square closed. Marie the Second moved her good-luck place, the site of informal services and benevolence, to Bayou St. John. On Friday afternoons she gathered everyone in a large circle at water's edge, prayed, and sang the theme song, "*We all go die in the water, it's true, we all go die in the water.*" At a special moment in the song, she signaled the participants, and those who wished swam, bathed, and were baptized in the waters of the bayou. People called it the "Cure Place" or the "Wishing Spot"—there they found something to eat and drink, coins to spend, and prayers for healing or good fortune. Unlike the ritual extravaganzas at the lakefront in June, the benevolent bathing parties on Bayou St. John occurred on Friday afternoons year-round and passed unnoticed in the press.

Marie's all-night gatherings with fires, feasting, dancing, and drums, however, were difficult to hide—especially at midsummer. The Voodoos had probably been meeting without notice along Lake Pontchartrain since the 1830s and 1840s. Then, at some point before the Civil War, Marie began to move her festivities to the village of Milneburg, a booming port and resort community and the most integrated and lively place in Reconstruction New Orleans—a place heir to the music and dances of Congo Square. The Pontchartrain Railroad, appropriately nicknamed the Smoky Mary, had opened in 1831 and linked the French Quarter with the lakefront beaches. Its tracks ran beside Elysian Fields, in classical mythology, the abode of the blessed after death, a place of bliss and happiness.

Marie the Second, a "widow" who had never been a wife, had rented a whitewashed cottage at the lakefront during the dreadful 1850s, perhaps after her father's and lover's deaths. She found more privacy at the end of the rail line than she did on St. Ann Street, where her children, her mother, her sister Philomène, nieces, nephews, George Legendre and his brothers, and a constant stream of guests filled the small house. But people gossiped even more about her, with even less evidence. They said the Voodoo queen was a notorious madam of a whorehouse and that her *maison blanche* or "white house" at the lake was a latter-day Quadroon ballroom where white men danced with women of color. It did not help Marie the Second's reputation that she counseled businesswomen who ran houses of pleasure and employment and offered them Voodoo charms and prayers or that both she and her mother had reason to sympathize with lovers who found each other across race, class, or religious boundaries. Women of various colors ran houses of prostitution at the lakefront; they have been successful sexual entrepreneurs in every era of New Orleans' history. But Marie chose the white cottage on the lakefront for reasons that had nothing to do with sex.

Milneburg was one of the great pleasure resorts in the South before the Civil War and a summer spa where tourists and citizens alike escaped the heat and contagion of the city. On the beach, taverns, bathhouses, and a grand hotel provided playgrounds for the elite. Restaurants earned the village an international reputation in a city already famous for its cuisine. Milneburg was also a hole in the net of slavery before Emancipation, and later, an insult to the racial rules of Reconstruction. There, white and black met as equals. Light-skinned people left the French Quarter as "colored" and arrived at the shores of the lake as "white." A white newspaper reporter, however, complained that the reverse had happened to him. The Smoky

Mary's sooty exhaust had turned him "black enough for admittance to the voudous or the Legislature."

A second Milneburg emerged after the Civil War. The lakefront became less the glittering playground for the well-to-do and more a funky people's place—fewer fine French soups and more gumbo, fewer classical quartets and more jazzy pickup bands. "A new and strange kind of music was beginning to be played there. To those who could remember the older Milneburg, the new sound was disturbing." Trombones and snare drums replaced guitars and violins. Visitors spoke of "blatant, raucous noises and revelries" and "swaying, swaggering dances. Others called it discordant ragtime and yearned for the tender rhythm of the waltz. But these raucous sounds were, of course, the sounds of early jazz, sounds that were to be the real glory of Milneburg and keep its name alive long after the place itself had passed from the map."

From the end of the Civil War until the early 1920s—in pre-radio and pre-recording days—live bands played at Milneburg every night. Blues man Danny Barker performed there in the early twentieth century; black and white bands, he said, battled or *bucked* each other from opposite camps as part of picnics and family outings. Sidney Bechet, composer and clarinetist, claimed that Milneburg deserved far more credit for hiring pioneer jazzmen than the whorehouses of Storyville did. On the lake from Milneburg to Spanish Fort, a musician could sit in, make a few bucks in tips, and practice with the big guys. The king himself, Louis Armstrong, played in Milneburg as part of a band from the Colored Waifs' Home for Boys.

In time, storms and hurricanes damaged the docks, piers, and bathhouses. In the 1920s city authorities evicted the residents of Milneburg, tore down their camps, and built a sea wall about a half-mile out on the water side. One day, jazz composer Jelly Roll Morton and some friends watched trucks haul earth to fill in between the old shore and the new seawall. They wrote a tribute, an obituary, to the delights of Milneburg and a woman named "Eliza the Shimmie Queen." The song, "Milenburg Joys"—named for the site of so much pleasure, its proper name spelled in a flexible New Orleans way—became a hit, a jazz standard. Eliza was one of the Voodoo leaders who worked with Marie the Second; the song suggests that Marie-style parties and dancing went on there much of the time and that at the lakefront camps Marie found the first and last love of her life—the freedom to dance.

> And ev'ry night with all her might, She does a dance that's hard to beat.
> The way she syncopates don't leave nothing out.
> You should hear this baby shout.
> Chorus: Rock my soul with the Milenburg Joys.
>         Play 'em Daddy, don't refuse.
>         Separate me from the weary blues. Hey! Hey! Hey!

After the Civil War, New Orleans' newspapers began to associate the women of Voodoo and their midsummer rituals with the intense racial conflicts of Reconstruction. In June of 1870, *Times'* reporters found Eliza and Marie "in their queenly glories, and homage paid to them, not only by their colored subjects, but also by a numerous crowd of well-known gentlemen from the city, who go out for curiosity and admiration of certain little yellow amendments to the Constitution." The *Bee* reported that hundreds of "heathenish Negroes," including Marie Laveau, Eliza Nicaud, and other black women, had gathered at the lakefront for the usual "disgusting rites." The *Bee* questioned what a "civilized community" could do to prevent the "intolerable excesses to which their ignorance and fanaticism lead." Then the editor of the paper blamed the Voodoos for the chronic misfortunes of the upper class—*you just can't find decent help anymore*. "Voudou devotees profess to practice witchcraft and in one instance where it is claimed to have been practiced at a gentleman's residence in this city we hear that he has been unable to procure colored servants ever since."

An editorial in the *Picayune* ranted about the Voodoos and resumed their charge that the cult drove innocent white women mad. "A young white girl, partially insane, was found in the midst of an assembly of Fetish worshipers chanting a horrible jargon, which they watched the progress of some strange rite of their curious and singular religion." Then the gentleman of the press added a new accusation. The Voodoos do human sacrifice. "Annually, the believers in this strange superstition indulge in strange orgies with singing and dancing and sacrifices which sometimes include human victims."

Human sacrifice is the ultimate ethnic accusation—an unfortunate infection of the human imagination about the "Other." Just after the midsummer ceremonies of 1870, the baby daughter of a prominent Anglo family in New Orleans was kidnapped. Last seen with her nursemaid—the woman was no doubt a Voodoo, reasoned the press—the poor child was destined to be "sacrificed to the Snake-God." Another reporter swore that he had "the word of a Voudou priestess that there are occasions which require the sacrifice of a new born infant in order to accomplish the purposes of this savage superstition."

Each year, by contrast, the city's newspapers printed large invitations to and announcements about the St. John's Day picnics and gatherings of white Masonic groups, veterans' associations, and benevolent societies. They compared the interracial, party-loving Voodoos unfavorably with the white community who celebrated St. John's Day in sedate daytime meetings or family picnics.

Marie the Second did not preside over the festivities in 1873. The *Picayune* said that she was "too old to attend." The *Herald* heard that the Voodoo queen had become religious—"the celebrated Marie Laveau, the former Queen of the Voudous, was not in attendance, she, in her honor be it said, having joined the church." Both newspapers were wrong.

The following June, Marie the Second, the still beautiful dancer who rarely went to church, decided to challenge and confront the newspapers, to tease or trick journalists who thought she was old and pious. On June 21, 1874, she issued a tongue-in-cheek invitation to newspaper reporters and citizens of the city to attend her midsummer's night party at Lake Pontchartrain. She and a colleague, Zelina, sent a letter in the style of invitation to a Mardi Gras ball to a regular column in the *Times*.

"Dear roundabout: Our yearly celebration of St. John's day (Voudou festival) at the old Lake End, will come off Wednesday night, the 24th inst. You and your friends are heartily invited to partake in the festivities, which will take place after the hour of ten p.m. near Marie Lavaux's old place, White House. In the name of the Queen, Her Secretary. ZELINA

Don't forget to come, Grand Voudou. Bring this card with you."

Then Marie the Second added a postscript: "P.S. If you guys on the *Times* are so influential, why don't you ask the Pontchartrain Railroad to reschedule its train to the lake. Then everybody can stay out late, have a great time, and still catch a ride home."

Two days later, on the morning of June 23, the *Times* printed the revised train schedule so that "thousands of curious sight-seers" could attend Marie's party. "In accordance with the long established custom, tonight— St. John's Eve, and tomorrow night, St. John's night—will be marked as the occasions of demonstrations by the Voudous, whose midnight orgies are at once among the most singular and striking spectacles of this or any other century." At last—reporters at the city's news desks promised them- selves—they would set eyes on the legendary queen of the Voodoos.

Three newspapers—the *Times,* the *Picayune,* and the *Commercial Bulletin*— sent reporters to the lakefront for the St. John's celebrations. Some newsmen got drunk. Others fell into slimy swamp waters. The people they questioned lied to them or laughed at them. One reporter did not know how to catch the Smoky Mary or find Milneburg on a map. Not one journalist found any woman who resembled the Marie of his imagination. To the *Times* reporter, however, that was proof that the "Voudous are no more, and their mys- terious ceremonies on St. John's eve and night at Milneburg have degenerated into a time of unrestrained license for the negroes, when they can get drunk and indulge in their idiotic pranks without fear of interference from the police." There were no religious activities—however revolting to refined sensibilities. It was just a wild party, the journalist sighed.

To the dismay of a second *Times'* reporter, both the Smoky Mary and the lakefront beaches were integrated, bursting with music and dancing. "Fully one-half of the passengers were negroes, and of these two-thirds were females of the lowest order. The most ardent defender of civil rights and social equality, were he black or white, would have blushed to have witnessed the many touching and affectionate illustrations of his pet theories. Men, women and children in all degrees of elegant attire, reeled and ranted and yelled through the uneven measures of the meanest music and lowest negro dance it was ever our ill fortune to witness."

"Marie is not out tonight," a woman in the group told the second man from the *Times*. "This St. John's Eve and we gonna have a great time tomorrow night. The queen, she come then."

The reporter for the *Bulletin* hired a carriage. From the main road he could see distant bonfires, dancing shadows thrown against the night sky. But, as his carriage neared, the music ceased, the fires were quenched, and the forms and shapes disappeared. Empty-handed and bitter, he returned the same muddy way he came.

A reporter for the *Republican*, however, took neither the Smoky Mary nor a hired carriage. He listened to and believed a different set of rumors— Marie the Second planned a hoax; she laid down a false scent and left fake clues. The newsman "was as eager to go as anyone else, but a well-informed friend held him back with the remark that he would thereby expend several hours in making an A No. 1 'gooney' of himself, and not get voudooed either. Those who did go found some bonfires, evidence of destroyed whiskey, a ballroom half-filled with bacchantes. But the voudou queen was invisible."

Journalists and their editors were chronically confused. When and where, exactly, did the Voodoos under Marie Laveau's leadership meet? If the reporters could not find them, were they there? Did people lie to or tease reporters about Marie Laveau's arrival or her presence at the ceremonies? Did the newsmen know what she looked like? More to the point, did reporters know the difference between a rousing New Orleans party and a Voodoo ritual?

Marie the Second used her organizational skills and spiritual contacts to lead the weekly good-fortune ritual baths on Bayou St. John and throw the yearly parties at the lake—parties that foreshadowed the annual Jazz and Heritage Festival. She served good liquor and fine food at her gatherings. The citizens of the city danced free—free of tight clothes, tight social rules, and the restraints of Reconstruction. And when the media of her time stalked her, she and John "hoodooed" them.

## Coda

Still smarting from the St. John's Eve disaster of 1874, all but one of the newspapers the following year gave up their summertime search for the queen of the Voodoos. In June of 1875 a young reporter from the *Picayune* visited Marie the First, the aged Widow Paris, at her St. Ann Street home. Their conversation is repeated word for word as he himself reported it.

"Bonjour, Monsieur."

"Bonjour, Mama Marie." He greeted her in the manner white Americans had adopted for black women—just "Mama" and a first name.

Madame Laveau, three-quarters of a century old, sat in her yard below a trellis laced with summer vines. On one side of her chair was a small altar. She wore a plain dark dress with a brooch at the neck; a white handkerchief rested on her black hair. The cane she held in one hand confirmed what people in New Orleans had been saying for several years—the Widow Paris, ailing or infirm, no longer walked the streets of the French Quarter.

The French-speaking reporter wanted to know about Voodoo; his colleagues on the *Picayune* called it "fetish devil worship of heathen Africa." They told him that the alleged Voodoo queens led dances at the lakefront— "bestial performances" and "the wildest and most hellish orgies." What do you have to do with such matters, the newsman asked the Widow Paris.

"Ah! So, Monsieur. I am no Voudou now. I am a believer in the holy faith." She kissed a small cross she held in her hand.

"Well, Mama. You can tell me something of them, can you not?"

"Not much, now, Monsieur. Last year I was not there. This year Eliza, a black woman, was the Queen. She lives on the lake shore 'way beyond Milneburg. It is a bad thing—a very bad thing."

Later generations of writers reported their conversation as the solemn truth. See, they declare, Marie Laveau, the Widow Paris, kissed her rosary and denounced the Voodoos. She repented of her lurid past and returned to proper Catholic piety.

The reporter continued to question the Widow Paris; he translated what she told him and put the exchange into his own words. "After a little conversation in which it was elicited that she had no more belief in the faith, and that the principal portion of the voudou worshipers were negroes, though there were some whites, it was understood that of late years the faith had somewhat degenerated, though it was still extensively practiced. It used to be the custom, also, long ago, to sacrifice little 'picaninnies,' but, of late years, the law was too strong and the people too poor to do this, and they had to be satisfied with a chicken, which was tossed into the pot, feathers and all, alive, and which, with the other ingredients, formed a kind of stew, which, if the faithful drank kept them from the evil eye for a year."

But Marie the First told the newsman that Voodoo had changed and adapted much faster than the *Picayune*. She fed him reckless gossip about chickens and evil eyes; the human sacrifice story was ludicrous—but he fell for all of it. He contradicted himself at every turn—the faith is withered and weakened, the faith is alive and well. I think she ran circles around him and anyone else who fell for her "repentance" act.

The *Picayune* reporter concluded his midsummer's tale: the glory of the Voodoo rites has vanished, only a remnant of its former heathen splendor remains. Then he added Marie Laveau's last statement.

"Monsieur, we've obtained a license for next year's St. John's Eve from the authorities."

A direct quote from the Widow Paris: the Voodoos can and will meet on their sacred holiday; the press may or may not be able to find them. High John the Conqueror—trickster, devil—must have been hiding near the garden vines on St. Ann Street. I can see the gleam in Marie Laveau's eye.

# Chapter 11

## A Tale of Two Sisters

COMMENCE! WE SPEAK THROUGH TEARS.

COMMENCE, S'IL VOUS PLAIT, MADAME, CALL THE GREAT DRUM!

—SYBIL KEIN, "TO THE WIDOW PARIS"

The physician from the health department of New Orleans knocked on the door of 152 St. Ann early that September morning. The women who opened the old door to him were dressed in Creole mourning clothes, the linen handkerchiefs they pulled from hidden pockets soaked with their tears. She passed away at four o'clock in the morning, they told him. He questioned them. No, she was not married, and yes, she had been born in New Orleans, they answered. What did she die of? How long had she been ill? To himself he added the silent questions his profession demanded, had she died of something contagious, something that might signal an epidemic? Had she been murdered?

After examining her body, the doctor determined that the cause of death was an abscess of her liver, although no medical tests of the period could have confirmed this diagnosis. September was yellow fever season; the disease cycles through the livers of afflicted people and turns their skin yellow—but so does an abscessed liver. Their conversation and the documents he filled out were in French three quarters of a century after Louisiana had become American. We're Creoles, free people of color, the women told him. The doctor translated into the only categories the bureaucracy he served could understand; at three different places in the short form, he stipulated that the deceased was "Colored."

Later that morning a priest from nearby St. Augustine's Catholic Church came to the Laveau-Glapion home with his own paperwork and prayers for the deceased woman. He examined the handwritten death certificate from the city's physician, copied down the information he would need for the church's records, and added the burial notice: the deceased was to be interred in the "high tomb of the family of the Widow Paris" in St. Louis Cemetery One. The custodian of the cemetery would need priestly certification to open the marble-fronted tomb.

The following morning, September 10, 1871, family members walked across Rampart Street, past Congo Square, and into St. Louis One, and left there the earthly body of twenty-six-year-old Aldina Crocker. The Widow Paris swore to the physician and to the priest—these facts are carefully recorded in the civil and church documents—that the deceased had been the daughter of one "Marie Laveau" and that she herself was the young woman's grandmother. Although the paperwork of death had improved by 1871, it answers only the questions of their time, not of ours. It leaves the grief of such a loss to our imagination and forces the question—where was Aldina's mother, Marie Eucharist?

Aldina had lived on St. Ann Street with her grandmother, the seventy-year-old Widow Paris, her aunt Philomène, her brother, Victor Pierre, and assorted cousins and boarders. Under ordinary circumstances, one might assume that a daughter's death had cast her mother into despair and that a levelheaded grandmother who had nursed the sick and dying all her life carried out the death duties. But, by the height of Reconstruction, Marie the Second, in her mid-forties, was an enigma. She did not sign her only daughter's death certificate. She proved difficult to locate in her own time—doubly so for those who have searched for her after that.

No newspapers, histories, or *gumbo ya-ya* confirm the existence of a woman named Aldina, probably born in 1845, a granddaughter and a daughter to the leaders of Voodoo—perhaps their hope of spiritual continuity. Nor did the family carve an inscription for her on the high tomb in St. Louis One. I have no doubt that Aldina rests there with eight other members of her family; the paper trail is clear. But the Paris-Glapion-Legendre household had fallen on hard times and could not afford to hire a stonecutter to mark her passing.

∿

The most stable person on St. Ann Street was Philomène. She owned the house; she had installed a husband, their children, and members of his family there, and she had inherited her mother's nursing skills. After Aldina's death, the Widow Paris—last glimpsed in May of 1871 at midnight Mass at Parish Prison praying for two men who were scheduled to hang—did not appear in public again. Aldina died in the fall of that year, and after that her grandmother became deeply housebound; newspaper reporters found her confined to her yard in 1875 and to her bed in 1879. But no one could find Marie the Second on St. Ann in the French Quarter, in her residence on Love Street in the Faubourg Marigny, or at her "white house" beyond the last stop of the Smoky Mary Railroad.

On New Year's Eve, 1879, two reporters from the *Daily States* knocked on the door of the St. Ann house at midnight—their idea of paying respects to the reputation for the mysterious and occult the house had earned by then, and to the only leader of the Voodoos they could identify. Philomène, "a middle-aged, light-visaged woman, a lady in all her motions and conversation," opened the door and introduced them to Glapion, her teenage son. The reporters could hear music and the sounds of dancing from a well-lighted house behind the front courtyard. The young people are having a party, she explained, and ushered them into a room "completely filled with furniture. A large walnut bedstead took up two-thirds of the floor, while a commode, a wash-stand, a trunk or so, a table and a huge protruding chimney piece occupied one-half the remaining space." Outside, the music quieted, and those who had been celebrating the passage of the old year crowded into the room and filled the entire space surrounding the bed. "The air became hot and stifling," the newsmen noted, "but here we were in the presence of ancient majesty, and could afford to bear with the discomfort."

Marie Laveau, the Widow Paris, in a white dress, her streaked black hair curled about her temples, rested beneath an old quilt divided into squares, each block decorated with flags. The reporter noticed "the glittering penetrating sparkle of small, coal black eyes" as she "lay there watching with ever restless eyes the crowd gathered around her." The older journalist spoke French to the Widow Paris and translated the conversation for his younger associate. She told the crowd around her bed about Père Antoine's benevolent smile that blessed the work they did together and the January day in 1815 she saw General Jackson enter the square that bears his name for the celebration of victory at the Battle of New Orleans. The younger journalist, however, heard only an "old lady speaking in a far-away feeble tone, but showing that she had her wits about her. Nothing really important was elicited."

The older journalist had better manners and more patience. At the end of the interview, he took Madame Laveau's outstretched hand, and inquired gently,

"Mama, here is some money. Glapion shall go to the French Market in the morning and get you something nice to eat. What shall he get for you?"

"In a deep, sepulchral voice came back the dissyllabic answer. 'Gumbo.'"

The Widow Paris lived another year and a half. Any mock mysteries about her date of death or where she lies buried are settled forever. She died in her own bed on June 15, 1881. Philomène who nursed her mother through the last years described her last moments. "On Wednesday the invalid sank into the sleep, which knows no waking. Those whom she had befriended crowded into the little room where she was exposed, in order to obtain a last look at the features, smiling even in death, of her who had been so kind to them." She lay in state briefly on June 16, and was buried that evening. A death certificate states that "Dame Christophe Glapion"—in death Philomène turned her mother into a respectable married lady—was buried in the middle vault of her own tomb in St. Louis One. Philomène said, "her remains were followed to the grave by a large concourse of people, the most prominent and the most humble joining in paying their last respects to the dead"—yet no eyewitnesses have ever surfaced to speak of that historic moment.

Newspapers in New Orleans ran obituaries that weekend and through the midsummer's nights of St. John's Eve that followed. The *Democrat* called the Widow Paris an "old negro creole character" who made love charms that brought lovers together and knew drugs that kept them apart. Thousands sought her for advice, good fortune, and revenge. "Much evil dies with her, but should we not add, a little poetry."

∿

Three weeks after the burial of the Widow Paris, the New Orleans City Council voted to "improve" and "develop" Congo Square once again. Contractors whom the councilmen hired agreed to remove the rusty old chain railing, "which, instead of being a protection and an ornament, really mars its beauty." They planned to gravel the walks, to trim and whitewash the trees, and to "make the square as attractive as any in the city." The Square, they noted, had been "a meeting place" at the edge of town where men and women from many parts of Africa "were want to meet and dance their native dances." The renovators chopped down the old oak tree, the place of Creole benevolence where Marie the Second had danced and her followers left food, drink, and coins for poor people in a poor city.

∿

The four adult women of the St. Ann Street household had survived the slavery system, an enemy occupation of their city, and a war that had divided, bankrupted, and ripped apart many families. But the so-called peace and freedom that followed were harder to bear. The troubled times began with a three-hour "riot" on July 30, 1866, that swept households like theirs into violent murders and the costs of racial resistance. Creoles of color called the tragic events an "absolute Massacre" because, of the forty to fifty men who died and the six times that many who were wounded, most were unarmed free people of color, a tragic cross-section of the tormented Creole community. The immediate cause of the 1866 confrontation was a constitutional convention that recognized the equality of blacks—by this time Creoles of color were included in the all-purpose racial category—and granted them rights to vote, hold public office, and be treated without discrimination as full citizens of a recently reunited country. Whites, particularly former Confederate soldiers and sympathizers, opposed all political or social policies that allowed formerly enslaved people equality within custom or the law and were willing to go into battle once more. Despite their bloody victory that day, however, it would take white supremacists another decade to undo the federally-imposed regulations of Reconstruction, to institute full segregation, and to find the means to put women like Marie the Second in their place.

For Aldina the deaths of July 30, 1866, added to those of friends in the Louisiana Native Guards and other military units, meant she had even fewer men within her narrowing social circles to marry. She may have lost a fiancé in the war; she may not have found a man within the diminished and demoralized ranks of Creoles or contemplated an Anglo, immigrant, or freedman. Men of her social class who had trouble finding and keeping jobs in the postwar economy were not in a marrying mood.

The Widow Paris dressed in extended Creole mourning—somber grays, soft lilacs, and dark-as-night colors—for the remainder of her life.

For the two sisters, Marie Eucharist and Philomène, however, that July day—the bloodiest episode of racial violence and resistance in the United States during Reconstruction—changed everything. Philomène, who already bore the brunt of American laws against cohabitation and interracial marriage, began to turn away from her Creole connections and to concentrate on safer and more neutral identities—conventional Catholic daughter, wife, and mother. Although she still called herself Madame Legendre, her husband George made it appear in official documents that he had moved away from St. Ann Street, a strategy that protected his family, as his father-in-law had tried to do. His male relatives no longer lived with them, and the household plunged into urban poverty. Although Philomène did not consider passing, she suspected that her children would; and so she whitewashed or rebuffed anything that might appear controversial or dangerous about their lives—particularly her mother's Voodoo activities and the very existence of her older sister. No one ever saw Philomène wearing a *tignon* again.

Marie the Second, in sharp contrast, shouldered the burdens of spiritual leadership amid the dying breaths of Creole nationalism; she wore—even flaunted—a high-tied *tignon* and gold jewelry and walked, many witnesses swore, as though she and her people still owned the city. With the end of the Civil War in 1865 and the full onset of Reconstruction, however, New Orleans was no longer a wealthy, glittering scene. It was a backwater of American economic life—a city that sang the blues. The social season of nightly amusements was diminished and tawdry. Hairdressers like Marie the Second were no longer on call at the fashionable hotels of the French Quarter and Garden District. In the genteel poverty that marked households in the Creole and American sections of town, women had to do their own hair.

How much influence could either Marie Laveau bring to bear on courts, judges, or lawyers who spoke English? *Gris-gris* was difficult to make work on Northerners; it was impossible to "fix" federal troops. How could Marie the First help "her people" or "be with the people in all things," as Philomène had said of her mother, if there were fewer Creoles each year? In 1860, the U.S. census counted almost 170,000 inhabitants of New Orleans; 10 percent were free people of color. In 1870, the city's population fell just short of 200,000, but no slaves or free people of color were left to be tallied. One out of four people in New Orleans were, however, counted as "colored." Creoles were pushed into the undiscriminating, yet fully discriminated against, classification: a suspected "one drop of black blood" turned a person into a Negro.

Creole racial flexibility gave way to Anglo-American apartheid. Although people in the South newly freed from slavery looked to Reconstruction as a time of opportunity, for Creoles who had been free and prosperous before the war and who dreamed of cultural leadership in a multiracial and multicultural society after the war, postwar life was hell. The 1873 "race riot" in Colfax, Louisiana, and the "Battle of Liberty Place" in New Orleans in 1874 that followed the 1866 massacre have been commemorated into the twenty-first century with demonstrations and arrests.

In the climate of violence and intimidation, Creoles of color like Marie the Second had every reason to be dispirited. Many who survived the war lost their will to live in its aftermath. Some killed themselves. Aristide Mary, a man of political standing before Reconstruction, was refused admittance to the Opera House. He failed in his attempt to block the Louisiana legislature from segregating state universities. In 1892, the Louisiana State Supreme Court ruled against Homer Plessy, a New Orleans' Creole of color, in the landmark case that would establish Jim Crow and "separate but equal" as the law of the land. Aristide Mary shot himself. So did John Racquet Clay and Jean Baptiste Jourdain—using guns they were forbidden by law to own. François Lacroix's son was killed in the "Riot" of 1866; the father died of a broken heart in 1875.

Creole philanthropists, poets, and perhaps Voodoo queens like Marie the Second, surrendered to the malaise. Free people of color fashioned many responses. They reworked nostalgic memories of their lost status. They left town. They went into internal and psychological exile, filled with frustration, futility, and self-destruction. The Civil War had produced neither liberty nor equality for Creoles of color. "It brought decline, division, and a desperate search for solace and seclusion." Before the Civil War they "were more strongly united by the bonds of love" and "our community took on an air of honest industry and mutual cordiality," said a Creole historian. After the war, "far from seeking deliverance," they lived "in a moral depression that seems to represent the last degree of impotence."

Marie the Second's life was unraveling. The newspapers were filled with anti-Voodoo outbursts that extended increasingly to her. "There can be no possible doubt that Voudouists have unnatural powers," the *Picayune* claimed in 1869. Deluded and neurotic white women sought Voodoo counseling to help them with their love lives. For example, "a young lady of remarkable sagacity, but at present bewitched ... fell in love, and procured the services of a Voudou to assist her in bringing to her feet the object of her love." And when the Voodoos were not bewitching their innocent white neighbors, they were robbing them. "A soldier named John Pirie was drugged and robbed in the Voudou den of Eliza Nicaud of $600 in money and a draft for $1,000.

The sable Nicaud is a high priestess of the Voudous, and is of high repute among the believers in that strange superstition." This is the same Eliza who danced with Marie the Second on St. John's Eve in 1871—"Eliza the Shimmie Queen" immortalized in the jazz song, "Milenburg Joys."

On May 24, 1871, the *Times* reported that "Mrs. Glapion, 152 St. Anne Street," the daughter of Marie Laveau, brought civil charges against a Mrs. Leblanc, 149 St. Anne Street, whom she said had provoked, insulted, and abused her. Mrs. Leblanc, "who had found some arrangements in the real voudou style on her doorsteps, had accused Mrs. Glapion and her family of having put those naughty things there, stating that her husband, who had to remove them, was sick since, and her daughter, who had only stepped over them, had also enjoyed but very poor health." There are no existing records of the "unusual array of witnesses and rich testimony" the newspaper claims took place at the hearing. The judge called Voodoo "a foolish thing," and required Mrs. Leblanc to furnish a peacekeeping bond.

Three months later the *Picayune* carried a story about an argument between Marie Laveau "and Dr. Jim, the great Physician, who is supposed by his disciples to hold in his hands the issues of life and death. Their violent discussions a few nights since demanded the interposition of the police, and a number of them were arrested; nevertheless, it had no effect in allaying the fever of excitement, and the conflict is still waged with vehement antipathy." Jim Alexander had initiated Marie the Second into Voodoo, taught her many secrets, and then had seen her surpass him in spiritual work and reputation. Both incidents, the feud with her neighbor and the turmoil with her teacher—whatever these stories mean or whoever was in the wrong—happened in the spring and summer of 1871, a summer that ended in Aldina's death.

The week Aldina died the *Picayune* placed Voodoo practitioners at the top of their list of causes for the city's postwar problems. The newspaper pointed out the staggering poverty and social dislocation among the newly freed black people and poor people of color whom "unscrupulous queens" had duped and tricked out of what little cash they had—"Voudou victims," the editorial said. The *Picayune* proposed a simple solution for scoundrels like Marie the Second—whoever built and profited from a Voodoo trade should be taken away and lynched, hanged in a public place.

Just after her triumphal appearance at the midsummer festivities of 1872, nine months after her daughter's death, the *Times* reported that the Voodoo queen had been "working some spell" on a man who confronted her with a cheese knife at the corner of Barracks and Burgundy, and "called her to account, whereupon a quarrel ensued, in which all the Voudous of the neighborhood participated." The police came and the crowd dispersed.

A year and a half after Aldina's death, the *Times* buried this short article on page six: "Marie Laveau, the Voudou Queen, made her advent as a spectator yesterday in the lobby of the Criminal Court, and attracted special attention by her weird appearance. She was dressed in all the soiled and dingy frippery of an impecunious princess, with her rather commanding form encircled by a red shawl, and a faded yellow Madras, wrapped in the form of a turban around her head and in her face there was an expression of the supernatural. She finally disappeared from the court room, whether astraddle of broomstick, or otherwise." In June 1873, two months after this article appeared, the *Times* reported that Marie Laveau the Second had been too ill to attend the St. John's Eve ceremonies at the lakefront.

In 1874, Marie the Second pulled the fraying strands of her life together and staged the great St. John's Eve Hoax to confront and challenge the newspapers' obsession with her. Although no one saw her, newspaper reporters certainly "believed" in her existence. After 1874, however, local reporters never spotted Marie the Second again. Neither Philomène nor the Widow Paris ever referred to her in the interviews they granted the press. On top of the tribulations of Reconstruction in the dispirited Creole community, Aldina's death crowned all other losses with a mother's grief. The weight of Voodoo leadership in such terrible times fell harder on Marie the Second than it had on her mother. I think it killed her.

Marie Laveau the Second vanished. I have not discovered a trustworthy date of death, a cause of death, a gravesite, or any believable report of her passing in the historic or folklore records. After the summer of 1874, I cannot find Marie the Second in a priestess's role, in a personal relationship, or in the public eye. She was not among those who gathered at her mother's dying pillow—Philomène told the *Picayune* reporter that the Widow Paris had left only one surviving child. If a death certificate ever existed, it has disappeared like many documents that bear the Laveau name. A neighbor said, "Marie Glapion was an outcast from her family. You see, that Madame Legendre, her sister, was so stuck up that she done denied her." Another backed her up: "Old Madame Legendre wouldn't have nothing to do with her sister even when she died."

Five months after the funeral of Marie the First, Victor Pierre Christophe Dieudonné Duminy de Glapion went to the Civil District Court of the Parish of Orleans and claimed that his mother, Marie the Second, was dead. On November 29, 1881, he swore an oath that he was "the sole and only heir at law" of his mother, Heloise Eucharist Glapion. He asked for legal possession of the house on Love Street, by then called Rampart. The court granted his petition.

On first reading this set of papers, I assumed Marie the Second died sometime between her mother's death in June and November of that same year. The year and a day rule meant the family could not have buried her in the high tomb of the Widow Paris with her parents, brother, and three of her Crocker children—the gravesite could not have been reopened for another internment until June 1882. My theory made sense of the persistent legend that Marie the Second is buried in St. Louis Cemetery Two, Square Three, where many famous Creoles of color lie. Her baby brother François, various Crockers including Pierre and his brother Bazile, several Marie Laveaus from collateral branches of the large family, and other relatives are buried there. People leave offerings at an oven grave on the outer wall. A brochure for a "Black History Tour" of St. Louis Two says, "Folk tradition has decreed this vault to be the final resting place of the voodoo queen who was the daughter of the Widow Paris, buried in St. Louis I cemetery."

But before the courts granted Victor Pierre Crocker's petition to be declared Eucharist Glapion's legal son and only heir, they demanded proof. How do we know, they asked, that you are her son, that she was your mother, and that she is really dead? A woman named "Mrs. Marie Philomène

Glapion, natural aunt of the petitioner above named" appeared before the civil authorities who deposed her and took down her sworn testimony. "I am the god-mother of Victor Pierre Crocker; I live in New Orleans, and I was there at the family home on St. Ann Street when his mother, my sister, gave birth to him in November, 1853, and again in early 1854 when she herself presented him to a priest for his baptism." Written, sworn testimony of two childhood friends of the deceased confirmed these facts. In nineteenth-century New Orleans, a baptism, sworn to and witnessed by three people, was proof of a person's birth and identity.

Philomène continued. "And furthermore, I swear that my sister used the name Eucharist Glapion. I swear that she was my natural sister, that she never married, and that she died without a will in June of 1862."

Victor Pierre Crocker and his aunt Philomène went to court in 1881, swore to and signed an oath that Eucharist Heloise Glapion—Marie the Second—had died in 1862. Victor Pierre needed to establish his legal existence and relationship to his deceased mother. He had no birth or baptismal certificates just as thousands who died in the yellow fever epidemic just before his birth had no death certificates. But what purpose did the tall tale with its deceptive date serve? I have to presume that Marie the Second died sometime after 1874 or 1875, when she was last glimpsed, and before her mother's death in 1881. Maybe the circumstances of her demise were so traumatic that family members managed to conceal them—she went crazy and her family locked her away somewhere, or she committed suicide or moved away as so many Creoles of color did. If Marie the Second's son and sister needed to cover up a disappearance or a disgrace, they picked the most convenient time in New Orleans' history in which to hide someone's death. In June of 1862, Federal troops who occupied the city collected or filed few vital statistics.

The signed documents of 1881 fail to convince me that Marie the Second died in 1862. They do, however, prove that Philomène and Victor Pierre inherited the family's propensity to manipulate written documents for their own purposes. Their intentions, as well as the location, condition, or whereabouts of Marie the Second during this time, remain the real mysteries. These documents are the only direct or written evidence about the death of Marie the

Second, and the only time Philomène ever acknowledged her sister in a public record. Yet newspaper articles after 1862, extensive WPA testimonies in the 1930s, Luke Turner's disclosures to Zora Neale Hurston, and some odd court dockets offset the documents that Philomène and Pierre signed. As a matter of public record, Eucharist Glapion appeared in two civil suits—one in 1865 and the other in 1866. City officials cited her for unpaid taxes on the Love Street house and fined her $3.50 each time. In New Orleans dead people are allowed to vote in most elections—but they do not have to pay real estate taxes.

In January of 1882, two months after he and his aunt signed the documents, Victor Pierre "Peter" Crocker, a barber, sold his mother's house on Love Street.

It is impossible to satisfy all the people who have opinions about the death and burial of Marie the Second. The *gumbo ya-ya* and the tales the interviewers of the WPA Federal Writers' Project collected place the Voodoo queen in graves all over the city. A staff member threw up her hands in despair: "Every other negro has a different burial place for Marie Laveau. No one person has ever been buried in so many places as the queen of the voodoos."

One citizen said, "At first she was buried in St. Louis Cemetery Two by Claiborne Street. Sure, I been to where she was, I used to go there when people wanted to wish at her grave. On Wednesday and Friday, you couldn't hardly get near for the crowd. They always put in the iron slats, $1.15, 'cause she always wanted money, and bottles of wine, preserves, pralines, and most everything, and they burned candles. Then they moved her away. They took most everything—throwed graveyard dust in too. Nobody knew why."

Marie Brown, who knew the family well, repeated the reburial tale with supporting details, "Marie Laveau was buried in St. Louis Number Two, on the Claiborne Street side. When they cut away a part of the wall, her bones had to go too, so they moved 'em to Girod Cemetery."

"Are you certain?" the interviewers from the Federal Writers' Project asked.

"Didn't I tole you where she was? She in Girod Cemetery!"

"They" moved her bones to the Girod Street cemetery, which is now buried beneath the New Orleans Superdome. Locals who knew people who saw the construction workers on the project tell me that the men tossed skulls to each other, laughed as the bones piled up, and failed to save markers or statuary. Those who constructed the stadium did not "decommission" the cemetery or otherwise pay their respects to those buried there. The *gumbo ya-ya* says that Marie the Second is not happy about this desecration of a graveyard, that the stadium is cursed as a result, and that the Saints' football team loses many games because they have not properly soothed the spirits who live in the now-buried city of the dead.

Marie the Second's disappearance and her lack of a proper burial have given rise to wild rumors—her enemies poisoned her; her family and friends shunned her; she died of a broken heart. Some say that Marie the Second was buried in St. Louis One, "but her spirit wouldn't behave. Madame Legendre and the other relatives got ashamed—you know how stuck up they was—so they moved her to Holt Cemetery and buried her there without no mark on her grave." Meanwhile, many in New Orleans believed that the spirit of Marie Laveau still walked the streets. "Once when I was in a drug store on Rampart Street, a woman come in. A man was standing near me. She walks around him, turns around," and in response to an offhand remark he made, "slaps the life out of him, then jumps over the fence—flip, fly— onto a tomb and disappears."

Marie Brown was eighty-six when the staff of the Writers' Project visited her. "No, I don't know where she died, an' I never heard anything 'bout a funeral. I been living in this neighborhood 75 years and it look like I would know something. The earth swallowed her up."

Marie Laveau was well-known in town, an eighty-seven-year-old woman said. "Maybe she was spirited away."

This much I know—wherever Marie the Second lies, she does not rest easy.

～

Five years after the Widow Paris's death, with the disappearance of Marie the Second still a mystery, a reporter from the *Picayune* barged into the

St. Ann Street household. He found Philomène, her two daughters, and a grandchild there. "Every one of the group was comely. Madame Legendre, although her heavy mass of hair is turning as white as that of her mother, still shows the sign of beauty which she inherited. Tall, majestic, graceful, the eye still flashing fire, and with firm step, notwithstanding months of illness, she rules her household."

The *Picayune* reporter baited Philomène with an article about the legendary queen of the Voodoos that Creole writer George Washington Cable had published in a national magazine. He read parts of it aloud to the women: "The worship of Voodoo is paid to a snake kept in a box. The worshipers are not merely a sect, but in some rude, savage way also an order. The queen is still a person of great note. She reigns as long as she continues to live."

"It's a lie. It's a lie."

Philomène interrupted the *Picayune* reporter with angry, scornful laughs. As she paced up and down the well-scrubbed plank floors with quick, sharp steps, she tried to express herself first in English, and, failing that, fell back on scorching French. The reporter who made no attempt to repeat her exact words captured her indignation.

"Snake in a box indeed! What for they say that about her when she is dead. She was too good. What did she know about a snake in a box?" Philomène, teeth clenched and lips quivering, stepped up her ferocious pacing up and down the narrow room.

"Can we not stop this? The courts must protect us. People come here and see nothing. They see nothing but ladies, and then they go off and tell lies. My mother never did them any harm, and then they go off and write bad things about her. What they know? There are some men in this town who knew my mother and who have power. I will go and see them, and they will not drag her name around and lie about her anymore."

"But you cannot stop them from talking far away from here," said the reporter.

"Yes, but I can tell them that they lie," Philomène replied.

"I know what we will do," Madame Legendre grew quiet and addressed her daughters. "Hereafter we will let no one in. They had that excuse, that the house was so old, that they wanted to see it. When they were polite we let them in."

Philomène's parents, Marie Laveau and Christophe Glapion, had sheltered strangers, visitors, and people without a place to stay. But in the five years since her mother's death, visitors showed up, many late at night, and demanded to be admitted. Philomène's home on St. Ann had become a Voodoo shrine, a place of pilgrimage to the legendary Marie Laveau whose very existence her daughter denied.

Philomène was a loving and competent nurse for her own mother as she aged and died. The liver disease that took Aldina's life may have made her an invalid in its final stages, and Philomène probably had to care for her older sister, Marie the Second, as she grew sicker and more despondent. Then she took in her mother-in-law, Emily Legendre, a widow, and cared for her too. Thanks to Philomène's stewardship, the house on St. Ann Street—though falling down from lack of maintenance as so many old houses in New Orleans were, then as now—remained female-focused, multigenerational, multiracial, and multicultural.

"When we get money it will be an old house no more," Philomène fantasized. "We will tear it down and build a new one. Then there will be nothing for them to see." Noime Legendre, one of her daughters present that day, fulfilled the prophesy. She sold the house on St. Ann a few weeks after her mother's death in 1897; the new owners demolished it.

Philomène Legendre continued to swear at the *Picayune* reporter in her French-accented English; she folded and refolded the cashmere shawl that rested on the back of an old rocking chair. The queen of England sent my mother this shawl, she said. Marie Laveau was a great woman—the French patriot, the Marquis de Lafayette, kissed her hand, and she waltzed with William Claiborne, the first American governor of Louisiana. There were never any spirited dances in Congo Square—no snakes in boxes. My mother never repented of cults and orgies; there was nothing that happened to regret or recant. I go to church each day to pray, just as my mother did.

No matter how provoked or pained Philomène may have been, however, not one word she said acknowledged her older sister, Marie the Second.

Then, in answer to a question the *Picayune* reporter never thought to ask, Philomène blurted out her last secret—a poignant longing across the rhythmic divide of culture and citizenship.

"Nobody ever see her dancing like that paper say. People have come here to see her and they never saw anything wrong. I could never dance."

*I could never dance.* Sweet Philomène. She could not marry or be buried beside a man she loved—her children passed for white and moved out of the community of their birth forever. Named for an obscure Catholic martyr and saint, dutiful Philomène kept the shrine on St. Ann Street, barred forever from the soul of Voodoo. Unlike her grandmother, her mother, her sister, and so many friends, she never danced in double-headed ecstasy.

# Chapter 12

## The Last Queen of the Voodoos
## Returns from the Dead

*THE SPIRIT HITS THEM AND THEY FOLLOW.*

—LOUIS ARMSTRONG

In the season when hurricanes mass off the coast of Africa and sweep across the Atlantic, when crepe myrtle trees explode in blowzy balls, and when heat-weary citizens sit on their stoops, the brick-scoured front steps of their cottages, the streets of New Orleans buzzed with enthralled tales of what had happened to Marie Laveau. From Frenchmen and Desire to St. Charles and Annunciation, from the neighborhoods of Tremé and Marigny to the Seventh and the Ninth Wards, the latest *gumbo ya-ya* spread like the floodwaters of the Mississippi when they escaped their levees.

Did you hear? "Marie Laveau was in her house out by the lake when the storm come up. She was giving a big Voodoo dance. The storm swept her house away and her and all them hoodoos with her."

Yes, that's what I heard too. "Marie was drowned when she got caught in a tree."

Each person embellished the story as they passed it on to the next. "She was dead when they found her. Her body floated in to shore and her eyes was closed and her hands folded jest like she was already laid out at her wake."

If Marie the Second perished in a storm on Lake Pontchartrain and her body was never recovered, the absence of a burial plot or memorial plaque for her makes sense. Yes, there was a big storm; summers in New Orleans are full of them. But, as the story spread, many citizens of New Orleans swore to their neighbors that Marie Laveau had conquered the waves and the winds, even death itself, to make a supernatural reappearance. "She got washed away in a big storm, but she never died. She floated five days on a log and was swept in to shore. She never even suffered from exposure. She was too powerful to let nothin' hurt her. She lived for years after that."

Young girls at impressionable ages overheard the stories their mothers, aunts, and grandmothers were telling in the neighborhood. One went to fish at Bayou St. John three days after St. John's Eve. "It was all over town that Marie Laveau was drowned, but I didn't know much about her and so I didn't pay it much mind." When the child reached her favorite place, she saw a waterlogged woman floating among the willow trees at the edge of the water. "All of a sudden I heard her moan, so I bent down and spoke to her." The child pushed aside the blue veil that covered the woman's face and lifted the box she clutched so tightly. "Her eyes opened up. She looked straight into my face and, let me tell you, I never seen such eyes. They were beautiful and they went straight through you."

"I love you, my child, and I don't love many people. I am Marie Laveau."

"But they say you're dead." The child began to shake.

"I know," she replied. "Marie Laveau's been dead before." And then Marie laughed, "I'm a strong woman. You come see me sometime."

Marie Dede, a colleague of the Laveaus and great-granddaughter of Sanité Dede, offered a breathless tale and the only dates within range of probability. "June 24th—that was in 1873—I'll never forget that. Marie Laveau and all her queens and kings was at the lake doing their hoodoo dance and singing in Creole, 'I wants to die in that lake.' And a storm came up and threw her in the lake and everybody thought she was drowned—but they found her floating on the water and they caught her and brought her on the shore and rolled her to bring her through—but she didn't die— she lived for about seven years after that. She died in 1880."

When Zora Neale Hurston asked Luke Turner what had happened to his great-aunt, he replied. "Three days Marie, she set at the Altar with the great sun candle burning and shining in her face. She set the water upon the Altar and turned to the window, and looked upon the lake. The sky grew dark. The lightning raced to the seventeen quarters of the heavens and the lake heaved like a mighty herd of cattle rolling in a pasture. The house shook with the earth. . . . Some who loved her hurried out to Bayou St. John and tried to enter the house but she try hard to send them off. They beat upon the door, but she will not open. The terrible strong wind at last tore the house away and set it in the lake. The thunder and lightning grow greater. Then the loving ones find a boat and went out to where her house floats on one side and break a window to bring her out, but she begs, 'No! Please, no,' she tell them. 'I want to die here in the lake,' but they would not permit her. She did not wish their destruction, so she let herself be drawn away from her altar in the lake. And the wind, the thunder and lightning, and the water all ceased the moment she set foot on dry land."

The gossip spread from the Creole stoops of downtown to the pillared porches of uptown, and elite white families repeated similar stories about the Voodoo queen to each other. A journalist heard the tales as a child and, grown to manhood, connected Marie the Second's death to a violent hurricane that hit New Orleans in 1884. She "was then living in a shanty on Lake Pontchartrain. The force of the wind was so great that her cabin was wrenched from its foundations and thrown into the angry waters. Obliged to seek shelter on the roof, she remained for several hours, discouraging the attempts of her would-be rescuers, and telling them, 'I want to die in that lake.'" Marie finally accepted help, and the rescuers removed her from the roof, "none too soon, for the cabin she was so loath to leave was completely shattered by the waves a few moments later."

Marie's song—"I want to die in the lake"—can be interpreted as suicide or self-destruction as well as spiritual death and rebirth through baptism. From the folk narratives, we might also conclude that Marie the Second did not die in a fierce storm on Lake Pontchartrain; she died in her own bed, wherever that was, sometime in the decade between her daughter's death in 1871 and her mother's death in 1881, whether she planned to or not. Perhaps Philomène, out of respect for Marie the Second's privacy, and out of a reasonable fear of Voodoo notoriety, nursed her older sister through a terminal illness. Then Philomène, with the help of her nephew, Victor Pierre, buried Marie Eucharist under a false name in a crypt with no markings; she knew how to manipulate or evade the authorities.

People who believed Marie the Second, the initiated child of lightning and thunder, had a spiritual relationship with storms must have known something. Weather reports after the end of the Civil War support the gossip on the streets—the sun always shone on the St. John's festivities. The weather was sometimes humid, but otherwise perfect, every St. John's Eve and St. John's Day from 1869 to 1881. That year—the first in which neither of the Laveaus was alive to calm the weather—it stormed.

With the deaths of both Marie Laveaus at the beginning of the new racial order in the United States, the spiritual and ceremonial world of New Orleans shifted its shape once again. The great serpent spirit, *Le Grand Zombi*, left the city when the last Laveau did. *Sainte Marie* and the spirit of Père Antoine-Antonio-St. Ant'ny retreated to the sanctuary of their altars, and Reverend Mothers gave birth to "spiritual churches." St. John the Baptist and High John the Conqueror yielded to a new set of spirits—the first, Black Hawk, was a militant and rebellious warrior who came to fight the battles that Reconstruction and segregation had brought to people of color in New Orleans. The second spirit was a monstrous evil through and through.

For decades after Marie the Second's disappearance, the politicians of New Orleans feared that she was still alive or that her spirit had outlived her body and returned to inspire other women to sway the outcomes of love, luck, and the law in their favor. In 1896 Sidney Story, a New Orleans councilman, wrote a city ordinance that attempted to restrict prostitution to a thirty-eight-block area between Canal Street and St. Louis Cemetery Two. The locals laughed at Story's attempt to regulate sex and named the red-light district after him—Storyville. To his dismay, the name stuck. The fabled red-light district—filled with Victorian mansions, madams, hot jazz, and thousands of working women—was just across the street from the wall of oven tombs in St. Louis Cemetery Two in which some say Marie the Second lies buried.

The following year, Councilman Story introduced another ordinance designed to control a different set of unruly women. The New Orleans City Council passed similar statutes in 1916, again in 1924, and a number of times after that—these laws are still in force in subsequent reincarnations. The 1897 regulation and the ones that followed prohibited trance artists, "voodoos," and similar tricksters from operating in the city. They outlawed fortune-telling, matchmaking, influencing matchmaking, making "fabulous statements" to influence others, taking money for readings, and related activities. The city council's fear of Voodoo queens and similar spiritual practitioners are left-handed compliments to Marie the Second. The city council could not outlaw the spirits, even the alcoholic kind. They could not ban a religion or stop the sales of sex. But in their frustrated efforts to stamp out "voodoo," they succeeded in defining it forever.

City Ordinance No. 3164—passed on February 2, 1916, Marie the Second's eighty-ninth birthday—is an epitaph for the tomb she does not have, a tribute to her spiritual powers as white men continued to define them. "All persons known as mediums, clairvoyants, fortune-tellers and others" who accept payment for reading palms, star charts and astrological signs, telling or pretending to tell fortunes either with cards, hands, water, letters or other devices or methods; all persons who promise to "settle lover's quarrels, bring the separated together, cause speedy marriages, locate buried or hidden treasures, jewels, wills, bonds, etc., remove evil influence and give luck, to effect marriages, heal sicknesses, reveal secrets, foretell the result of lawsuits, business transactions, investments of whatever nature, wills, deeds, mortgages; lost or absent friends or relatives, to reveal, move and avoid domestic troubles; bring together the bitterest enemies" and convert them into staunch friends shall be arrested, tried, fined, and, if guilty, sentenced to imprisonment.

At the close of Reconstruction in 1877, press and police escalated their attacks on the women of Voodoo. When they could no longer arrest them for heresy or illegal assembly, they harassed them for telling fortunes and using their psychic gifts to make money. Practitioners by the dozens migrated to

Algiers; from their place of exile they could see the rooftops of the French Quarter on the opposite bank of the Mississippi River. In the late 1920s Zora Neale Hurston stayed in Algiers to be near the exiled priestesses, watching out for and bearing witness to the still active police persecution of them. The Laveaus had trained most of women on both sides of the river, and the banished women continued in their footsteps, telling Zora and the other folklore collectors of the 1930s about the miracles their mentors had performed.

Marie Laveau and the ghosts of Voodoo also lived on in the Spiritual Churches, small groups "founded on traditions deriving from native African spirit worship (and its New World offspring, Voodoo), south African Zionism, native American Indian belief, fundamental Christianity, and an almost medieval Catholicism." New Orleans is the Jerusalem and Rome of the spiritual church movement; both Zora Neale Hurston and the interviewers of the Federal Writers' Project recognized the connection between nineteenth-century Voodoo and the twentieth-century Spiritual Churches; both passed through the prism of Creole Catholicism and African American or Afro-Creole music, dance, and ritual.

One Friday evening, in the old Tremé neighborhood near Congo Square, I park around the corner from a converted double shotgun house that serves as sanctuary for one of the Spiritual Churches. The week before, I spoke to the bishop of the congregation, a quiet man, older than I, who questioned me about my intentions in seeking permission to attend their services. At the cottage door a woman dressed in white welcomes men in work clothes and serious suits, women dressed like her or in tropical laces and fancy hats, and children of all ages. She looks closely into my eyes, appears to listen to an unseen voice or to smell something out of the ordinary. Do you understand why you are here? Do you understand how the spirits will come? she asks gently. Like the bishop, she invites me to observe and to participate as the spirit moves me in the baptisms scheduled for that evening.

It is easier to feel Marie Laveau and the spirits of Voodoo in this warm, candlelit sanctuary than it is in libraries and archives—but I remind myself of the dangers that lurk on that path. The leaders of this little Spiritual church and the others meeting throughout town point with pride to their

Catholic roots and their African ancestors; they honor Native American warriors like Black Hawk and his spirit of resistance to injustice and discrimination. But they cannot afford to acknowledge their kinship and family connections to Voodoo or Hoodoo; they can pay only indirect homage to "Mother Laveau." Sometimes journalists, photographers, or television crews request permission to record the services, music, and spirit possessions. Anthropologists and spiritual-seekers like me want to learn, to write, to understand. But each of us promises to take them at their word—"The Holy Spirit Forces lead us." We don't do Voodoo.

"What we do comes out of the Bible," a lady-bishop says to those who ask. "People can be brought down or made sick—so we don't tell about our spirit guides." Yes, she admits, "there is a lot of Hoodoo going around. But I don't want to be worried about it."

In an atmosphere that cannot be rushed, for which no schedule is posted, people drift in and greet old friends and visitors in a mood of generous anticipation. The hand-lettered sign with a Bible verse on it—*God is a spirit and those who worship Him must worship Him in spirit and in truth*—and the deep baptismal pool—*rebirth and resurrection in the beauty of holiness*—conjure up my primitive Christian roots and infuse my research with new interpretations. The women who prepare the altars fill the available spaces with flags, pictures of saints, statues of respected Indian chiefs, crucifixes, and rosaries. They move around holy water, rare liqueurs, perfume, incense, and dozens of candles until the effect pleases them, and add handwritten petitions or thank-you notes to various spirits. Everywhere I turn my eyes, Catholic saints— Expedite, Patrick, Michael, Joseph, Raymond, and Peter—rest amid the offerings that summon their help. On the altar there is a popular reproduction of a painting of a woman of color with *tignon* and a grave gaze— most assume she is Marie herself. Yet, no matter how many times the altars are built and rebuilt, no matter what the members of the congregation tell visitors about their ancestors, a serpent still snakes its way among the offerings, and "our Lady," lovely lady dressed in blue, will have gifts at her feet.

"Make a joyful noise unto the Lord," the singers shout to the band as they decide what to play—complex Afro-Caribbean polyrhythms, gospel rock, New Orleans jazz, rhythm and blues, or the fundamentalist hymns of my childhood. I can hear Louis Armstrong say *we play life*. To the mounting rhythm of tambourines, rattles, piano, saxophone, beating feet and clapping hands, the consciousness changes; we are "slain in the spirit," "falling out." A lady-bishop told a photographer-artist what the woman in white told me, "When you feel like dancing, you dance. When you feel like shouting, you shout. When you feel the visitation of the spirit, you do whatever you feel like doing and it's all right. You can't really explain the spirit. You get a little closer to God, and you dig a little deeper into the mysteries."

At these services the spirits choose whom they will, whose body and soul they will bless, and in the late nineteenth century, after the lives of the Laveaus had ended, they chose a woman named Leafy Anderson. They instructed her to leave Chicago and move to New Orleans. Neither Creole nor Catholic, Anderson's healing services drew enormous crowds and created legal problems for her. Police reported that she was practicing Hoodoo, witchcraft, and fortune-telling; they followed and harassed her. But she gained protection from the law the way Marie Laveau the First and Second did—by calling in powerful, protective spirits. Mother Anderson also prayed, fasted, "read" the judge, and offered sizable sums of money in return for the licenses and permits to build her first church. Hundreds more Spiritual Churches have followed the first one she built; all have been free of legal persecution. The city ordinances passed against the likes of Marie Laveau excluded the meeting places of the Spiritual Churches and spared their leaders, the reverend mothers, successors of Voodoo, who were doing exactly what the ordinances prohibited and more. Like Leafy Anderson, women of color in the Spiritual Churches of the twentieth century call themselves spiritual advisors, palm readers, fortune-tellers, psychics, prophets, healers, and reverend mothers. Each has her own unique relationships with saints, spirits, and ancestors.

Mother Leafy Anderson worked with the spirits of Queen Esther, Father John, and the most influential of all—a Native American revolutionary leader named Black Hawk. Queen Esther was as revolutionary and royal a woman as can be found in the Judeo-Christian faiths. Many Spiritual churches use the name "Israelites" in their name. They identify with the historic oppression of Jews, their struggles with slavery, the deliverance of Moses, and historic forms of racial injustice and intolerance. If Queen Esther led her people out of the hands of tyranny once before, she can help them again. Reverend Mother Anderson said that Father John was a spirit who had come to her—a great doctor, minister, and guide. Father John—sometimes pronounced "Jones"—could be the descendent of Voodoo's Dr. John, Hoodoo's High John, or the Creole's St. John the Baptist. His spirit is in a popular patent medicine, "Father John's," said to cure colds, coughs, sore throats, and other ailments. There are always musicians and healers in New Orleans with names like Dr. John and Deacon John.

Black Hawk was the first post-Laveau spirit to make his lively presence known throughout the city. He was a "natural man"—a person who had once lived, someone who had kinfolks, a history, and reasons to resist. Born in the upper Mississippi valley, Black Hawk grew up among the Sauk and Fox nations. During the war of 1812 he sided with the British against the Americans. He insisted that the intruders and occupiers had stolen his people's land, and he organized a resistance movement that ended in the Black Hawk War of 1832. The U.S. Army massacred most of his followers and shortly after that captured and jailed Black Hawk. Black Hawk knew what prison meant to people of color; he understood the price defiance carried.

In New Orleans, people call on the Native American's vigilance and protection; *Black Hawk has my back, I go to him for peace and justice,* they tell me. In life, Black Hawk led a rebellion against American authorities. In spirit form, Black Hawk deals in survival for people of color just as St. Raymond-Maroon, the patron saint of Louisiana runaways, did. Native Americans offered Africans respect, protection, and sanctuary from the earliest days of the colony. Africans, Creoles, and Native Americans in New Orleans resisted slavery together, traded with, and married each other. Like the mother of the first Marie Laveau and grandmother to the second, they practiced benevolence, herbal healing, and spirit contact.

As the authorities in the late nineteenth century forced women of color to hide their spiritual lives, black men replaced black women as ritual leaders in the public dances. In 1872, when the Louisiana state legislature made it

Figure 6. A member of a Mardis Gras Indian marching society sews, sings, and dances in honor of Marie Laveau. (photograph copyright © Jeffrey Ehrenreich, New Orleans)

legal to mask on Mardi Gras day, many blacks began to dress in bright head-dresses, breastplates, armbands, and sequined displays. Men took to the streets in brilliant, hand-sown costumes of feathers and sequins that honor Black Hawk and many other Native American warriors. Today, the spirits of Black Hawk and Marie Laveau infuse the costumes, dances, songs, and street parades whenever the Mardi Gras Indians mask and march. Their elaborate costumes of feathers and beads are moving altars to the spirits.

～

In the troubled decades after 1877 when Reconstruction ended—and for the first time in this book—an evil spirit came upon the people. Neither

Catholic nor Creole, the spirit came in the body of a large, noisy bird with nasty social habits, a malevolent entity born in New Orleans, grown to malignant manhood in the South. Neither Marie Laveau the First or the Second conjured him up or danced to possession with him. The Voodoos never honored him with dressed candles and holy water; indeed, all the charms, spells, rituals, and their abilities to foretell the future, failed to protect them from him. As always in New Orleans, the music tells the story.

"For almost a century, the minstrel show would be the most popular form of entertainment in America, a ritualized blend of lively music, knockabout comedy, sophisticated elegance, the reinforcement of ugly and persistent stereotypes—and simultaneous unabashed enthusiasm for the music and dance of the country's most despised minority. The first big minstrel hit was written down and performed by a white man in blackface named Thomas Dartmouth 'Daddy' Rice—who said *he'd* first heard it being sung by a black stable hand cleaning out a horse's stall. Rice named the tune after the stable hand—Jim Crow."

*Jim Crow.* The song came to life in New Orleans. First performed in New York in 1833, it sparked a huge love affair, a craze among European Americans for African American song and dance—for the minstrel shows and face paint that fed the national manias about racial differences. Over time, the title of the song attached itself to the legal and customary practices of separation between races in the United States. All the laws, customs, and the social habits of segregation and discrimination against people of color after Reconstruction ended were summarized in the name of "Jim Crow"—the red, white, and blue bird of American apartheid.

In 1890 the Louisiana state legislature passed a Jim Crow law requiring that blacks and whites travel in separate railroad cars within the state. Two years later, a Creole from New Orleans named Homer Plessy boarded an excursion train and with calm deliberation sat down in the "Whites Only" car. Plessy was, in his words, seven-eighths white and one-eighth black. He could pass; he had passed before the law made him choose. Homer Plessy was arrested, tried, and convicted of the crime of riding in a whites-only railroad car. His trial case went to the United States Supreme Court, and, in

1896, the case of *Plessy vs. Ferguson* confirmed segregation as the supreme law of the land. The judges held that the provision of "separate but equal" accommodations for blacks on railroad trains did not violate the "equal protection of the laws" provision of the Fourteenth Amendment to the Constitution. Jim Crow and his spirit of racial division dominated the economic, social, political, and spiritual life of the nation for the next sixty years.

Once again, we hear the music of New Orleans. Like both Laveaus, Jelly Roll Morton, born Ferdinand La Menthe, was a light-skinned, French-speaking Catholic Creole who lived in multiracial "downtown." His grandmother kicked him out of her house for making "common" music with the sons of slaves and for listening to the sounds of the streets in the segregated American "uptown." But Morton kept playing music with his dark-skinned African American friends and "a half century later the lineage of every fine musician can still be traced back to the handful of half-caste Creoles who performed the original act of creation. All these men knew each other."

Jelly Roll Morton became the greatest jazz composer in American history; for him, jazz had the same ancestors as Voodoo did. "So tolerant New Orleans absorbed slowly over the centuries Iberian, African, Cuban, Parisian, Martiniquan, and American musical influences. All these flavors may be found in jazz, for jazz is a sort of musical gumbo. But the taster, the stirrer, the pot-watcher for this gumbo was the New Orleans colored Creole. Their capital was New Orleans, where for a hundred years they raised the most beautiful girls, who cooked up the tastiest dishes and were courted with the hottest music of any place in the Mississippi Valley." They produced "a new music of and by New Orleans—a wordless Creole counterpoint of protest and of pride."

Creole musicians like Jelly Roll Morton set celebration and resistance to music. Creole activists like Homer Plessy fought the evil spirit of Jim Crow. And Marie the Second, last of the Creole conjurers, put a curse on those who hurt her people. She may have vanished, but she did not go quietly. Of the thirty Voodoo Psalms she gave to her grand-nephew Luke Turner, who passed them on to Zora Neale Hurston, one is incomparable. The eleventh prayer is a lament for what is lost forever and a damnation called down upon wicked people—whomever they may be.

In her book, *Mules and Men,* Hurston tells how she learned this curse-prayer. Luke Turner had just quoted the spiritual petition of a woman who had enemies. "By the time that Turner had finished his recitation he wasn't too conscious of me. In fact he gave me the feeling that he was just speaking, but not for my benefit. He was away off somewhere. He made a final dramatic gesture with open hands and hushed for a minute. Then he sank deeper into himself and went on: 'But when she put the last curse on a person, it would be better if that man was dead, yes.' With an impatient gesture he signaled me not to interrupt him."

In a quiet voice Luke told Zora how Marie the Second set up an altar to curse her enemies. We are left to guess who her foes were—I nominate businessmen who profited from the slave trade and the politicians and judges who called down Jim Crow and the doctrine of separate-but-equal. The prayer-curse is too powerful for ordinary double-crosses, unfaithful lovers, biased newspapers, or the ordinary frictions of urban life.

To make the curse work, Marie Laveau prepared black candles, "dressed" or washed in strong vinegar. She took a new needle and wrote the names of persons to be cursed on the candles; then she "placed fifteen cents in the lap of Death upon the altar to pay the spirit to obey her orders." With the ritual preparations made and the candles lighted, the priestess placed her hands flat upon the altar:

> *To The Man God: O great One,* I have been sorely tried by my enemies and have been blasphemed and lied against. My good thoughts and my honest actions have been turned to bad actions and dishonest ideas. My home has been disrespected, my children have been cursed and ill treated. My dear ones have been backbitten and their virtue questioned. O Lord, I beg that this that I ask for my enemies shall come to pass.
>
> That the South Wind shall scorch their bodies and make them wither, and shall not be tempered to them. That the North Wind shall freeze their blood and numb their muscles, and that it shall not be tempered to them. That the West Wind shall blow away their life's breath and will not leave their hair grow, and that their nails shall fall off and their bones shall crumble. That the East Wind shall make their minds grow dark, their sight shall fail, and their seed dry up so that they shall not multiply.

O Lord, I pray that their fathers and mothers from their furtherest generation will not intercede for them before the great throne, and the wombs of their women shall not bear fruit except for strangers, and that they shall become extinct; I pray that the children who may come shall be weak of mind and paralyzed of limb, and that they themselves shall curse them in their turn for ever turning the breath of life in their bodies. I pray that disease and death shall be forever with them and that their worldly goods shall not prosper, and that their crops shall not multiply, and that their cows, their sheep and their hogs and all their living beasts and fowl will die of starvation and thirst.

I pray that their house shall be un-roofed and that the rain, the thunder and the lighting shall find the innermost recess of their home, and that the foundation shall crumble and the flood tear it asunder. I pray that the sun shall not shed its rays of prosperity on them, and that instead it shall beat down on them and burn them up and destroy them. I pray that the moon shall not give them peace, but instead shall deride them and decry them and cause their minds to shrivel. I pray that their friends shall betray them and cause them loss of power and loss of their gold and silver, and that their enemies shall smite them both hip and thigh until they beg for mercy which will not be given them. I pray that their tongues shall forget how to speak in sweet words, and that it shall be paralyzed, and that all about them will be desolation, pestilence and death.

O great Lord, I ask you for all these things because they have dragged me in the dust and destroyed my good name, have broken my heart and caused me to curse the day that I was born. So Be It.

Jim Crow earned this terrible curse—he killed the Creole vision of a caste-free society that the Laveaus embodied, and brought a race-conscious social order out of the ashes of Civil War and Reconstruction. The U.S. Supreme Court reversed *Plessy v. Ferguson* in 1954 in the case of *Brown v. Board of Education*, and Homer Plessy, Creole of color, rests in a high tomb near Marie the First in St. Louis Cemetery One. Marie the Second understood and accepted the spiritual consequences of her terrible pronouncement. To curse others is to be cursed in return. In the inevitable logic of Voodoo, what goes round comes round. That principle may, in the final years and moments of Marie's life, explain what happened to her.

When Luke finished the curse-prayer, he sat without moving. Late one night, Marie she come to my house, Turner whispered to Hurston. She dragged me from my bed. The great rattlesnake "that had come to her a little one when she was also young" had finished its work and was preparing to die. It had refused all food from its altar and was singing its death song.

"'Look well, Turner,' she told me. 'No one shall hear and see such as this for many centuries.' She went to her Great Altar and made great ceremony. The snake finished his song and seemed to sleep. She drove me back to my bed and went again to her Altar. The next morning the great snake was not at his altar. His hide was before the Great Altar stuffed with spices and things of power. Never did I know what become of his flesh. This is his skin that I wear about my shoulders whenever I reach for power."

Luke Turner saw Marie Laveau for the last time on the night of the great storm at the lake. When the sky darkened and the waters rolled, Luke and her followers rescued her—she let herself be drawn from the lake that night to protect the men from the furies of the storm, he said. The wind, thunder, and lightning ceased when she stepped onto the beach. Yes, she survived; she harnessed the power of the winds that night. But, later, alone and in the still darkness, bereft of her sustaining spirits, her life turned to ashes, Marie Laveau chose to leave.

"That night she also sing a song and is dead, yes." Her grand-nephew took a deep, painful breath. "So I have the snake skin and do works with the power she leave me."

## Epilogue

Early on the morning of April 1, 1957, Robert Tallant, author of the misguided but best-selling book, *Voodoo in New Orleans*, entered his bachelor kitchen and selected a clean, clear glass from his cabinet. He held it under the faucet as it filled. He took three sips and dropped dead on the floor. New Orleans' water doesn't usually kill that fast.

His aunt, alarmed that he failed to answer the phone when she called, used her own key to enter his apartment. She saw his body and the broken pieces of glass on the floor. At his premature death, Tallant was forty-eight years old and a reporter for the *States-Item*. A rival newspaper, the *Times-Picayune*, reported that an autopsy showed Tallant had probably died from "natural causes"—a hemorrhage of his stomach. Neither paper observed that he was an alcoholic who had been warned not to trash Voodoo.

On June 24, 1999, the *Times-Picayune* sent a reporter to do a feature story on the Voodoos and their St. John's Day celebrations. The newsman was better informed than the journalists of the nineteenth century—he did not say "primitive," "cultic," or "superstitious." He knew better than to mention near-naked women or throbbing drums. But he was unaware of his colleagues' difficulties in tracking down the legendary Marie the Second at midsummer; he had no idea that men like him had left their footprints in High John's territory more than a century earlier. A gray-haired man who looked trustworthy but did not give his name approached the newsman in the lobby of a downtown hotel where a head-washing ceremony in honor of St. John was under way. He told the reporter that the real New Orleans Voodoo would take place later that evening at Holt Cemetery. The newsman went in good faith—"but a 20-minute search of the cemetery in the darkness later—a creepy experience to be sure—revealed nothing."

The reporter did, however, interview a contemporary priestess or *manbo*, Sallie Ann Glassman, who had led both the gathering at the International House on the June 24, and a sunset service at Bayou St. John the night before. Under her leadership, the spirit of Marie Laveau—merged mother and daughter—had returned to New Orleans to dance again on St. John's Eve. The reporter, who did not see what happened that night and did not know the Laveau's relationship to St. John the Baptist, asked Glassman what Marie Laveau was like. What did a self-styled "nice Jewish girl from Maine," a priestess trained in Haiti, learn from the spirit of a Creole Catholic of nineteenth-century New Orleans? Sallie Ann replied, "Marie Laveau doesn't like people who stand back at a distance, and are judgmental. And she doesn't like militaristic drumming. She likes a more fluid, loping, sensuous beat. She really didn't like the television news crews that came out to the bayou because they heard there was a satanic ceremony going on." And furthermore, Glassman added, Marie Laveau does not like newspaper reporters much either.

The merged Marie Laveau whom Sallie Ann Glassman met in spirit form sounds like the same women I found in libraries and archives. "Marie is doing a primal seductive dance with history and race," said her contemporary counterpart. "As priestess, her experience is of intensely sacred personal isolation. She walks through crowds of people, but is not one of them. She is terribly lonely in this isolation, even though surrounded by followers and accompanied by Spirit. She only feels connection with her own life through her children, who make her life actual and real to her. Still, though, she lives in the shadow of her own myth. Marie Laveau operates on many levels, most of which are misinterpreted, and all of which cause her much pain."

So the tale of the enchanted priestesses of New Orleans Voodoo ends on the footbridge over Bayou St. John on the last Eve of St. John in the twentieth century—twilight, June 23, 1999. The calm waterway reflects without blemish or break the ancient magnolias and raised houses that line Moss Street on either side. Beyond the arched iron pedestrian bridge on which we stand are the ancient live oaks of the city's largest park, and in the opposite direction is the silhouetted skyline of New Orleans. At the middle of the bridge stands a three-tiered altar covered in white cloth. Brilliant candles pierce the dusk; they illuminate a statue of *Sainte Marie*, the Good Mother who brings safety and quick comfort, and shine upon a vision-inspired painting of Marie Laveau hanging against the rusted railings of the bridge. The candlelight tracks the path of painted snakes that slither up a tall pillar to the sky.

Residents from the neighborhood association who are sponsoring a potluck dinner and ceremonial in honor of St. John, curious spectators, and those like me who love to see a new generation of women pick up their rattles and dance, greet each other. The altar that members of the band and the chorus have prepared speaks of the Voodoo worldview of abundance and homage and of Marie's favorite things—blue and white candles, bath salts, fresh flowers, jeweled combs, French pastries, worn rosaries, and handmade *gris-gris* bags. Voodoo is different in each setting, with each priestess, with each spirit honored—different in New Orleans than in

Haiti, different in New York than in New Orleans. Each altar, each ritual, serves a distinctive intention. That night and everything that will happen belong to Marie Laveau.

The barefoot priestess, Sallie Ann Glassman, wears a white dress and a white handkerchief, almost a *tignon*, on her head. She slips off her shoes and picks up a bowl. "Perhaps Marie Laveau's spirit will come into someone here tonight," she speaks in a soft voice to those gathered on the footbridge. "Spirit possession is an honor for you, a gift to all of us. If Marie borrows your body for her performance tonight, you will recognize her. You will not feel afraid; she will teach you and you will know that we can take care of you when you meet her face to face."

Then the priestess signals the drummers to begin the beat the spirits crave. The choir and the dancers move one by one, in respect and intention, to place their offerings in the front of the altar. As the drumbeat builds, I leave my gift—a pair of gold earrings I have worn in Marie's honor— amidst the abundance of the altar. The lead drummer follows the priestess's signals; he improvises and synchronizes the songs that draw Marie to Bayou St. John that night. With great care and concentration, she trickles small handfuls of white corn meal onto the wooden deck of the bridge to form a *Vèvè*, a symbolic design that merges Marie Laveau's initials, a curvilinear cross like those in the cities of the dead, and the Voodoo queen's signature X mark, the sign of freedom. The beat of the drums opens the path, candles burning with supernatural flame beside a handmade altar light the way—we welcome her home, body and soul.

The *gumbo ya-ya* is right: there is only one Marie Laveau. Through the power of intention, dancing and drumming, the two priestesses merge into one, then return to New Orleans, drawn back to where their earthly bodies experienced ecstasy, pain, and death. When those of us who are still alive honor our ancestors—once living people who have passed through the initiation that death of the body brings—we join them in a community of spirits and saints.

Some people in New Orleans can see Marie Laveau or sense her presence at the marches of the Mardi Gras Indians, in the cities of the dead, in candles that burn with heightened brightness, or in sudden storms that bring soft, dry breezes and lift the spirits of citizens. They say Marie helps and protects them, and they honor her on midsummer's nights and at the Feast of All Saints. Others she visits in dreams, visions, and in possession; when this happens Marie bids them dance from the bottom of their soul, dance for healing songs and stories, dance for hope and mercy. Many leave offerings in front of the high tomb in the old St. Louis Cemetery One; others place gifts for her near the oven vault in St. Louis Two. When I pass the shrine to the Widow Paris, born Laveau, I think of the family buried there, members who lie elsewhere, one who disappeared, and some who have passed from the community forever. If Marie Laveau has the power to bestow blessings—and many swear she does—then I ask for racial justice and for the health and safety of all our children. In gratitude, I light a candle and leave a tribute—coins in multiples of fifteen cents, a bouquet of fresh flowers or some fine French chocolate.

The Call:       *Keep on keepin' on. Everything gonna be all right.*
The Response:   *Thank you kind spirit.*

—Benediction and Blessing in a Spiritual Church,
New Orleans, 1999.

# Postscript: Events in the Lives of the Marie Laveaus

| | |
|---|---|
| 1699 | Colony of Louisiana founded |
| 1719 | *L'Aurore*, first French slave-trade ship arrives |
| 1727 | Ursuline Sisters arrive |
| 1763 | Spanish colonial administration begins |
| 1775 | Charles Trudeau Laveaux, Marie the First's father, born |
| 1776 | American Revolution begins |
| 1781 | Fray Antonio de Sedella arrives |
| 1786 | "Proclamation for Good Government" requires free women of color to wear *tignons* |
| 1789 | French Revolution begins |
| 1789 | St. Louis Cemetery One is dedicated |
| 1791 | St. Domingue-Haitian Revolution begins |
| 1795 | Fray Antonio de Sedella turns into Père Antoine |
| 1796 | First official outbreak of yellow fever |
| 1801 | September 10: Marie Laveau the First born |
| 1803 | Louisiana Purchase: New Orleans becomes part of the United States |
| 1804 | January 3: Marie Laveaux (Auguste) born |
| 1808 | Orleans Territory Act requires "race" on legal proceedings for free people of color |
| 1809 | 10,000 exiles/refugees from St. Domingue-Haiti arrive in New Orleans |
| 1811 | Yellow fever spike |
| 1811 | St. John the Baptist Parish: largest slave uprising in U.S. history |
| 1812 | Statehood for Louisiana |
| 1812 | Henriette Delille born |

| | |
|---|---|
| 1815 | January 8: Battle of New Orleans ends War of 1812 |
| 1815 | January 23: Victory Celebration in the French Quarter |
| 1815 | April 4: Marie Louise Darcantel (Marie the First's half-sister) marries Louis Foucher |
| 1817 | Yellow fever spike |
| 1817 | October 22: Will of Darcantel brothers acknowledges Marguerite Darcantel |
| 1809-17 | City ordinances place limitations on gatherings in Congo Square |
| 1818 | September 3: Marie Laveaux (Marie the First's half sister) marries François Auguste |
| 1819 | July 27: Marriage contract for Marie Laveau and Jacques Paris |
| 1819 | August 4: Marie Laveau the First marries Jacques Paris |
| 1819 | Yellow fever spike |
| 1822 | Yellow fever spike |
| 1823 | St. Louis Cemetery Two is dedicated |
| 1823 | French Market opens |
| 1823 | Pharmacy on Chartres Street opens |
| 1825 | Sanité Dede's Voudou ritual and initiation ceremony |
| 1827 | Civil Codes restrict interracial marriage and inheritance |
| 1827 | February 2: Marie Eucharist Heloise (Marie the Second) born to Christophe and Marie |
| 1827 | October 21: Mortuary Chapel of St. Anthony dedicated |
| 1828 | August 19: Marie Eucharist baptized at St. Louis Cathedral |
| 1829 | January 19–23: Père Antoine dies, lies in state, and is buried |
| 1829 | August 10: Marie Louise Caroline born to Christophe and Marie |
| 1829 | September 10: Marie Louise Caroline baptized at St. Louis Cathedral |
| 1829 | December 9: Marie Louise Caroline dies at five months of age |
| 1829 | Yellow fever spikes |
| 1831 | Nat Turner's Rebellion |
| 1831 | Civil Codes on emancipation, manumission, interracial marriage and inheritance strengthened |
| 1831 | Pontchartrain Railroad, the "Smoky Mary," runs from French Quarter to Milneburg |
| 1832 | Major cholera epidemic |
| 1832 | July 25: Donation of Love St. property to Marie Eucharist |
| 1832 | September 21: Christophe Glapion bids on St. Ann Street property |
| 1832 | September 28: Marie Laveau mortgages Love St. house with her father |
| 1832 | September 28: Christophe Glapion purchases St. Ann St. property |

| | |
|---|---|
| 1833 | September 22: François Auguste born to Christophe and Marie |
| 1834 | May 13: François Auguste baptized |
| 1834 | May 18: François Auguste dies, eight months old |
| 1834 | Parish Prison in Tremé built |
| 1835 | March 6: Marie Philomène born |
| 1836 | Archange, son of Marie and Christophe born |
| 1836 | April 1: Marie Philomène baptized |
| 1838 | May: Case of *"Statu libre"* for Alexandrine, a.k.a. Ninine |
| 1838 | August: Case of *"Statu libre"* for Irma |
| 1838 | June 8: Christophe Glapion "sells" St. Ann Street property for usufruct rights |
| 1839 | September 23: Donation of St. Ann Street property to Philomène and Archange |
| 1837 | Howard Association formed |
| 1839 | June 22: Marie Laveaux (Auguste) dies in Paris |
| 1839 | October 29: Reburied in New Orleans |
| 1842 | Legislative acts prohibit free people of color from entering Louisiana |
| 1842 | St. Augustine's Roman Catholic Church for Creoles of color is dedicated in Tremé |
| 1842 | Henriette Delille founds the Sisters of the Holy Family |
| 1843 | December: Congo Square closed for Sunday afternoon gatherings of people of color |
| 1844 | Joseph Eugene Crocker born to Marie the Second and Pierre Crocker |
| 1845 | January 6: Archange Glapion dies, buried in St. Louis Cemetery One |
| 1845 | May 5: Joseph Eugene Crocker dies, buried in St. Louis Cemetery One |
| 1845 | Aldina Crocker born to Marie the Second and Pierre Crocker |
| 1845 | June: Congo Square reopens for gatherings of people of color |
| 1848 | Case of *"Statu libre"* for Juliette a.k.a. Nounoute |
| 1850 | January 8: Esmeralda Crocker, daughter of Marie the Second and Pierre Crocker, dies |
| 1850 | July 9: Marie Glapion baptized in St. Louis Cathedral, one year old |
| 1850 | Summer: Case of the "Voudou Virgin" |
| 1852 | Louisiana legislature further restricts emancipation and manumission |
| 1852 | July 2: Execution of Jean Adams and Anthony Delille in Parish Prison |
| 1853 | Summer–Fall: Largest epidemic of yellow fever in U.S. history |
| 1853 | November 8: Victor Pierre Christophe Duminy Dieudonné de Glapion born to Marie the Second and Pierre Crocker |
| 1855 | Louisiana legislature restricts freedom of assembly for free people of color |

| | |
|---|---|
| 1855 | June 26: Christophe Duminy de Glapion dies, buried in St. Louis Cemetery One |
| 1856 | City council closes Congo Square, bans street parties, marches, music in public places |
| 1857 | Louisiana legislature prohibits all emancipation or manumission of slaves |
| 1858 | City ordinances prohibit freedoms of speech, assembly, religion to free people of color |
| 1859 | March: Executions of Haas, Smith, and Lindsay in Parish Prison |
| 1859 | July: Execution of James Mullen in Parish Prison |
| 1859 | Louisiana legislature orders all free people of color to become slaves |
| 1860 | June: Eugene Pepe-Adams dies in Parish Prison |
| 1860 | August: Antoine Cambre dies in Parish Prison |
| 1862 | Union fleet captures New Orleans; Reconstruction begins |
| 1862 | June 7: Public execution of William Mumford |
| 1862 | November 16: Henriette Delille, founder of the Sisters of the Holy Family, dies |
| 1863 | July 29: Funeral of Captain André Cailloux |
| 1866 | 13th, 14th, and 15th Amendments to Constitution change legal status of enslaved peoples in the United States |
| 1866 | January 29: Eugenie Legendre, daughter of Philomène Glapion and George Legendre dies, one month old |
| 1866 | July 30: Anglo "Race Riot"—Creole "Massacre" in New Orleans |
| 1870 | February 12: Joseph Legendre, son of Philomène Glapion and George Legendre dies, one month old |
| 1870 | May: Execution of John Bazar canceled |
| 1871 | May: Execution of Abril and Bayona at Parish Prison; Widow Paris last seen in public |
| 1871 | June: Marie the Second conducts St. John's Eve celebrations with Queen Eliza |
| 1871 | September 10: A. Aldina Crocker, age 26, buried in St. Louis One |
| 1872 | June: Marie the Second conducts St. John's Eve celebrations at Lake Pontchartrain |
| 1873 | April: Marie the Second last seen in public |
| 1874 | June: Year of the Great St. John's Eve Hoax |
| 1874 | September 14: Battle of Liberty Place, New Orleans |
| 1875 | June 25: *Picayune* interview with Widow Paris at St. Ann Street |

| 1877 | Reconstruction ends; Jim Crow begins |
|---|---|
| 1879 | December 31: *Daily States* interview with Widow Paris [published June 17, 1881] |
| 1881 | June 16: Marie Laveau, the Widow Paris, dies; buried in St. Louis One |
| 1881 | July: Congo Square renovated |
| 1881 | November 29: Victor Pierre Crocker has his mother, Marie the Second, declared dead |
| 1882 | January: Victor Pierre Crocker sells house on Love Street |
| 1885 | George Washington Cable publishes *Century* article on Voudou |
| 1886 | April 11: *Picayune* interview with Philomène Glapion Legendre |
| 1896 | May 19: Supreme Court decision, *Plessy v. Ferguson* |
| 1897 | Councilman Story writes an ordinance to control women who take money for sex and an ordinance to control women who take money for spiritual activities |
| 1897 | June 11: Marie Philomène Glapion dies; buried in St. Louis One |
| 1897 | September 18: Noime Legendre sells house on St. Ann Street |
| 1916 | February 2: City Ordinance #3164 prohibits sale of spiritual services |
| 1920 | Reverend Mother Lacey Anderson charters the Spiritual Churches in New Orleans |
| 1928 | Summer: Zora Neale Hurston arrives in New Orleans |
| 1930 | Spring: Zora Neale Hurston completes fieldwork in New Orleans |
| 1931 | Zora Neale Hurston publishes "Hoodoo in America" in *Journal of American Folklore* |
| 1932 | March 15: Last trip of the "Smoky Mary" to Milneburg |
| 1935 | October: Federal Writers' Project begins |
| 1935 | Zora Neale Hurston publishes *Mules and Men* |
| 1942 | December: Federal Writers' Project ends |
| 1947 | Robert Tallant publishes *Voodoo in New Orleans* |
| 1956 | Supreme Court decision, *Brown v. Board of Education* |
| 1957 | April 1: Robert Tallant dies |
| 1999 | June 23: St. John's Eve Voodoo gathering on Bayou St. John; Marie Laveau returns to New Orleans |

# Notes

---

## Abbreviations Used in Notes

**COB:** Conveyance Office Book. New Orleans Public Library; New Orleans Notarial Archives.

**Hurston 1990:** Zora Neale Hurston, *Mules and Men*, New York: HarperPerennial, 1990 [orig. pub. J. B. Lippincott, 1935].

**Hurston 1931:** Zora Neale Hurston, "Hoodoo in America." *Journal of American Folklore* 44 (174):317–417.

**Hyatt 1970; 1973; 1978:** Harry Middleton Hyatt, *Hoodoo-Conjuration-Witchcraft-Rootwork*. Memoirs of the Alma Egan Hyatt Foundation. Hannibal, Mo.: Western Publishing, Inc., Vols. 1, 2, 1970; Vols. 3, 4, 1973; Vol. 5, 1978.

**MCC-UNO:** Marcus B. Christian Collection, Archives and Manuscripts, Special Collections Department, Earl K. Long Library, University of New Orleans. New Orleans, Louisiana.

**Tallant 1998:** Robert Tallant, *Voodoo in New Orleans*. New Orleans: Pelican, 1998.

**WPA-FWP/NSU:** Works Progress Administration, Federal Writers' Project, Cammie G. Henry Research Center, Eugene P. Watson Memorial Library, Northwestern State University, Natchitoches, Louisiana [including unpublished manuscripts by Catherine Dillon, hereafter referred to as Dillon manuscripts].

**WPA-LWP/BR:** Works Progress Administration, Louisiana Writers' Project, State Library of Louisiana. Baton Rouge, Louisiana.

All newspaper titles are from New Orleans unless otherwise indicated.

## Introduction

XIII   *"Blacks and whites ..."* Henry Castellanos, *New Orleans As It Was: Episodes of Louisiana Life.* 2nd ed. (New Orleans: L. Graham, 1895), 99.

XIV   *"neurotic and repressed white women ..."* Herbert Asbury, *Informal History of the New Orleans Underground* (Garden City, N.Y.: Garden City Publications, 1938), 256.

xiv Creole: see Arnold Hirsch and Joseph Logsdon, eds., *Creole New Orleans: Race and Americanization* (Baton Rouge: Louisiana State University Press, 1992); Virginia R. Dominquez, *White by Definition: Social Classification in Creole Louisiana* (New Brunswick, N.J.: Rutgers University Press, 1994); and Sybil Kein, ed., *Creole: The History and Legacy of Louisiana's Free People of Color* (Baton Rouge: Louisiana State University, 2000).

xvi "magical means of transforming reality." Theophus Smith, *Conjuring Culture: Biblical Formations of Black America* (New York: Oxford University Press, 1994), 4.

# Chapter 1

3 "*She come walkin'* ..." Tom Bragg, WPA-FWP/NSU; Tallant 1998:56. The raw transcripts from WPA Federal Writers' Project contain typographical errors, nonstandard dialect representations, and idiosyncratic spellings. I have edited them lightly with the goal of retaining the original flavor, narrative flow, and spontaneity.

4 "Congo Square ..." Jerah Johnson, *Congo Square in New Orleans* (New Orleans: Louisiana Landmarks Society, 1995); George Washington Cable, *The Dance in Place Congo and Creole Slave Songs*, 3rd ed. (New Orleans: Faruk von Turk, 1976); Benjamin Latrobe, *Impressions Respecting New Orleans: Diary & Sketches 1818–1820* (New York: Columbia University, 1951), 46–51; and Folder, "Congo Square," WPA-FWP/NSU.

4 For the closing and reopening of Congo Square, see Johnson 1995:44–47; Cable 1976; Kmen 1972; and Dillon manuscripts, "Place Congo," "The Law's Long Arm: The Suppression of Voodoo," WPA-FWP/NSU.

4 "*People complained* ..." Ramon Rivaros, WPA-FWP/NSU; WPA-LWP/BR.

4 "*Marie Laveau brought* ..." Eugene Fritz, WPA-FWP/NSU; WPA-LWP/BR.

5 "*Sometimes them policemens* ..." Tom Bragg, WPA-FWP/NSU; Tallant 1998:57.

5 "*Marie danced with a snake* ..." Eugene Fritz, WPA-FWP/NSU; WPA-LWP/BR.

5 "Marie signaled the ..." For the contributions of the dances in Congo Square to the development of American dance, see Johnson 1995:4; Asbury 1938:252; Lynne Fauley Emery, *Black Dance From 1619 to Today*, 2nd ed. (Princeton, N.J.: Dance Horizons Press, 1988), 54–56; Henry A. Kmen, "The Roots of Jazz and the Dance in Place Congo: A Reappraisal,"

*Yearbook, Anuario* 8, 1972; Gary Donaldson, "A Window on Slave Culture: Dances at Congo Square in New Orleans, 1800–1862," *Journal of Negro History* 69, 2 (1984); David Estes, "Traditional Dances and Processions of Blacks in New Orleans as Witnessed by Antebellum Travelers," *Louisiana Folklore Miscellany* 6, 3 (1990); John Q. Anderson, "The New Orleans Voodoo Ritual Dance and its Twentieth Century Survivals," *Southern Folklore Quarterly* 24 (1960); and Jacqui Malone, *Steppin' on the Blues: The Visible Rhythms of African American Dance* (Urbana and Chicago: University of Illinois, 1996).

5    *"extended by the corners ..."* Latrobe 1951:49.

5    *"slow, slow vehemence ..."* Cable 1976:519.

6    *"long-drawn human cry ..."* Cable 1976:520.

6    *"Danse Calinda ..."* Cable 1976:26. Sixteen stanzas of *Danse Calinda* are quoted in the *New Orleans Guide Book* prepared for the Cotton Centennial Exposition in 1885; Emilie LeJeune, "Creole Folk Songs," *Louisiana Historical Quarterly* 2:456–58, 1919:457. "The Calinda is the song most often mentioned in connection with Congo Square and Marie Laveau," Folder "Congo Square," WPA-FWP/NSU, no pgs.

6    *"Nothing is more dreaded ..."* Antoine Page DuPratz, *History of Louisiana*, vol. 2 (Baton Rouge: Louisiana State University Press, 1975), 270.

6    *"twenty different dancing groups ..."* Christian Schultz, *Travels on an Inland Voyage*, vol. 2 (New York: Isaac Riley, 1810), 197.

6    *"a rapid jig"* to *"... in its glory."* James Creecy, *Scenes in the South and Other Miscellaneous Pieces* (Philadelphia: Lippincott, 1860), 20–21.

6    *"I have never seen ..."* Latrobe 1951:51.000 *"tall, well-knit Senegalese ..."* to *"... came from Africa."* Cable 1976:522–23.

7    *"L'appe vini ..."* Chorus of a folk song about Marie Laveau; the WPA Federal Writers' Project collected a number of versions in both Louisiana Creole and French, each with different phrases, words, and spellings. Usage in the nineteenth century and among interviewers, transcribers, or typists on the WPA project in the twentieth was not standardized. I selected one version of the song from the archives; Dr. Sybil Kein, scholar of Louisiana Creole French, graciously translated it.

7    "Spirit possession is ..." See Joseph M. Murphy, *Working with the Spirit: Ceremonies of the African Diaspora* (Boston: Beacon Press, 1994); Erika Bourguignon, *Possession* (Prospect Heights, Ill.: Waveland Press, 1991); Glenn Hinson, *Fire in My Bones: Transcendence and the Holy Spirit in African American Gospel* (Philadelphia: University of Pennsylvania Press, 2000); Judy Rosenthal, *Possession, Ecstasy, and Law in Ewe Voodoo* (Charlottesville: University Press of

Virginia, 1998); Jim Wafer, *The Taste of Blood: Spirit Possession in Brazilian Candomblé*, (Philadelphia: University of Pennsylvania Press, 1991); and Zora Neale Hurston, "Shouting," "Conversions and Visions," "Characteristics of Negro Expression," "Spirituals and Neo-Spirituals," in Nancy Cunard, ed., *Negro, An Anthology* (New York: Frederick Ungar, 1970).

7    "*When she got in . . .*" Tom Bragg, WPA-FWP/NSU; Tallant 1998:57.

8    "*Now for the fantastic . . .*" Cable 1976:7.

8    "*The sudden entrance . . .*" to "*. . . of the vortex.*" *Times*, June 26, 1872.

8    "*she talked to herself . . .*" Fredrika Bremer, quoted in Frank deCaro and Roseann Jordan, eds., *Louisiana Sojourns: Travelers' Tales and Literary Journeys* (Baton Rouge: Louisiana State University Press, 1998), 535.

8    "*natural supremacy . . .*" Cable 1976:26.

9    "After 1820 . . ." *Louisiana Gazette*, August 16, 1820, "*idolatrous worship of an African deity called Vaudoo*" is one of the first published references to the Voodoo organizations.

10   "*long raven locks . . .*" James Buckingham, *The Slave States of America*, vol. 1 (London: Fisher, Son, and Co., 1842), 36.

10   "Marie the First was born . . ." Two documents place her birth in 1800 or 1801: (1) New Orleans Office of Recorder or Births and Deaths, Vincent Ramos, Recorder, Book #4, 1832–1838:159 [daughter Philomène's birth registration]; and (2) New Orleans Notarial Archives, H. Lavergne, Notary, Contract of Marriage, July 27, 1819 [which states the Marie Laveau was still a minor in 1819]. Working within this framework, researcher Ina Fandrich found a baptismal certificate with a birth date of September 10, 1801, in the Catholic Archdiocesan Archives: *Times-Picayune*, February 17, 2002.

10   "Travelers were right . . ." For the relationship of slavery and gender in colonial Louisiana, see Laura Foner, "The Free People of Color in Louisiana and St. Dominque: A Comparative Portrait of Two Three-Caste Slave Societies," *Journal of Social History* 3 (1970); Gwendolyn Midlo Hall, "African Women in French and Spanish Louisiana: Origins, Roles, Family, Work, Treatment," in Catherine Clinton and Michele Gillespie, eds., *The Devil's Lane: Sex and Race in the Early South* (New York: Oxford University Press, 1997); Kimberley S. Hanger, *Bounded Lives, Bounded Places: Free Black Society in Colonial New Orleans, 1769–1803* (Durham and London: Duke University Press, 1997); "Coping in a Complex World: Free Black Women in Colonial New Orleans," in Clinton and Gillespie, eds., 1997; "The Fortunes of Women in America: Spanish New Orleans's Free Women of African Descent and their Relations with Slave Women," in Patricia Morton, ed.,

*Discovering the Women in Slavery: Emancipating Perspectives on the American Past* (Athens: University of Georgia Press, 1996); and "Protecting Property, Family, and Self: The *Mujeres Libres* of Colonial New Orleans," *Revista/Review Interamericana*, 1992a; *A Medley of Cultures: Louisiana History at the Cabildo* (New Orleans: Louisiana Museum Foundation, 1996); Virginia Meacham Gould, *In Full Enjoyment of Their Liberty: The Free Women of Color of the Gulf Ports of New Orleans, Mobile, and Pensacola, 1769–1860* (Ph.D. dissertation, Emory University, 1991); and "'A Chaos of Iniquity and Discord:' Slave and Free Women of Color in the Spanish Ports of New Orleans, Mobile, and Pensacola," in Clinton and Gillespie, eds., 1997.

10    twenty-three ships: Gwendolyn Midlo Hall, *Africans in Colonial Louisiana: The Development of Afro-Creole Culture in the Eighteenth Century* (Baton Rouge: Louisiana State University Press, 1992a); and "The Formation of Afro-Creole Culture," in Hirsch and Logsdon, eds., 1992b.

10    "The majority of the . . ." Hall, 1992a:381; Hall 1992b:70.

11    "The next largest group . . ." Gwendolyn Midlo Hall, CD-Rom: *Databases for the Study of Afro-Louisiana History and Genealogy, 1699–1860*, 2000; Hall 1992a, 1992b; John K. Thornton, *The Kongolese St. Anthony: Dona Beatriz Kimpa Vita and the Antonian Movement, 1684–1706* (Cambridge: Cambridge University Press, 1998); "On the Trail of Voodoo: African Christianity in Africa and the Americas," *Americas* 44, 3 (1987–88); and "The Development of the African Catholic Church in the Kingdom of Kongo, 1491–1750," *Journal of African History* 25 (1984).

11    Marie Laveau's Kongolese ancestor: Hurston 1931:326.

11    *ngangas* in Kongo: see Thornton 1998.

11    "wanga" or "oanga," "wangateurs": WPA-FWP/NSU; WPA-LWP/BR.

12    Population statistics: Dominquez 1994:116.

13    African significance of **X** marks: Carolyn Morrow Long, *Spiritual Merchants: Religion, Magic, and Commerce* (Knoxville: University of Tennessee Press, 2000), 8, 25.

14    *"When Marie's son-in-law . . ."* to *". . . in that yard"*: Marie Dede. Similar stories appear in the testimonies of Anita Fonvergne, Oscar Felix, and Ramond Rivaros: WPA-FWP/NSU; WPA-LWP/BR.

14    Story of Guinea peppers and the St. Ann house: Tallant 1998:58.

16    *"All in all . . ."* *Picayune*, June 17, 1881

16    *"stuffing our contemporaries . . ."* *New Orleans Times Democrat*, June 18, 1881.

17    WPA Federal Writers' Project in Louisiana: Ronnie Clayton, *A History of the Federal Writers' Project in Louisiana* (Ph.D. dissertation, Louisiana State

University, 1974); Clayton, *Mother-Wit: The Ex-Slave Narratives of the Louisiana Writers' Project* (New York: Peter Lang, 1990); Clayton, "The Federal Writers' Project for Blacks in Louisiana," *Louisiana History* 19, 3 (1978); Donald Hatley, "A Preliminary Guide to Folklore in the Louisiana Writers' Project, *Louisiana Folklore Miscellany* 6, 3 (1986–87); and Joan Redding, "The Dillard Project: The Black Unit of the Louisiana Writers' Project," *Louisiana History* 32 (1991).

17    "... blood drinking and group sex." Tallant 1998:55. Author's paraphrase.

18    "*Marie Laveau? Sure ...*" James St. Ann, WPA-FWP/NSU; WPA-LWP/BR.

18    "*When I remember ...*" Tony Miller, WPA-FWP/NSU; WPA-LWP/BR; Tallant 1998:75.

18    "*always wore diamond ...*" Charles Raphael: WPA-FWP/NSU; WPA-LWP/BR.

18    "*Marie Laveau? Who, that she-devil ...*" Marie Brown, WPA-FWP/NSU; WPA-LWP/BR; Clayton 1990:34–35.

18    "*I don't know nothing ...*" Marguerite Gitson, WPA-FWP/NSU; WPA-LWP/BR.

19    Commentary on the Spanish administration and *tignons*: Charles Gayerrè, *History of Louisiana* vol. 1, (New Orleans: Pelican, 1974); Charles Roussève, *The Negro in Louisiana* (New Orleans: Xavier University Press, 1937); and Gould 1991.

## Chapter 2

21    "*Marie Laveau was ...*" Castellanos 1895:97.

21    "*dressed in black ...*" to "*... silver shell.*" Latrobe 1951:121.

22    "*exceeding crowded ...*" Latrobe 1951:114.

22    "*chanted the service ...*" to "*... more diabolical*" Latrobe 1951:61.

23    Catholicism in Louisiana had unique characteristics: see Caryn Cossé Bell, *Revolution, Romanticism, and the Afro-Creole Protest Tradition in Louisiana, 1718–1868* (Baton Rouge: Louisiana State University, 1997); Roger Baudier, *The Catholic Church in Louisiana* (New Orleans, 1939); and Glen R. Conrad, ed., *Cross, Crozier, and Crucible: A Volume Celebrating the Bicentennial of a Catholic Diocese in Louisiana* (New Orleans, 1993).

23    "*Besides being charitable ...*" *Picayune*, June 17, 1881.

23    Père Antoine: Clarence W. Bishpam, "Fray Antonio de Sedella: An Appreciation," *Louisiana Historical Quarterly* 2 (1919); Charles Edwards O'Neill, "A Quarter Marked by Sundry Peculiarities: New Orleans, Lay

Trustees, and Pére Antoine," *Catholic Historical Review* (1990); and Edgar J. Bruns, "Annotating for Posterity: The Sacramental Records of Father Antonio de Sedella" in Conrad 1993.

23  *"scourge of the Church"* to *". . . unto himself."* O'Neill, 1990:261.

24  *"knew Father Antoine . . ."* *Picayune*, June 17, 1881. For striking parallel examples of the distinctive partnerships and alliances between women of color and white clergymen in New Orleans, see Emily Clark and Virginia Meacham Gould, "The Feminine Face of Afro-Catholicism in New Orleans, 1727–1852," *William and Mary Quarterly* 59, 2 (April 2002).

24  Antoine's influence on court cases: Judith K. Schafer, "'Open and Notorious Concubinage': The Emancipation of Slave Mistresses by Will and Supreme Court in Antebellum Louisiana," *Louisiana History* 28 (1987).

24  *"new Babylon . . ."* to *". . . on earth."* Baudier 1939:275; Bell 1997:71.

25  The gossip about Pére Antoine and his Masonic connections runs throughout the published works on his life cited above.

25  Ursulines: Emily Clark, *A New World Community: The New Orleans Ursulines and Colonial Society, 1727–1803* (Ph.D. dissertation, Tulane University, 1998).

25  Religious instruction and devotional habits of women: Virginia Meacham Gould and Charles E. Nolan, eds., *No Cross, No Crown: Black Nuns in Nineteenth Century New Orleans* (Bloomington: Indiana University Press, 2001); Gould and Nolan, *Henriette Delille: "Servant of Slaves,"* (New Orleans: Sisters of the Holy Family, 1999); Mackie Blanton and Gayle K. Nolan, "Creole Lenten Devotions" in Conrad 1993; Patricia Rickles, "The Folklore of Sacraments and Sacramentals in South Louisiana," *Louisiana Folklore Miscellany* 2 (1965); and Dolores Egger Labbé, "Helpers in the Gospel: Women and Religious in Louisiana, 1800–1830," *Mid-America: An Historical Review* 79, 2 (1997); and Clark and Gould 2002.

25  Many catechisms were in common use in the nineteenth century; I have cited: *Catéchisme de La Louisiane,* Prepared for Monseigneur Joseph Rosati of St. Louis in the Diocese of Nouvelle Orléans; prepared for the diocese of Louisiana in France (Paris, 1839); and *Missel de la Très Sainte Vierge,* No. 32 (Archevéché De Paris 1891); both from the Historic New Orleans Collection. The translations are mine.

26  The story of the Ursuline nuns' prayers for victory is retold at a special Mass every January 8.

26  *"And suddenly from . . ."* Acts 2:1–4. *Bible.*

27  Zora Neale Hurston: Robert Hemenway, *Zora Neale Hurston: A Literary Biography* (Urbana: University of Illinois, 1980); Houston A. Baker, Jr.,

*Workings of the Spirit: The Poetics of Afro-American Women's Writing* (Chicago: University of Chicago, 1991); Valerie Boyd, *Wrapped in Rainbows: The Life of Zora Neale Hurston* (New York: Scribner, 2003); Carla Kaplan, collector and editor, *Zora Neale Hurston: A Life in Letters* (New York: Doubleday, 2002); and Gwendolyn Mikell, "The Anthropological Imagination of Zora Neale Hurston," *Western Journal of Black Studies* 7, 1 (1983).

28   "*O good mother, I come . . .*" to "*. . . of your friends. So Be It.*" Hurston 1931:334.

28   "*O good mother, I come . . .*" to "*. . . care and worry. So Be It.*" Hurston 1931:338.

29   "In African traditions . . ." Luisah Teish, *Jambalaya: The Natural Woman's Book of Personal Charms and Practical Rituals* (New York: HarperCollins, 1985).

29   "She appears as Erzulie . . ." the Haitian female spirit, see Sallie Ann Glassman, *Vodou Visions: An Encounter with Divine Mystery* (New York: Villard, 2000); Michel Laguerre, *Voodoo Heritage* (Beverly Hills: Sage, 1980); and Milo Rigaud, *Secrets of Voodoo* (New York: Pocket Books, 1971).

29   "*the boy . . .*" and chorus, "*Lovely lady . . .*" Art, Aaron, Charles, and Cyril Neville with David Ritz, *The Brothers: An Autobiography* (Boston: Little, Brown, 2000), 306.

30   Dede's initiation ceremony, dated approximately 1825, though problematic, is the only account from that period. J.W. Buel, *Metropolitan Live Unveiled* (St. Louis: Historical Publishing Co., 1882). Quotes and paraphrases are from pages 518–30.

32   "Master magic" and African consciousness in the New World: see Lawrence W. Levine, *Black Culture and Black Consciousness: Afro-American Folk Thought from Slavery to Freedom* (New York: Oxford University Press, 1977); Robert Farris Thompson, *Flash of the Spirit: African and Afro-American Art and Philosophy* (New York: Random House, 1983); Joseph Holloway, ed., *Africanisms in American Culture* (Bloomington: Indiana University Press, 1990); Andrew Apter, "Herskovits's Heritage: Rethinking Syncretism in the African Diaspora," *Diaspora* 1, 3 (1991); and Ina Fandrich, *The Mysterious Voodoo Queen Marie Laveaux: A Study of Power and Female Leadership in Nineteenth-Century New Orleans* (Ph.D. dissertation, Temple University, 1994).

32   Court cases: Laura Porteous, "The Gris-Gris Case," *Louisiana Historical Quarterly* 17, 1 (1934); Marcus B. Christian, manuscript, *A Black History of Louisiana*, chapter, "Voodooism and Mumbo-Jumbo," no pg., MCC-UNO; and DuPratz 1975.

33   "The ten thousand . . ." *Mayor's Report*, City of New Orleans, January 18, 1810; French exiles: see Paul F. Lachance, "The 1809 Immigration of Saint-Domingue Refugees to New Orleans: Reception, Integration and

Impact," *Louisiana Historical Quarterly* 29 (1988); "The Foreign French," in Hirsch and Logsdon 1992; and Thomas Fiehrer, "Saint-Domingue/Haiti: Louisiana's Caribbean Connection," *Louisiana History* 30 (1989).

## Chapter 3

34   *"Marie knew all about …"* Jennie Collins, WPA-FWP/NSU; WPA-LWP/BR; Tallant 1998:106.

36   Marriage of Marie Laveau and Jacques Paris: New Orleans Notarial Archives, H. Lavergne, Notary, Contract of Marriage, July 27, 1819; and *St. Louis Cathedral Book of Marriages of Persons of Color*, vol. I, 1777–1830, August 4, 1819, Book 1, Folio 60-A.

36   *Plaçage:* The quasi-marital institution of *plaçage* in New Orleans is best seen by looking directly at the lives of free women of color and their survival tactics, rather than older sources which discount women's agency and range of movement or which emphasized "quadroon" women as property and sexual objects. In this regard, female scholars historians have created a major new corpus of scholarship on career, marriage, and family building strategies for women, particularly women of color. See Joan M. Martin, *"Plaçage* and the Louisiana *Gens de Couleur Libre:* How Race and Sex Defined the Lifestyles of Free Women of Color," in Kein 2000; Hall 1997; Dominquez 1994; Gould 1991; 1997a; Hanger 1997, 1997b, 1996a, and 1992.

37   Henriette Delille: Gould and Nolan 1999; Gould and Nolan 2001.

37   Marriage of Marie Laveau's maternal half-sister, Marie Louise Darcantel to Louis Foucher: *St. Louis Cathedral Book of Marriages of Persons of Color*, vol. 1, 1777–1830, April 4, 1815:110. Marriage of Marie Laveau's paternal half-sister: New Orleans Notarial Archives, Narcisse Broutin, Notary, Contract of Marriage for François Auguste and Marie Laveaux, September 3, 1818.

38   Charles Laveaux: A wide assortment of civil records testify to Laveaux's prosperity and business connections within the Creole community, WPA/FWP-NSU; see also Roulhac Toledano, Sally Kittredge Evans, and Mary Lou Christovich, *New Orleans Architecture*, vol. 4, *The Creole Faubourgs* (New Orleans: Pelican, 1974), 34.

38   Undated, unpaged notes about Madame Parizien, Dillon manuscript, "The Menage Laveau," WPA/FWP-NSU.

39   Baroness Micaela Almonaster de Pontalba: Christine Vella, *Intimate Enemies: The Two Worlds of the Baroness de Pontalba* (Baton Rouge: Louisiana State University, 1997).

39    *"Did you ever see . . ."* *New Orleans Times*, November 25, 1887.

40    *"Besides being . . ."* *Picayune*, June 17, 1881.

40    Marguerite Darcantel and Voodoo: "many people said she [Marie the Second] would never be a hoodoo doctor like her mother and grandma before her." Hurston 1990:192.

40    Darcantel will: New Orleans Public Library, City of New Orleans, Records of Wills, Henry Darcantel, October 22, 1817. Darcantel is sometimes spelled D'Arcantel or D'arcantel.

40    "New Orleans was a deadly place . . ." John Duffy, *The Rudolph Matas History of Medicine in Louisiana*, vol. 1, vol. 2 (Baton Rouge: Louisiana State University, 1958, 1962); and Katherine Bankole, *Slavery and Medicine: Enslavement and Medical Practices in Antebellum Louisiana* (New York: Garland, 1998).

41    *"These far-famed nurses . . ."* Alexander Walker, *Life of Andrew Jackson* (New York: Derby and Jackson, 1858), 346; also see Grace King, *New Orleans: The Place and the People* (New York: Macmillan, 1926), 249; and Rodolphe Lucien Desdunes, *Our People and Our History* (Baton Rouge: Louisiana State University, 1973), 97.

41    Amputations: Rudolph Matas Papers, Medical School Library, Tulane University, New Orleans, Louisiana.

42    Sources on materials, chemicals, compounds, herbs, or other materials available to nurses: Long 2001, chs. 3 and 4; Hurston 1990:227–85, and Hurston 1931:411–17. The *materia medica* of Voodoo-Hoodoo runs throughout Harry Middleton Hyatt, *Hoodoo-Conjuration-Witchcraft-Rootwork*, all five volumes, 1970–78. Files of the WPA Federal Writers' Project contain thousands of references to folk medicine and conjure in Louisiana, WPA-FWP/NSU. WPA-LWP/BR.

42    Louis Dufilho's apothecary at 514 Rue Chartres is now the New Orleans Pharmacy Museum. For a visitor's description of the pharmacy in Laveau's time, see deCaro 1998:86.

43    *"the skill of their women . . ."* Buel 1882:535.

43    Creole life in early nineteenth century. George Washington Cable, *The Creoles of Louisiana* (New York: Charles Scribner's Sons, 1884); Erastus Paul Puckett, *The Free Negro in New Orleans, 1803–1850* (M.A. thesis, Tulane University, 1907); Leonard P. Curry, *The Free Black in Urban America, 1800–1850* (Chicago: University of Chicago, 1981); Mary Gehman, *The Free People of Color in New Orleans* (New Orleans: Margaret Media, 1994); Sally Kittredge Evans, "Free Persons of Color," in Toledano, Evans, and Christovich 1974:25–36; Hirsch and Logsdon 1992; and Kein 2000.

44 *"When Marie was twenty-five . . ."* Picayune, June 17, 1991.

44 Military records for Christophe Glapion: Jane Lucas DeGrummond and Ronald R. Morazan, *The Baratarians and the Battle of New Orleans with Biographical Sketches of the Veterans of the Battalions of Orleans, 1814–1815* (Baton Rouge: Legacy Publications, 1979), 27, and cross-references [spelled Capion]; Muster Roll of Captain Henry de St. G?me, Company of Dragoons, 16 December 1814 to 28 February 1815, shows both Glapion's military service and his race.

44 "Sons of Freedom": Roland C. McConnell, "Louisiana's Black Military History, 1729–1865" in Robert R. Macdonald, John R. Kemp, and Edward F. Haas, eds., *Louisiana's Black Heritage* (New Orleans: Louisiana State Museum, 1979); and Roland C. McConnell, *Negro Troops of Antebellum Louisiana: A History of the Battalion of Free Men of Color* (Baton Rouge: Louisiana State University, 1968).

45 *"Christophe Glapion's family . . ."* The name in various spellings appears in many colonial documents. The Federal Writers' Project records list the "white" associations of the founding members of the Glapion family, WPA-FWP/NSU; WPA-LWP/BR; Clark, 1998, mentions the social prominence and race of the women in the Glapion family.

45 Racial rules in Louisiana: See Dominquez 1994, for analysis of "race" and "blood."

47 Marie Heloise Eucharist Glapion: "GLAPION, Marie Heloise, 1827, *St. Louis Cathedral Book of Baptisms for People of Color,* Reg. 21–folio 220. (Col.) illeg. daughter of Christophe Glapion and Marie Laveau. Father signed record." "Marie Heloise Glapion, daughter of Christophe Glapion and Marie Laveau, baptized August 21, 1828. St. Louis Cathedral, Book 21A, 1827–1829, p. 290, #1232." Typed notes in WPA-LWP/BR.

## Chapter 4

49 *"You sprinkle Holy Water . . ."* Hyatt, vol. 1, 1970:879.

49 Pére Antoine's death and funeral: *Louisiana Courier,* January 20, 21, and 23, 1829; Celestine Chambon, *The St. Louis Cathedral and Its Neighbors* (New Orleans: Louisiana State Museum, 1938); Baudier 1939; Bishram 1919; and Castellanos 1895.

50 Story of Dona Beatriz: Thornton 1998.

51 "Hail Anthony" prayer: Thornton 1998:216.

51 *"so that the spirits of . . ."* Hurston 1931:339.

51    *"St. Ant'ny, open dis do'"* Hyatt, vol. 3, 1973:1913. For examples and analysis of New Orleans Hoodoo-Voodoo from Hyatt's work, see Michael Edward Bell, *Pattern, Structure, and Logic in Afro-American Hoodoo Performance* (Ph.D. dissertation, Indiana University, 1970).

52    *"You take care of the saint . . ."* Teish 1985:129.

52    *"The Dead have achieved . . ."* Glassman 2000:14.

52    *"benevolent conjuration"* Charles Raphael, WPA-FWP/NSU.

53    St. Maroon, the patron saint of runaways in Louisiana, Tallant 1998:204.

53    *"You go to the saint store . . ."* Hyatt, vol. 1, 1970:878.

53    *"Once you is gris-grised . . ."* Octavia Williams, WPA-FWP/NSU.

54    *"Everything has not always . . ."* Dillon Folder, "Folklore/La. Catholic Customs and Traditions, St. Expedite," WPA-FWP/NSU.

54    *"St. Peter cursed . . ."* Hyatt, vol. 2, 1970:1819.

55    *"St. Peter? He's good . . ."* Hyatt, vol. 1, 1970:874.

55    *"If I wanted St. Peter . . ."* Hyatt, vol. 1, 1970:876.

55    *"If you a man . . ."* Hyatt, vol. 3, 1973:1913. St. Rita poem.

56    *"Yeah, he's another one . . ."* Hyatt, vol. 2, 1970:1230. St. Michael.

56    *"In the name of . . ."* Hyatt, vol. 2, 1970:1407, St. Michael Curse-Prayer.

56    *"On your left leg . . ."* Hurston 1931:343.

57    *"She fix up . . ."* Hyatt, vol. 2, 1970:1648. St. Roch.

57    "St. John was the patron saint . . ." Blanton and Nolan, Conrad 1993.

58    "In many parts of Africa . . ." Teish 1985; Laguerre 1980; and Rigaud 1971. Significance of St. John's Eve in Haiti, see Hurston, *Tell My Horse: Voodoo and Life in Haiti and Jamaica* (New York: J.P. Lippincott, 1938).

58    *"had come from Africa . . ."* Zora Neale Hurston, "High John De Conquer," *The Complete Stories* (New York: HarperPerennial, 1996), 140. Orig. pub. *The American Mercury*, July 1943.

59    *"The thousands upon . . ."* Hurston 1996:148.

59    "When I play dice . . ." paraphrased from "The Gambling Hand," Hurston 1931:328.

59    *"For yourself . . ."* to *". . . same time. So Be It ."* Hurston 1931:355.

60    *"Marie Laveau? My god, yes . . ."* Harrison Camille, WPA-FWP/NSU; WPA-LWP/BR. Clayton 1990: 40.

60    *"lips smeared with blood . . ."* Tallant 1998:66.

60    "But the European devil . . ." Hurston 1996:139–48.

61    Woman-led religions: see Karen McCarthy Brown, *Mama Lola: A Vodou Priestess in Brooklyn* (Berkeley: University of California Press, 2001); Ruth Landes, *The City of Women* (Albuquerque: University of New Mexico,

1994); and Susan Sered, *Priestess, Mother, Sacred Sister: Religions Dominated by Woman* (New York: Oxford University Press, 1994). Women's spiritual leadership in New Orleans, see Clark and Gould 2002.

61 *"root doctor . . ."* to *". . . loved ones."* Glassman 2000:21.

62 Celestin Glapion: see Dillon manuscript, "The Menage Laveau," WPA-FWP/NSU; and WPA-LWP/BR.

62 Marie Laveaux Auguste: *Will of Marie Françoise Dupart Laveaux*, New Orleans Notarial Archives, L.T. Caire, vol. 6, #56, January 19, 1829; Marie Auguste's debts: *Louisiana Courier*, November 24, 1819; August 27, 1828; Marie Auguste's estate: *Louisiana Courier*, February 14, 1842; Dillon manuscript, "The Menage Laveau," WPA-FWP/NSU; and for coffin story, Fandrich, 1994:251 and notes.

63 Henriette Delille: Gould and Nolan 1999; Gould and Nolan 2001; and M. Boniface Adams, "The Gift of Religious Leadership: Henriette Delille and the Foundation of the Holy Family Sisters," in Conrad 1993.

63 Benevolent societies, Masonic orders, and voluntary mutual aid associations: Claude Jacobs, "Benevolent Societies of New Orleans Blacks during the Late Nineteenth and Early Twentieth Centuries," *Louisiana History* 28 (1988); Bell 1997; and Kein 2000.

64 *"Marie negritte*, slave of the Widow Paris born Marie Laveau, F. D. C. L.," May 12, 1838. St. Louis Cemetery One. *Book of Funerals*, 1835–1843, Folio 98; #247.

64 *Society of the Ladies of the Tignon*, the *Society of Mother Hens and Baby Hens*, Edward Ashley, WPA-FWP/NSU; WPA-LWP/BR; *Ladies and their Sacred Friends*: Alexander Augustin, WPA-FWP/NSU; WPA-LWP/BR.

# Chapter 5

65 *"The steps of her house . . ."* James St. Ann, WPA-FWP/NSU; WPA-LWP/BR.

65 High walnut bed mentioned: *Daily States*, June 17, 1881.

66 *"She was a pretty woman . . ."* Tallant 1998:54–55.

66 *"Fifteen children were . . ."* Picayune, June 17, 1881.

66 "Between 1827 and 1836 . . ." See Genealogy for Marie Laveau and Christophe Glapion's children. Although civil and church records often do not agree with each other, or are incomplete, they do seem to confirm these five children.

68 The donation of the Love St. property to Eucharist Glapion: New Orleans Notarial Archives, L.T. Caire, #763, July 25, 1832; and COB, vol. 11, January

12, 1833. Notaries: The New Orleans Notarial Archive is the only such repository for records of public notaries in the United States. Established after the Civil War to house colonial and antebellum records, the archives hold approximately forty million pages of signed acts from three centuries of notary activities. In Roman law and civil law, a notary witnessed most private contracts, guaranteed the intentions of the parties present, and filed a copy of transactions such as wills, successions, acts of sale, marriage contracts, mortgages, loans, building contracts, powers of attorney, inventories of estates, family meetings, meetings on debts and bankruptcy, law suits, and individual declarations of intent. The heritage of civil law in Louisiana is similar to France under the Napoleonic Codes and differs sharply from English common law traditions in the rest of the United States; Edward F. Haas, ed., *Louisiana's Legal Heritage* (Pensacola, Fla.: Perdido Bay Press, 1983).

68  Purchase of St. Ann St. house: New Orleans Notarial Archives, Octave de Armas, *Succession of Catherine Henry, f. w. c.*; September 28, 1832, Vol. 16 #482. "A certain lot of ground situated in Saint Ann Street between Burgundy and Rampart Strs measuring 37½ ft. X 80 ft. in depth together with the buildings thereon, which was adjudicated to" Christophe Glapion; including Glapion's bid at auction on September 21. COB 12/246, September 28, 1832.

68  Mortgage on the Love St. property: New Orleans Notarial Archives, T. Seghers, #396, September 28, 1832, and #461, December 5, 1832.

68  "*Marie Laveau was born . . .*" *Picayune*, June 17, 1881.

69  St. Ann St. house transactions of 1838–1839: New Orleans Notarial Archives, T.S. Seghers, July 30, 1836; June 8, 1838; September 23, 1839; L.T. Caire, February 24, 1827; State of Louisiana, C.V. Foulon, Sale–Original Act, June 8, 1838–translated by WPA-FWP/NSU.

71  Death certificates for Joseph and Esmeralda Crocker: New Orleans Public Library, Orleans Parish, Records of Births and Deaths: *Death Certificate for Joseph Eugene Crocker*, May 5, 1845. *Death Certificate for Esmeralda Crocker*, January 8, 1850.

71  Bazile Crocker: Desdunes 1973:77.

71  Name of Marie the Second's son: Civil District Court, Judgement #4597. *Succession of Eloise Euchariste or Euchariste Glapion.* Nov. 28th 1881. H. Miester, Dy. Clk.

71  Pierre Crocker's involvement in Glapion's death: Judicial Archives, Second District Court, *Succession of Christophe D. Glapion. No. 9168. Vol. IV*; Public Library, Parish of Orleans, Office of Recorder of Births and Deaths, *Death Certificate for Christophe Glapion*, June 29, 1855.

71 Records for Pierre Crocker: New Orleans city directories from the nineteenth-century tracks official addresses, residences, and occupations of the Crocker men. Also see New Orleans Public Library, *Successions*: Crocker, Widow, P. #17,513; Crocker, Mrs. B. #9496; Crocker, Bazile #41,045. Obituaries: Bazile Crocker, *New Orleans Bee*, January 30, 1879. Pierre Crocker, *Louisiana Courier*, July 10, 1857, *Bee*, July 10, 1857. The baptismal records of St. Louis Cathedral record Pierre and Rose Gignac Crocker's children. See also Roulhac Toledano and Mary Louise Christovich, *New Orleans Architecture, Vol. 6: Faubourg Treme and the Bayou Road* (New Orleans, LA: Pelican, 1980), 87. Both Bazile and Pierre Crocker owned slaves, at least two of whom they buried in family plots in St. Louis Cemetery One.

72 Baptismal certificate for Marie Glapion: St. Louis Cathedral, *Book of Baptisms for People of Color*, vol. 32(2):353, July 9, 1850.

73 *"Marie called herself a . . ."* Theresa Kavanaugh, WPA-FWP/NSU; WPA-LWP/BR.

73 *"Marie Laveau gained entree . . ."* Dillon ms., Folder # 317: "Marie Laveau II," WPA-FWP/NSU, no pages.

73 *"Nowhere do hearts betray . . ."* Eliza Potter, *A Hairdresser's Experiences in the High Life* (Cincinnati, Ohio: Privately pub., 1859), iv.

73 Story of Monsieur Preval's wife and mistress reconstructed from Potter 1859:166; the name Preval comes from published verses of the *Calinda*.

74 *Calinda*: Folder: "Survey of Folklore," WPA-FWP/NSU; Emilie Lejeune, "Creole Folk Songs," *Louisiana Historical Quarterly*, vol. 2, 1919.

75 *"She also made . . ."* Dillon ms. Folder # 317: "Marie Laveau II," WPA-FWP/NSU.

75 *"for it was now . . ."* Tallant 1998:54.

76 Glapion's pension: DeGrummond and Morazan 1979:27 and Appendixes as cited.

76 Christophe Glapion's mother: New Orleans Public Library. *Succession of Madame Lalande Ferrière Glapion (Jeanne Sophie)*, Dec. 7, 1835. VCH 160, vol. 5:161.

76 *"Marie used to trade . . ."* Marie Dede. WPA-FWP/NSU; WPA-LWP/BR

77 *"After dark, you might . . ."* John Kendall, "Old New Orleans Houses and the People Who Lived in Them," *Louisiana Historical Quarterly* 20, 3 (1937), 799.

## Chapter 6

78 Description of French Market: William H. Coleman, *Historic Sketch Book and Guide to New Orleans and Its Environs* (New York: Coleman, 1885).

79 Description of slave-sale cottages: Walter Johnson, *Soul by Soul: Life Inside the Antebellum Slave Market* (Cambridge, Mass.: Harvard University Press, 1999).

80 *"men wore good ..."* Robert Reinders, "Slavery in New Orleans in the Decade before the Civil War." *Mid-America* 44, 4 (1962), 212.

80 *"The girl—who ..."* Georges J. Joyaux, "Forest's *Voyage aux Etats-Unis de l'Amérique en 1831*," *Louisiana Historic Quarterly* 39, 4 (1956), 467.

80 Ordinance prohibiting sidewalk displays: *Orleanian*, January 20, 1852.

80 *"I stopped ..."* to *"... bought and sold."* Potter 1859:171–74.

81 *"Before the war ..."* Dr. Bass, *New Orleans States*, August 26, 1881.

81 *"negro fetishism"* Dr. Samuel Cartwright. *Sunday Delta*, January 27, 1861.

81 *"mystical connection between ..."* Dr. Samuel Cartwright. *Sunday Delta*, March 17, 1861.

82 "New Orleans was a metropolitan magnet ..." see John Hope Franklin and Loren Schweninger, *Runaway Slaves: Rebels on the Plantation* (New York: Oxford University Press, 1999), 136; John W. Blassingame, ed., *Slave Testimony: Two Centuries of Letters, Speeches, Interviews, and Autobiographies* (Baton Rouge: Louisiana State University Press, 1977); and Judith K. Schafer, "New Orleans Slavery in 1850 as Seen in Advertisements," *Journal of Southern History* 47, 1 (1981).

82 *"The whites were neither ..."* Levine 1977:74. See also Jessie Gaston Mulira, "The Case of Voodoo in New Orleans," in Holloway 1990:34–68, for Voodoo militarism or social activism in both Haiti and Louisiana.

83 *"Carry to river at twelve ..."* Hurston 1931:389.

83 *"Take a toad ..."* Hurston 1931:377.

83 *"They git cayenne pepper ..."* Hyatt, vol. 2, 1970:1232.

83 *"Get some of that fast-foot powder ..."* Hyatt, vol. 2, 1970:1823.

83 Marie the Second's night-time excursions: Tallant 1998:94.

84 Nat Turner: Judith Schafer, "The Immediate Impact of Nat Turner's Insurrection on New Orleans," *Louisiana History* 21 (1980).

84 Alexandrine: New Orleans Notarial Archives, *"Statue libre,"* L.T. Caire, vol. 65A, #407, May 19, 1838; #408, May 19, 1838. Free people of color owned slaves in antebellum Louisiana; many had to invest their limited capital in the purchase of relatives and friends, even potential spouses: Judith K. Schafer, *Slavery, the Civil Law and the Supreme Court of Louisiana* (Baton Rouge: Louisiana State University, 1994); James Hardy, "A Slave Sale in Antebellum New Orleans," *Southern Studies* 23 (1984); Reinders 1962b; Puckett 1907; Curry 1981; and Gould, 1991.

85    Relationship of Spanish colonial practices to manumission, emancipa-
      tion, and self-purchase for women of color: Hanger, 1997a, 1997b, 1996,
      and 1992; Gould, 1997a, 1991.

86    For relationships of women of color to slavery and concubinage in ante-
      bellum New Orleans; see Virginia Meacham Gould, "'The House that
      Was Never a Home': Slave Family and Household Organization in New
      Orleans, 1820–1850," *Slavery and Abolition* 18, 2 (1997b); "'If I Can't Have My
      Rights, I Can Have My Pleasures, And If They Won't Give Me Wages,
      I Can Take Them': Gender and Slave Labor in Antebellum New Orleans,"
      Morton 1996:179–201; and Schafer 1987.

86    Price of women: a "mulatto girl" sold for $7,000 *Picayune*, February 14,
      1837; a "mulatto girl" sold for $8,000 *Bee*, October 16, 1841.

86    Case of Irma: New Orleans Notarial Archives, Sale of Irma, *Statu libre*,
      L.T. Caire vol. 66A, #593, #594, August 10, 1838.

87    Case of Juliette a.k.a. Nounoute: New Orleans Notarial Archives,
      J. Agaisse Vol. I, #48, Sale of Slave, *Statu libre*, Aug 17, 1843; P. Laresche, vol. 2,
      Sale of Slave, *Statue libre*, Nov. 15, 1847; J. Agaisse, vol. 6 #42, Sale of Slave,
      *Statu libre*, April 27, 1848; COB vol. 44:573–574; COB Vol. 45:209.

88    Case of Peter: New Orleans Notarial Archives, J. Agaisse #109, Sale of
      slave, October 24, 1849.

89    Founding of St. Augustine's Church: Brenda Marie Osbey, "Faubourg
      Treme: A Community in Transition. Part I: Early History." *New Orleans
      Tribune*, December 1990.

89    Congo Square: Johnson 1995; Emery 1988; Kmen 1972; Anderson 1960; and
      Malone 1966.

90    *Counja*, song: Folders, "Survey of Folklore," "Congo Square,"
      "Folklore/Voodoo," WPA-FWP/NSU; WPA-LWP/BR.

90    "*swaying, swinging, chanting …*" to "*… to it.*" Dillon manuscript, "Congo
      Square," WPA-FWP/NSU, no pgs.

90    *Calinda; Bamboula*: Folders, "Survey of Folklore," "Congo Square,"
      "Folklore/Voodoo," WPA-FWP/NSU; WPA-LWP/BR.

91    "*a great cauldron*" to "*… of magnetic shocks.*" Tallant 1998:13–14.

91    *Zambi Mpungu*, name of God in the Kikongo language of Central Africa:
      Thornton 1998, 1987, and 1984.

92    "In St. Domingue-Haiti …" Ethnobotanist Wade Davis investigated
      and documented cases of zombis in Haiti, *The Serpent and the Rainbow*
      (New York: Simon and Schuster, 1985).

# Chapter 7

93   *"I've seen people . . ."* Saxon, Tallant, and Dreyer 1998:349.

93   Creole mourning customs and funerals: Saxon et al., 1998, chapter 16; original files in WPA-FWP/NSU; WPA-LWP/BR; also see Sybil Kein, "The Celebration of Life in New Orleans Jazz Funerals," *Revue Française D'Etudes Americaines* 51 (1992). For account of an early Creole burial, see Latrobe 1951:82–86. Many documents and gravestones of that period use date of burial rather than date of death.

94   New Orleans cemeteries: see Mary Louise Christovich, ed., *New Orleans Architecture*, vol. 3, *The Cemeteries* (New Orleans: Pelican) 1997; Robert Florence, *City of the Dead: A Journey Through St. Louis Cemetery #1, New Orleans, Louisiana* (Lafayette, La.: Center for Louisiana Studies, 1996); Samuel Wilson, Jr., and Leonard Huber, *The St. Louis Cemeteries of New Orleans* (New Orleans: St. Louis Cathedral, 1963); Eric J. Brock, *New Orleans Cemeteries*, (Charleston, S.C.: Arcadia, 1999); and Patricia Brady, "Free Men of Color as Tomb Builders in the Nineteenth Century," in Conrad 1993.

95   Laveau-Paris tomb: The staff of the WPA Federal Writers' Project copied inscriptions from tombs in the city's most famous cemeteries, obituaries from newspapers, and death notices from the city's vital statistics records. This information is in various formats in the Williams Research Center, Historic New Orleans Collection; the Louisiana State Museum; the Amistad Collection and Special Collections at Tulane University; also WPA-FWP/NSU; WPA-LWP/BR.

96   "In central Africa . . ." Thornton 1998; 1987–88; 1984.

97   *"Black was the color of the living."* Thornton 1998:160.

97   Deaths of Laveau-Glapion children: François Auguste Glapion, died May 18, 1834. Cemetery Files, St. Louis #2. St. Louis Cathedral, Book of Baptisms for People of Color, vol. 23, p. 403, #2715. Marie Louise Caroline Glapion, St. Louis Cathedral, *Baptisms for People of Color*, September 10, 1829, vol. 22, p. 56, #317. St. Louis Cathedral, *Funerals for People of Color*, December 9, 1829, vol. 9, part 2, #8. Archange: New Orleans Public Library, Orleans Parish, Records of Births and Deaths. Death Certificate for Archange Glapion, January 8, 1845, vol. 10:297. Typed notes, WPA-FWP/NSU.

98   "In New Orleans, one out . . ." For estimates and analysis of the social conditions that led to high infant mortality, see John Duffy 1958, 1962; and Gould 1997a, 1997b.

98    For the relationship of child loss and maternal spirituality, see Sered 1994; and Ann Braude, *Radical Spirits: Spiritualism and Women's Rights in Nineteenth-Century America* (Boston: Beacon Press, 1989).

98    *"the willingness to interact ..."* Sered 1994:191–92.

99    *"Oh, my daughter, I have painfully ..."* Hurston 1931:345.

99    Statistics of 1853 epidemic: New Orleans City Council, *Report of the Sanitary Commission of New Orleans on the Epidemic of Yellow Fever of 1853*, 1854:460. See John Duffy, *Sword of Pestilence: The New Orleans Yellow Fever Epidemic of 1853*, (Baton Rouge: Louisiana State University, 1966); and Jo Ann Carrigan, *The Saffron Scourge: A History of Yellow Fever in Louisiana, 1796–1905* (Lafayette, La.: Center for Louisiana Studies, 1994).

100   Howard Association: see Laura Hanggi-Myers, "The Howard Association of New Orleans—Precursor to District Nursing," *Public Health Nursing* 12, 2 (1995); Flora Bassett Hildreth, *The Howard Association of New Orleans 1837–1878* (Ph.D. dissertation, University of California, Los Angeles, 1975); and "Early Red Cross: The Howard Association of New Orleans, 1837–1878," *Louisiana History* 20 (1979); and William L. Robinson, *Diary of a Samaritan* (New York: Harper Bros., 1860).

100   *"a committee of gentlemen ..."* New Orleans *Picayune*, June 17, 1881.

100   *"stood to their duties ..."*: John Kendall, "History and Incidents of the Plague in New Orleans," *Harper's Magazine* 7 (1853), 805. Italics mine.

100   *"Yellow Jack ..."* to *"... good health."* John Duffy, ed., *Parson Clapp of the Strangers' Church of New Orleans* (Baton Rouge: Louisiana State University, 1957), 130.

101   Birth of Victor Pierre: Civil District Court, Judgement #4597. *Succession of Eloise Euchariste or Euchariste Glapion.* Nov. 28th 1881. H. Miester, Dy. Clk.

102   Death of Christophe Glapion: New Orleans Public Library: Parish of Orleans, Office of the Recorder of Births and Deaths, *Death Certificate of Christophe Glapion*, June 29, 1855. St. Louis Cemetery No. 1, Succession of Christophe de Glapion. Internment Payment Records, #9168, p. 263; no. 737.

103   *"There is some old ..."* Succession of Christophe Glapion: New Orleans Judicial Archives, 2nd District Court, *Succession of Christophe D. Glapion*, no. 9168, vol. IV, August 19,1854, to October 15, 1856.

104   *"You will write your children ..."* Hurston 1931:329.

106   Philomène's infants: New Orleans Public Library, Orleans Parish, Records of Births and Deaths. Death Certificate, Joseph Legendre, February 12,

1870; vol. 32:225. St. Louis Cemetery # 1, Burial Certificate for Eugenie Legendre, Reg. No. 1865–69, Folio 146, January 29, 1866.

106   *"I knew a gentleman ..."* Potter 1859:176.

106   *"Mrs. Legendre, I ..."* Josephine Harrison, WPA-FWP/NSU; WPA-LWP/BR.

106   *"Yeah, her daughters ..."* Mary Washington, WPA-FWP/NSU; WPA-LWP/BR.

106   *"I saw her ..."* to *"... keep their secret."* Josephine Harrison, asterisked footnote: Dillon manuscript, Folder #317, "Marie Laveau II," WPA-FWP/NSU, no pages.

107   Passing: Arthé Anthony, "'Lost Boundaries': Racial Passing and Poverty in Segregated New Orleans," in Kein 2000.

## Chapter 8

108   Zora's question and Luke's answer are reconstructed from Hurston 1990:192.

109   *"there was a hollow tree ..."* Joseph Morris, WPA-FWP/NSU; WPA-LWP/BR. See also Charles Raphael, WPA-FWP/NSU.

109   *"Whenever there was food ..."* Oscar Felix, WPA-FWP/NSU. Oscar Felix's interviews are scattered: see WPA-FWP/NSU under name of "Nome"; Robert Tallant Collection, Amistad Research Center, Tulane University; Marcus Christian papers, MCC–UNO; Tallant fictionalized him under the name "Rooster," 1998, ch. 18.

109   *"No more dramatic ..."* Times-Democrat, August 1, 1891.

109   *"and the dancers ..."* Theresa Kavanaugh, WPA-FWP/NSU; WPA-LWP/BR.

110   Jim Alexander: Real name was Charles Lafontaine, died August 19, 1890, Long 2001:44, 272, n.23. Nathan Hobley's testimony, Clayton 1990:112–13. See Dillon manuscripts, "Folklore/Voodoo," "Other Famous Wangateurs," WPA-FWP/NSU; and WPA-LWP/BR.

110   *"Marie, she would rather ..."* Hurston 1990:192.

110   Arresting fortune-tellers: Kaplan 2003:127.

111   *"Turner again ..."* to *"... do not matter."* Hurston 1990:198. The italics are mine.

111   *"while my spirit went ..."* Hurston 1990:199.

111   Conversation: *"How must I come?"* to *"She is worthy."* Hurston 1990:200–201.

112   *"A knife flashed ..."* Hurston 1990:202.

113 *"never allowed you ..."* Raymond Rivaros, WPA-FWP/NSU; WPA-LWP/ BR.

114 Altars and the imagery of the Dead, Ancestors, and Spirits: Glassman 2000:26–29; Oscar Felix, illustration of his Marie-inspired altar, WPA-FWP/NSU.

114 *"used to have so ..."* Marie Dede, WPA-FWP/NSU; WPA-LWP/BR.

114 *"Before the ..."* Edward Ashley, WPA-FWP/NSU; WPA-LWP/BR.

115 *"a white sheet was ..."* Gerald July, WPA-FWP/NSU; WPA-LWP/BR; Tallant 1998:61.

115 *"Marie would call ..."* Raymond Rivaros, WPA-FWP/NSU; WPA-LWP/BR.

115 *"and when you left ..."* Edward Ashley, WPA-FWP/NSU; WPA-LWP/BR.

116 *"not a woman ..."* Hurston 1990:195.

116 *"Lay your burden ..."* to *"... abide in plenty. So Be It."* Hurston 1931:331.

116 *"And, my son, be sure ..."* to *"... closed in on you. So Be It."* Hurston 1931:329.

117 "Another woman ..." The Woman Who Wished to Be Uncrossed. Hurston 1931:333.

117 *"Oh, good mother, the evil spirit ..."* Hurston 1931:341.

117 *"I am disgusted ..."* to *"... prosperity. So Be It."* Hurston 1931:348.

119 "paraphernalia of conjure": Hurston 1990:277–85; and Hyatt, all volumes.

119 *"I'll tell you ..."* Harrison Camille, WPA-FWP/NSU; WPA-LWP/BR.

119 "Make nine bags ..." Hurston 1990:276; "measure his member" is widespread folklore in Louisiana, and widely available in other sources as well, see Hurston 1931, 1990; Hyatt, all volumes; and files of WPA-FWP/NSU; WPA-LWP/BR.

119 *"Love is at the bottom ..."* Hurston 1931:351.

119 *"He be lying in bed ..."* Hyatt, vol. 2, 1970:1824.

120 *"one of the daughters ..."* Josephine Jones, WPA-FWP/NSU; WPA-LWP/BR.

120 *"A poor woman came crying ..."* Ramon Rivaros, WPA-FWP/NSU; WPA-LWP/BR.

120 *"courthouse work"* to *"... prisoner."* Lala Hopkins, WPA-FWP/NSU; WPA-LWP/BR.

121 *"Now the learned ..."* to *"... good fortune."* Hurston 1931:343.

121 *"When the judge and the sheriff ..."* James St. Ann, WPA-FWP/NSU; WPA-LWP/BR.

122 *"They ran leaving ..."* Mrs. Dauphine, WPA-FWP/NSU; WPA-LWP/BR.

# Chapter 9

123    *"In the name of . . ."* Hyatt, vol. 2, 1970:1349.

124    *"The chimes of the . . ."* Castellanos 1895:108.

124    *"Although the rain . . ."* Picayune, July 3, 1852.

124    *"A tall woman . . ."* Tallant 1998:71.

124    *"An arrogant and consummate imposter"* Castellanos 1895:113.

124    *"this horrid execution . . ."* Castellanos 1895:110. The Louisiana legislature banned public executions that fall: *Historical Sketch Book & Guide to New Orleans* (New York: Coleman, 1885), 207.

125    *"Marie Laveau devoted . . ."* to *". . . Virgin Mary."* Asbury 1938:270.

125    *"Although Marie Laveau had taken . . ."* Picayune, April 11, 1886.

125    *"Whenever a prisoner . . ."* Picayune, June 17, 1881.

125    *"was convicted . . ."* Asbury 1938:275.

126    *"with most curious . . ."*; and James Mullen story: William Howard Russell, *My Diary North and South* (Boston, 1963), 244.

126    *"good Christian woman . . ."* Picayune, May 10, 1871.

127    Conversation: *"If you die . . ."* to *". . . give me the grace."* Sister Helen Prejean, *Dead Man Walking* (New York: Vintage, 1993), 37.

128    *"It was generally rumored . . ."* alleged conversation between Widow Paris and Antoine Cambre, Castellanos 1895:113; see also Dennis C. Rousey, *Policing the Southern City: New Orleans, 1805–1889* (Baton Rouge: Louisiana State University Press, 1996:87); and *State v. Antoine Cambre*, First District Court, Minute Books, Case No. 14369.

129    *"At breakfast time . . ."* Bee, August 8, 1860. Death and Inquest.

129    *"There has been a rumor . . ."* Bee, June 21, 1860; see also *State v. Eugene Pepe alias Eugene Adams*, First District Court, Docket Books, Case No. 14066.

129    *"Don't fool yourself . . ."* Hurston 1990:186.

129    *"And the man died . . "* Hurston 1990:196.

129    *"the dueling capital . . ."* Rousey 1996:80; crime rate, Rousey 1996:85.

130    *"nothing would ever . . ."* Russell 1863:244.

130    *"Marie Laveau was in . . ."* Joseph Alfred, WPA-FWP/NSU; WPA-LWP/BR.

130    *"Marie was smart . . ."* Nathan Hobley, WPA-LWP/BR; Dillon ms. "Marie Laveau II," no pages; WPA-FWP/NSU. Clayton, 1990:114, followed WPA instructions.

130    *"notorious thug"* James G. Hollandsworth, *An Absolute Massacre: The New Orleans Race Riot of July 30, 1866* (Baton Rouge: Louisiana State University, 2001), 185. Obituary of Lucien Adams, Picayune, March 2, 1900.

130 *"stopped by Marie ..."* Marguerite Gitson, WPA-FWP/NSU; WPA-LWP/BR.

131 *"Adams? Well, Marie ..."* Mary Washington, WPA-FWP/NSU; WPA-LWP/BR.

131 Thomas Adams, see Rousey 1996:115, 118, 122; Hollandsworth 2001:73, 88, 152.

131 New Orleans in the "Golden Age": Samuel Wilson, Jr., Patricia Brady, and Lynn Adams, *Queen of the South, New Orleans, 1853–1962,* (New Orleans: Historic New Orleans Collection and New York Public Library, 1999); with Video, 1999; Joseph Logsdon and Caryn Cossé Bell, "The Americanization of Black New Orleans," and Introduction, Part 3: "Franco-Africans and African Americans," in Hirsch and Logsdon 1992.

131 Population statistics: Dominguez 1994:116.

132 Problems for free people of color in antebellum New Orleans: Robert C. Reinders, "The Free Negro in the New Orleans Economy, 1850–1860," *Louisiana History* 6 (1965); and "The Decline of the New Orleans Free Negro in the Decade Before the Civil War," *Journal of Mississippi History* 24 (1962); and Loren Schweninger, "A Negro Sojourner in Antebellum New Orleans," *Louisiana History* 30 (1979).

132 *"Some of the ..."* to *"Dauphine."* True Delta, June 26, 1850. The first arrest reports of June 1850, included the name of Betsey Tolodano: "Report of the Night Watch, June 27, 1850, New Orleans, Louisiana," *Third Municipality Guard Mayor's Book 1838–1850,* vol. 7, May 25, 1848, to July 5, 1850, p. 496; see Fandrich 1994:215, 254–55, and notes.

132 "swore out a criminal warrant ..." Marie Laveau's suit to recover the statue is recorded in the "Judicial Record Books 1840–1852." *Third Municipality Recorder's Office,* vol. 3, p. 206; July 2, 1850. See Fandrich, above.

132 *"We saw the thing ..."* Picayune, July 3, 1850.

133 *"fair daughters ..."* Weekly Delta, July 8, 1850.

133 *"mysterious orders of Voudou"* Weekly Delta, July 15, 1850.

133 *"stout and intelligent ..."* Crescent, July 31, 1950.

133 Testimony of Toledano: *Picayune,* July 31, 1850.

134 "Virgin of Voudou," "compact crowd ..." to "... Egyptian mummy." *Weekly Delta,* August 12, 1850.

134 *"a young Quadroon ..."* Weekly Delta, August 12, 1850.

135 *"she stretch out ..."* Hurston 1990:193; see also Hurston 1931:327.

135 *"There can be no doubt ..."* Picayune, July 31, 1850.

135 "In 1852 the Louisiana legislature ..." Dillon manscript, "The Law's Long Arm: The Suppression of Voodoo," WPA-FWP/NSU.

136 "*a great and constantly ...*" New Orleans City Ordinance # 3847, April 7, 1858.

136 "The press grew more ..." Lawrence Dunbar Reddick, *The Negro in the New Orleans Press, 1850–1860: A Study in Attitudes and Propaganda,* (Ph.D. dissertation, University of Chicago, 1939).

136 "*Knowing ones*" to "*... kind of revelry.*" *Picayune,* July 12, 1859.

136 Creole spiritualism in New Orleans: see Bell 1997; women in the American Spiritualist Movement, see Braude 1989. Minutes of séances: "Spiritualist Registers," Rene Grandjean Collection, Archives and Manuscripts, Special Collections Department, Earl K. Long Library, University of New Orleans.

137 Occupation of New Orleans: Chester G. Hearn, *When the Devil Came Down to Dixie* (Baton Rouge: Louisiana State University, 1997); Mumford: Hearn 1997:134–38.

137 Cailloux's funeral: Stephen J. Ochs, *A Black Patriot and a White Priest: Andre Cailloux and Claude Paschal Maistre in Civil War New Orleans* (Baton Rouge: Louisiana State University Press, 2000), 1–8.

137 Louisiana Native Guards: Mary F. Berry, "Negro Troops in Blue and Gray: The Louisiana Native Guards, 1861–1863," *Louisiana History* 8 (1967).

139 "*Woman Order.*" Hearn 1997:103.

139 The women's parting curse on General Butler is paraphrased from Hearn 1997:220.

## Chapter 10

140 "*Then Marie Laveau comes out ...*" William Moore, WPA-FWP/NSU.

140 Songs and all quotes from Marie the Second are from *Times,* June 28, 1872; the song, "*Chauffez Ça,*" may have been another version of the *Counja,* Dillon manuscript, #118 (2); "Marie II"–Section 6, # 318; also "Congo Square," WPA-FWP/NSU. Typesetters of early periods had few diacritical markings; so I restored the cedilla to *ça.* I left intact their spelling of "*chauffez*" and "*fe*" and translated or interpreted the latter as "*fait,*" the imperative of the verb "*faire,*" to make or do. The WPA writers continued the nineteenth-century practice of spelling Marie the Second's title as "*Mam'zelle,*" an informal version of French "*Mademoiselle.*" I have followed their lead, and suggested translations of the song fragments that reflect Marie's personality, the temper of the times, the sung or improvised qualities of songs in the Louisiana Creole language.

140    *"They celebrated on . . ."* Oscar Felix, FWP-NSU.

143    *"four nude . . ."* *Times*, June 28, 1872.

143    *"On St. John's . . ."* Mattie O'Hara, WPA-FWP/NSU; WPA-LWP/BR; Tallant 1998:82.

143    *"You won't believe it . . ."* Raoul Desfresne, WPA-FWP/NSU; WPA-LWP/BR; Tallant 1998:79.

143    *"The dancers would stomp . . ."* Eugene Fritz, WPA-FWP/NSU; WPA-LWP/BR.

144    *"Man, I mean to tell you . . ."* William Moore, WPA-FWP/NSU; WPA-LWP/BR.

144    *"White ladies . . ."* to *". . . nowadays, no."* Raoul Desfresne, WPA-FWP/NSU; WPA-LWP/BR; Tallant 1998:79.

144    *"She had meetings . . ."* Louis Hopkins, WPA-FWP/NSU.

144    *"those around her . . ."* to *". . . nine days again."* Hurston 1990:193.

145    *"That stuff must . . ."* "Pops" Abou, WPA-FWP/NSU; WPA-LWP/BR; Tallant 1998:86.

145    Benevolent ceremonies and song on Bayou St. John: Alexander Augustin, Gloria White, WPA-FWP/NSU; WPA-LWP/BR; Tallant 1998:84; Dillon ms., #317, "Marie II," WPA-FWP/NSU; ritual baptisms, see Murphy 1994, chapter 6.

146    White House: Dillon manuscript, Folder #317, "Marie Laveau II, Section 6, no pages. WPA-FWP/NSU.

146    Milneburg: Angela Mohar, "Milneburg—The Lakefront's Golden Era," *Preservation in Print*, parts 1, 2 (1995), and James Baughman, "A Southern Spa: Ante-bellum Lake Pontchartrain," *Louisiana History* 3, 1 (1962).

147    *"black enough for . . ."* *Picayune*, June 26, 1871.

147    *"A new and strange kind . . ."* to *". . . from the map."* Henry A. Kmen, "The Joys of Milneburg," *New Orleans Magazine* (May, 1969), 19. Musicians at Milneburg: Kmen 1969:19–20.

147    *MILENBURG JOYS.* Words by Walter Melrose. Music by Leon Rappolo, Paul Mares, and Jelly Roll Morton. Melrose Music Company, Chicago, Illinois. 1925. Courtesy of Hogan Jazz Archives, Tulane University. Milneburg, the village at the lakefront, was named for Alexander Milne, Scottish immigrant and philanthropist. The song title follows the spelling and pronunciation given to it by Rappolo, Mares, and Morton.

148    *"in their queenly glories . . ."* *Times*, June 25, 1870.

148    *"heathenish Negroes"* to *". . . ever since."* *Bee*, June 25, 1870. Analysis of newspaper accounts in postwar press; see Blake Touchstone, "Voodoo in New

Orleans," *Louisiana History* 13, 4 (1972); and Barbara Rosendale Duggal, "Marie Laveau: The Voodoo Queen Repossessed," in Kein 2000.

148    *"A young white girl . . ."* to *". . . human victims." Picayune*, June 23, 1870.

149    *"sacrificed to the snake god" Times*, July 8; Molly Digby: *Times*, July 8, 9, 10, 1870.

149    *"the word of a Voudou . . ." Times*, July 17, 1870; *New York Herald*, August 12, 1870.

149    *"too old to attend . . ." Picayune*, June 24, 1873.

149    *"the celebrated Marie Laveau . . ." Herald*, June 24, 1873.

149    Invitation: *Times*, June 21, 1874.

150    *"Voudous are no more . . ." Times*, June 26, 1874.

150    *"Fully one-half . . ."* to *". . . come then." Times*, June 25, 1874.

151    *Commercial Bulletin*, June 25, 1874.

151    *" was as eager . . ." Republican*, June 25, 1874.

152    *Coda*, Conversation and all quotes *"Bonjour, Monsieur . . ."* to *". . . from the authorities." Picayune*, June 25, 1875.

## Chapter 11

154    *"Commence! We speak through tears. . . ."* Kein 1999:26.

155    Death records for Aldina Crocker [spelled Croker]: St. Louis Cemetery No. 1, Reg. No. 1810–73, Folio 215, Archives, Archdiocese of New Orleans. *Death Certificate of A. Aldina Croker* [sic]. New Orleans Public Library, Recorder of Births and Deaths, New Orleans Health Department, *Death Certificate of A. Aldina Croker* [sic], September 9, 1871, Vol. 52, Box 35, p. 245. The documents of A. Aldina Crocker's death agree with each other. The records of her birth, baptism, or other names she may have used are not as clear; see Long 2001:274.

156    "last glimpsed" *Picayune*, May 10, 1871.

156    "a middle-aged . . ." to ". . . answer. Gumbo." Interview: *Daily States*, June 17, 1881.

157    Death of the Widow Paris: New Orleans Public Library, St. Louis Cemetery No. 1. Burial Records, January 17, 1881–January 1883, # 487.

157    "On Wednesday the . . ." *Picayune*, June 17, 1881.

157    "her remains were followed . . ." *Picayune*, June 17, 1881.

158    "old negro character" to ". . . a little poetry." *Democrat*, June 17, 1881.

158    "which, instead of . . ." to ". . . native dancers." *Democrat*, July 8, 1881.

158    Riot-Massacre of 1866: James G. Hollandsworth, *An Absolute Massacre: The New Orleans Race Riot of July 30, 1866* (Baton Rouge: Louisiana State University Press, 2001), 129; Giles Vandal, *The New Orleans Riot of 1866: Anatomy of a Tragedy* (Lafayette, La.: Center for Louisiana Studies, 1983); and

"The Origins of the New Orleans Riot of 1866, Revisited." *Louisiana History* 22 (Spring 1981).

160 Reconstruction: David C. Rankin, "The Impact of the Civil War on the Free Colored Community of New Orleans," *Perspectives on American History* 11 (1977–78); *The Forgotten People: Free People of Color in New Orleans, 1850–1870* (Ph.D. dissertation, The Johns Hopkins University, 1976); Loren Schweninger, "Antebellum Free People of Color in Postbellum Louisiana," *Louisiana History* 30 (1989); John W. Blassingame, *Black New Orleans, 1860–1880* (Chicago: University of Chicago Press, 1973); Charles Vincent, "Black Louisianians During the Civil War and Reconstruction: Aspects of their Struggles and Achievements," in Macdonald et al. 1979; Caroline Senter, "Creole Poets on the Verge of a Nation," in Kein 2000; Logsdon and Bell in Hirsch and Logsdon 1992; Dominguez 1994; Hanger 1996, chapters 8 and 9; and Roussève 1937.

160 Population statistics: Dominquez 1994:116.

161 Aristide Mary and other Creole men: Rankin 1977–78.

161 *"It brought decline . . ."* Rankin 1977–78:416.

161 *"were more . . ."* through *". . . degree of impotence."* Desdunes 1973:15–18.

161 *"There can be no . . ."* to *". . . of her love."* Picayune, February 28, 1869.

161 *"A soldier named . . ."* Picayune, March 17, 1871.

162 *"Mrs. Glapion . . ."* to *". . . foolish thing."* Times, May 24, 1871.

162 *"and Dr. Jim . . ."* Picayune, August 18, 1871.

162 *"unscrupulous queens"* and *"Voudou victims"* Picayune, September 15, 1871.

163 *"working some spell"* to *". . . participated."* Times, June 26, 1872.

163 *"Marie Laveau, the Voudou Queen . . ."* Times, April 3, 1873.

164 *"Marie Glapion was an outcast . . ."* Virgie Wilson, WPA-FWP/NSU; Tallant 1998:121.

164 *"Old Madame Legendre . . ."* Théophile Miche, WPA-FWP/NSU; Tallant 1998:128.

164 *"the sole and only heir at law"* Judgment No. 4597. Civil District Court. *Succession of Eloise Euchariste or Euchariste Glapion. Petition of heir to be put in possession.* Filed Nov. 28th 1881. H. Miester; also WPA-FWP/NSU.

164 *"Folk tradition . . ."* Raphael Cassimere, Jr., Danny Barker, Florence Borders, D. Clive Hardy, Joseph Logsdon, and Charles Roussève 1980. "New Orleans Black History Tour of St. Louis II Cemetery Square 3." Compiled by New Orleans NAACP.

164 *"Mrs. Marie Philomène Glapion . . ."* Civil District Court No. 4597, WPA-FWP/NSU.

166 Unpaid taxes: 6th District Court, Docket E #14103, 1865; 6th District Court, Docket F #16067, 1866; cited from Fandrich 1994:255, 310.

166 *"Every other negro . . ."* Dillon manuscript, Folder #317, "Marie Laveau II," Section 8, WPA-FWP/NSU.

166 *"At first she was buried . . ."* Sophie Rey, WPA-FWP/NSU.

166 *"Marie Laveau was buried . . ."* Marie Brown, WPA-FWP/NSU. Plans for St. Louis Cemetery Two shows that sections 10–50 of the wall were torn down to make room for an office and tool room, and remains transferred to St. Louis Cemetery Three on August 1, 1918; no records of individual graves; fire destroyed the records of Girod Street Cemetery for the years 1914–18, when reburials may have occurred, WPA-FWP/NSU.

166 New Orleans Saints' football team: The *gumbo ya-ya* about Marie the Second's reburial, an article about her in the *Times-Picayune* on December 17, 2000, and the Saints' uncanny football losses prompted the team to call on Ava Kay Jones, prominent African American lawyer and Yoruba-trained priestess of Vodou. She brought her snake, danced, and did ritual work at halftime on the fifty-yard line. The Saints won their first play-off game in thirty-four years, "The Curse is Lifted," *Times-Picayune*, December 31, 2000; also see Buddy Diliberto, *When the Saints Came Marching In* (New Orleans: Pelican, 2001).

167 *"but her spirit . . ."* Jimmie St. Clair, WPA-FWP/NSU; Tallant 1998:129–30.

167 *"Once when I was . . ."* James St. Ann, WPA-FWP/NSU.

167 *"No, I don't know . . ."* Marie Brown, WPA-FWP/NSU.

167 *"Maybe she was . . ."* Della Greenfield, WPA-FWP/NSU.

168 *"Every one of the group . . ."* and subsequent conversations, "Flagitious Fiction: Cable's Romance about Marie Laveau and the Voudous," *Picayune*, April 11, 1886.

168 *"The worship of Voodoo . . ."* Cable 1976:26; orig. pub. in *Century*, April 1885.

169 Sale of St. Ann Street: New Orleans Notarial Archives, A. Doriocourt, September 18, 1897. COB 170/73, September 18, 1897. Noime Legendre, "Mimi" or "Meme" in WPA interviews, married a white man, some said Jewish, with the last name of Santenac.

170 *"Nobody ever saw . . ."* *Picayune*, April 11, 1886.

## Chapter 12

171 *"The spirit hits them . . ."* Armstrong 1954:91.

171 *"Marie Laveau was in her . . ."* Louise Butler, WPA-LWP/BR; WPA-FWP/NSU. The narratives about Marie the Second's death or disappearance in

a storm at Lake Pontchartrain are scattered throughout the files of interviews from the Federal Writers' Project records: Drawer #16, #12-Folder
50, and Drawer # 6, Folders 30–37, WPA-LWP/BR; and Folders # 317,
318, 319, WPA-FWP/NSU. Tallant quoted many in *Voodoo in New Orleans*,
1998, chapter 15. New Orleanians continued to discuss the magical death
and resurrection stories; Creole poet and musician Sybil Kein heard the
near-drowning story from an aunt, and wrote a poem, "I Want to Die in
That Lake," 1999:29.

171    *"Marie was drowned . . ."* Sophie Rey, WPA-LWP/BR; WPA-FWP/NSU.

171    *"She was dead . . ."* Annabelle Kate Tricou, WPA-LWP/BR; WPA-FWP/NSU.

172    *"She got washed away . . ."* Alice Zeno, WPA-LWP/BR; WPA-FWP/NSU.

172    *"It was all . . ."* to *". . . sometime."* Louise Walters, WPA-LWP/BR; WPA-
FWP/NSU.

172    *"June 24th . . ."* Marie Dede, WPA-LWP/BR; WPA-FWP/NSU.

172    *Three days Marie . . ."* Hurston 1990:194.

173    *"was then living . . ."* William Nott, "Marie Laveau: Long High Priestess,"
*Times-Picayune*, November 19, 1922:7. Nott's article became the twentieth-
century model for journalists. The staff of the Federal Writers' Project
cited it as primary data.

174    Weather reports: *Picayune*, June 22, 23, 24, 1869 through 1881.

175    *"fabulous statements"* to *". . . bitterest enemies."* City Ordinance #3164; Dillon
manuscript, "The Law's Long Arm: The Suppressions of Voodoo," WPA-
FWP/NSU.

175    Zora Neale Hurston chose to live in Algiers for the presence of so much
Hoodoo-Voodoo activity; her letters mention police persecution of
practitioners, Kaplan 2002:127. The majority of the New Orleans
Hoodoo-Voodoo practitioners that Harry Middleton Hyatt interviewed
in the late 1930s and early 1940s were still living in Algiers.

176    *"founded on traditions . . ."* Michael P. Smith, *Spirit World: Photos and Journal*
(New Orleans: Pelican, 1992), 35. Spiritual Churches of New Orleans and
Mother Leafy Anderson: Claude F. Jacobs and Andrew J. Kaslow, *The
Spiritual Churches of New Orleans: Origins, Beliefs, and Rituals of an African-
American Religion* (Knoxville: University of Tennessee Press, 1991); Hans A.
Baer, *The Black Spiritual Movement: A Religious Response to Racism* (Knoxville:
University of Tennessee Press, 1984); Claude Jacobs, "Healing and
Prophesy in the Black Spiritual Churches: A Need for Reexamination,"
*Medical Anthropology* 12, 4 (1990); and "Spirit Guides and Possession in the

New Orleans Black Spiritual Churches," *Journal of American Folklore* 102 (1989).

177  "*The Holy Spirit . . .*" Smith 1992:46.

177  "*What we do comes . . .*" Smith 1992:57.

178  "*When you feel like . . .*" Smith 1992:53.

178  Black Hawk: Donald Jackson, *Black Hawk: An Autobiography* (Urbana: University of Illinois, 1955); Jason Berry, *The Spirit of Black Hawk: A Mystery of Africans and Indians* (Jackson: University Press of Mississippi, 1995); and WPA-FWP/NSU. Mother Anderson's relationship to Black Hawk, see Jacobs and Kaslow 1991.

179  Comparison of St. Maroon/St. Raymond and Black Hawk: Marcus B. Christian, "Voodooism and Mumbo-Jumbo: A Review of Robert Tallant's *The Voodoo Queen,*" *Phylon* 7, 3 (1949), 293.

181  "*For almost a century . . .*" Geoffrey C. Ward and Ken Burns, *Jazz: A History of America's Music* (New York: Alfred A. Knopf, 2001), 8.

181  Homer Plessy: Keith Weldon Medley, "The True Story of the Supreme Court Cast of Plessy vs. Ferguson," *New Orleans Tribune*, 12, 5 (May 1996); and "When Plessy Met Ferguson," *Cultural Vistas* (Winter 1996).

182  "*a half century later . . .*" Alan Lomax, *Mister Jelly Roll: The Fortunes of Jelly Roll Morton, New Orleans Creole and "Inventor of Jazz"* (New York: Grosset & Dunlap, 1950), xiv.

182  "*So tolerant New . . .*" to "*. . . of pride.*" Lomax 1950:xv.

183  "*By the time that Turner . . .*" to "*. . . obey her orders.*" Hurston 1990:196.

183  "*To The Man God . . .*" Hurston 1931:337. The curse-prayer is reprinted in full with this exception: the opening address to the Deity is from Hurston 1990:197.

185  "*that had come . . .*" to "*. . . for power.*" Hurston 1990:194.

185  "*That night she sing . . .*" Hurston 1990:195; "*So I have the snake . . .*" is a paraphrase.

185  Death of Robert Tallant: *Times-Picayune*, April 2, April 3, 1957; *New York Times*, April 3, 1957; *States-Item*, April 1, 1957.

186  "*But a 20-minute . . .*" *Times-Picayune*, June 30, 1999.

186  "*Marie Laveau doesn't like people . . .*" *Times-Picayune*, June 30, 1999.

187  "*Marie is doing a primal dance . .*" Glassman 2000:53.

# Sources

Adams, M. Boniface. 1993. The Gift of Religious Leadership: Henriette Delille and the Foundation of the Holy Family Sisters. In Glen R. Conrad, 360–74.

Anderson, John Q. 1960. The New Orleans Voodoo Ritual Dance and Its Twentieth Century Survivals. *Southern Folklore Quarterly* 24:135–43.

Anthony, Arthé A. 2000. "Lost Boundaries": Racial Passing and Poverty in Segregated New Orleans. In Kein, 2000. Reprinted from *Louisiana History* 36, 1995:291–312.

Apter, Andrew. 1991. Herskovits's Heritage: Rethinking Syncretism in the African Diaspora. *Diaspora* 1(3):235–60.

Armstrong, Louis. 1954. *Satchmo: My Life in New Orleans*. New York: Prentice-Hall.

Asbury, Herbert. 1938. *The French Quarter: An Informal History of the New Orleans Underworld*. Garden City, N.Y.: Garden City Publications.

Baer, Hans. 1984. *The Black Spiritual Movement: A Religious Response to Racism*. Knoxville: University of Tennessee Press.

Baker, Houston A., Jr. 1991. *Workings of the Spirit: The Poetics of Afro-American Women's Writing*. Chicago: University of Chicago Press.

Bankole, Katherine. 1998. *Slavery and Medicine: Enslavement and Medical Practices in Antebellum Louisiana*. New York: Garland.

Baudier, Roger. 1939. *The Catholic Church in Louisiana*. New Orleans.

Baughman, James P. 1962. A Southern Spa: Ante-bellum Lake Pontchartrain. *Louisiana History* 3(1):5–32.

Bell, Caryn Cossé. 1997. *Revolution, Romanticism, and the Afro-Creole Protest Tradition in Louisiana, 1718–1868*. Baton Rouge: Louisiana State University Press.

Bell, Michael Edward. 1970. Pattern, Structure, and Logic in Afro-American Hoodoo Performance. Ph.D. dissertation, Indiana University.

Berry, Jason. 1995. *The Spirit of Black Hawk: A Mystery of Africans and Indians*. Jackson: University Press of Mississippi.

Berry, Mary F. 1967. Negro Troops in Blue and Gray: The Louisiana Native Guards, 1861–1863. *Louisiana History* 8:165–90.

Bishpam, Clarence W. 1919. Fray Antonio de Sedella: An Appreciation. *Louisiana Historical Quarterly* 2:24–37, 369–92.

Blanton, Mackie J. V., and Gayle K. Nolan. 1993. Creole Lenten Devotions: Nineteenth-Century Practices and their Implications. In Glen R. Conrad, 525–39.

Blassingame, John W., ed. 1977. *Slave Testimony: Two Centuries of Letters, Speeches, Interviews, and Autobiographies.* Baton Rouge: Louisiana State University Press.

———. 1973. *Black New Orleans, 1860–1880.* Chicago: University of Chicago Press.

Bourguignon, Erika. 1991. *Possession.* Prospect Heights, Ill.: Waveland Press.

Boyd, Valerie. 2003. *Wrapped in Rainbows: The Life of Zora Neale Hurston.* New York: Scribner.

Brady, Patricia. 1993. Free Men of Color as Tomb Builders in the Nineteenth Century. In Conrad, 1993, 478–88.

Braude, Ann. 1989. *Radical Spirits: Spiritualism and Women's Rights in Nineteenth-Century America.* Boston: Beacon Press.

Brock, Eric 1999 *New Orleans Cemeteries: Images of America.* Charleston, S.C.: Arcadia.

Brown, Karen McCarthy. 2001. *Mama Lola: A Vodou Priestess in Brooklyn,* 2nd ed. Berkeley: University of California Press.

Bruns, J. Edgar. 1993. Annotating for Posterity: The Sacramental Records of Father Antonio de Sedella. In Conrad, 1993, 349–59.

Buckingham, James. 1842. *The Slave States of America,* vol. 1. London: Fisher, Son, & Co.

Buel, J. W. 1882. *Metropolitan Life Unveiled: Mysteries and Miseries of America's Great Cities.* St. Louis: Historical Publishing Co.

Cable, George Washington. 1884. *The Creoles of Louisiana.* New York: Charles Scribner's Sons.

———. 1976. *The Dance in Place Congo and Creole Slave Songs,* 3rd ed. New Orleans: Faruk von Turk.

Carrigan, Jo Ann. 1994. *The Saffron Scourge: A History of Yellow Fever in Louisiana, 1796–1905.* Lafayette, La.: Center for Louisiana Studies.

Cassimere, Raphael, Jr., Danny Barker, Florence Borders, D. Clive Hardy, Joseph Logsdon, and Charles Rousseve. 1980. "New Orleans Black History Tour of St. Louis II Cemetery Square 3." Compiled by New Orleans NAACP.

Castellanos, Henry C. 1895. *New Orleans As It Was: Episodes of Louisiana Life,* 2nd ed. New Orleans: L. Graham.

Chambon, Rt. Rev. Celestine. 1938. *The St. Louis Cathedral and Its Neighbors.* New Orleans: Louisiana State Museum Publications.

Christian, Marcus Bruce, 1946. Voodooism and Mumbo-Jumbo: A Review of Robert Tallant's *The Voodoo Queen. Phylon* 7(3):293–96.

Christovich, Mary Louise, ed. 1997. *New Orleans Architecture*, vol. 3: *The Cemeteries*. New Orleans: Pelican Publishing Company.

Clark, Emily. 1998. A New World Community: The New Orleans Ursulines and Colonial Society, 1727–1803. Ph.D. dissertation, Tulane University.

Clark, Emily, and Virginia Meacham Gould. 2002. The Feminine Face of Afro-Catholicism in New Orleans, 1727–1852. *William and Mary Quarterly*, 3rd series, 59(2):409–48.

Clayton, Ronnie W. 1990. *Mother Wit: The Ex-Slave Narratives of the Louisiana Writers' Project*. New York: Peter Lang.

———. 1978. The Federal Writers' Project for Blacks in Louisiana. *Louisiana History* 19(3):327–35.

———. 1974. *A History of the Federal Writers' Project in Louisiana*. Ph.D. dissertation, Louisiana State University.

Clinton, Catherine, and Michele Gillespie, eds. 1997. *The Devil's Lane: Sex and Race in the Early South*. New York: Oxford University Press.

Coleman, William H. 1885. *Historical Sketch Book and Guide to New Orleans and Environs*. New York: William Head Coleman.

Conrad, Glen R., ed. 1993. *Cross, Crozier, and Crucible: A Volume Celebrating the Bicentennial of a Catholic Diocese in Louisiana*. New Orleans.

———. 1988. *A Dictionary of Louisiana Biography*. New York: Louisiana Historical Association.

Creecy, James. 1860. *Scenes in the South and Other Miscellaneous Pieces*. Philadelphia: Lippincott.

Curry, Leonard P. 1981. *The Free Black in Urban America 1800–1850*. Chicago: University of Chicago Press.

Davis, Wade. 1985. *The Serpent and the Rainbow: A Harvard Scientist's Astonishing Journey into the Secret Societies of Haitian Voodoo, Zombis, and Magic*. New York: Simon and Schuster.

deCaro, Frank, ed., and Rosan Augusta Jordan, assoc. ed. 1998. *Louisiana Sojourns: Travelers' Tales and Literary Journeys*. Baton Rouge: Louisiana State University Press.

DeGrummond, Jane Lucas, and Ronald R. Morazan. 1979. *The Baratarians and the Battle of New Orleans with Biographical Sketches of the Veterans of the Battalion of Orleans. 1814–1815*. Baton Rouge, La.: Legacy Publications.

Desdunes, Rodolphe Lucien. 1973. *Our People and Our History*. Trans. Sr. Dorothea Olga McCants. Baton Rouge: Louisiana State University Press.

Diliberto, Buddy. 2001. *When the Saints Came Marching In.* Photographs, Michael C. Hebert. New Orleans: Pelican Publishing Company.

Domínguez, Virginia R. 1994. *White By Definition: Social Classification in Creole Louisiana.* New Brunswick, N.J.: Rutgers University Press.

Donaldson, Gary A. 1984. A Window on Slave Culture: Dances at Congo Square in New Orleans, 1800–1862. *Journal of Negro History* 69(2):63–72.

Duffy, John. 1966. *The Sword of Pestilence: The New Orleans Yellow Fever Epidemic of 1853.* Baton Rouge: Louisiana State University Press.

———. 1962. *The Rudolph Matas History of Medicine in Louisiana*, vol. 2. Baton Rouge: Louisiana State University Press.

———. 1958. *The Rudolph Matas History of Medicine in Louisiana*, vol. 1. Baton Rouge: Louisiana State University Press.

Duffy, John, ed. 1957. *Parson Clapp of the Stranger's Church of New Orleans.* Baton Rouge: Louisiana State University Press.

Duggal, Barbara Rosendale. 2000. Marie Laveau: The Voodoo Queen Repossessed. In Kein, 2000, 157–78.

DuPratz, Antoine S. LePage. 1975. *History of Louisiana.* Trans. T. Becket and P. A. DeHondt. London: Strand. Reprint, Joseph Tregle, ed. Baton Rouge: Louisiana State University Press.

Emery, Lynne Fauley. 1988. *Black Dance From 1619 to Today*, 2nd ed. Princeton, N.J.: Dance Horizons Press.

Estes, David C. 1990. Traditional Dances and Processions of Blacks in New Orleans as Witnessed by Antebellum Travelers. *Louisiana Folklore Miscellany* 6(3): 1–4.

Evans, Sally Kittredge. 1974. Free Persons of Color. In Toledano, Evans, and Christovich, 25–36.

Fandrich, Ina Johanna. 1994. The Mysterious Voodoo Queen Marie Laveaux: A Study of Power and Female Leadership in Nineteenth-Century New Orleans. Ph.D. dissertation, Temple University.

Federal Writers' Project of the Works Progress Administration. 1938. *New Orleans City Guide.*

Fiehrer, Thomas. 1989. Saint-Domingue/Haiti: Louisiana's Caribbean Connection. *Louisiana History* 30:419–37.

Florence, Robert. 1996. *City of the Dead: A Journey Through St. Louis Cemetery #1, New Orleans, Louisiana.* Lafayette, La.: The Center for Louisiana Studies.

Foner, Laura. 1970. The Free People of Color in Louisiana and St. Domingue: A Comparative Portrait of Two Three-Caste Slave Societies. *Journal of Social History* 3:406–30.

Franklin, John Hope, and Loren Schweninger. 1999. *Runaway Slaves: Rebels on the Plantation*. New York: Oxford University Press.

Gayarré, Charles. 1974. *History of Louisiana*. 4 vols. New Orleans: Pelican Publishing Co.

Gehman, Mary. 1994. *The Free People of Color in New Orleans: An Introduction*. New Orleans: Margaret Media.

Glassman, Sallie Ann. 2000. *Vodou Visions: An Encounter with Divine Mystery*. New York: Villard.

Gould, Virgina Meacham. 1997a. "A Chaos of Iniquity and Discord:" Slave and Free Women of Color in the Spanish Ports of New Orleans, Mobile, and Pensacola. In Clinton and Gillespie, 232–47.

―――. 1997b. "The House that Was Never a Home": Slave Family and Household Organization in New Orleans, 1820–50. *Slavery and Abolition* 18(2):90–103.

―――. 1996. "If I Can't Have My Rights, I Can Have My Pleasures, And If They Won't Give Me Wages, I Can Take Them": Gender and Slave Labor in Antebellum New Orleans. In Morton, 179–201.

―――. 1991. In Full Enjoyment of their Liberty: The Free Women of Color of the Gulf Ports of New Orleans, Mobile, and Pensacola, 1769–1860. Ph.D. dissertation, Emory University.

Gould, Virginia Meacham, and Charles E. Nolan. 1999. *Henriette Delille: "Servant of Slaves."* New Orleans: Sisters of the Holy Family.

Gould, Virginia Meacham, and Charles E. Nolan, eds. 2001. *No Cross, No Crown: Black Nuns in Nineteenth-Century New Orleans. The History of the Sisters of the Holy Family, Sister Mary Bernard Deggs*. Bloomington: Indiana University Press.

Haas, Edward F., ed. 1983. *Louisiana's Legal Heritage*. Pensacola, Fla.: Perdido Bay Press.

Hall, Gwendolyn Midlo. 1997. African Women in French and Spanish Louisiana: Origins, Roles, Family, Work, Treatment. In Clinton and Gillespie, 246–62.

―――. 1992a. *Africans in Colonial Louisiana: The Development of Afro-Creole Culture in the Eighteenth Century*. Baton Rouge: Louisiana State University Press.

―――. 1992b. The Formation of Afro-Creole Culture. In Hirsch and Logsdon, 58–87.

Hall, Gwendolyn Midlo, ed. 2000. *Databases for the Study of Afro-Louisiana History and Genealogy, 1699–1860*. CD-Rom. Computerized Information from Original Manuscript Sources. Baton Rouge: Louisiana State University Press.

Hanger, Kimberley S. 1997a. *Bounded Lives, Bounded Places: Free Black Society in Colonial New Orleans, 1769–1803*. Durham & London: Duke University Press.

————. 1997b. Coping in a Complex World: Free Black Women in Colonial New Orleans. In Clinton and Gillespie, 218–31.

————. 1996a. "The Fortunes of Women in America": Spanish New Orleans's Free Women of African Descent and their Relations with Slave Women. In Patricia Morton, ed., 153–78.

————. 1996b. *A Medley of Cultures: Louisiana History at the Cabildo.* New Orleans: Louisiana Museum Foundation.

————. 1992. Protecting Property, Family, and Self: The *Mujeres Libres* of Colonial New Orleans. *Revista/Review Interamericana* 22(1, 2) Spring:126–50.

Hanggi-Myers, Laura. 1995. The Howard Association of New Orleans— Precursor to District Nursing. *Public Health Nursing* 12(2):78–82.

Hardy, James D., Jr. 1984. A Slave Sale in Antebellum New Orleans. *Southern Studies*: 23:306–14.

Hatley, Donald W. 1986–87. A Preliminary Guide to Folklore in the Louisiana Federal Writers' Project. *Louisiana Folklore Miscellany* 6(2):8–14.

Hearn, Chester G. 1997. *When the Devil Came Down to Dixie.* Baton Rouge: Louisiana State University.

Hemenway, Robert E. 1980. *Zora Neale Hurston: A Literary Biography.* With a foreword by Alice Walker. Urbana: University of Illinois Press.

Hildreth, Flora Bassett. 1975. *The Howard Association of New Orleans 1837–1878.* Ph.D. dissertation, University of California, Los Angeles.

————. 1979. Early Red Cross: The Howard Association of New Orleans, 1837–1878. *Louisiana History* 20:49–75.

Hinson, Glenn. 2000. *Fire in My Bones: Transcendence and the Holy Spirit in African American Gospel.* Philadelphia: University of Pennsylvania Press.

Hirsch, Arnold R., and Joseph Logsdon, eds. 1992. *Creole New Orleans: Race and Americanization.* Baton Rouge: Louisiana State University Press.

Hollandsworth, James G. 2001. *An Absolute Massacre: The New Orleans Race Riot of July 30, 1866.* Baton Rouge: Louisiana State University Press.

Holloway, Joseph, ed. 1990. *Africanisms in American Culture.* Bloomington: Indiana University Press.

Hurston, Zora Neale. 1996. *The Complete Stories.* Introduction by Henry Louis Gates and Sieglinde Lewis. New York: HarperPerennial.

————. 1990. *Mules and Men.* New York: HarperPerennial.

————. 1970. Shouting. Conversions and Visions. Characteristics of Negro Expression. Spirituals and Neo-Spirituals. In *Negro, An Anthology.* Collected and edited by Nancy Cunard. New York: Frederick Ungar.

————. 1938. *Tell My Horse: Voodoo and Life in Haiti and Jamaica.* New York: J.B. Lippincott.

————. 1931. Hoodoo in America. *Journal of American Folklore* 44(174):317–417.

Hyatt, Harry Middleton. 1970. *Hoodoo-Conjuration-Witchcraft-Rootwork.* Memoirs of the Alma Egan Hyatt Foundation. Hannibal, Mo.: Western Publishing, Inc. Vols. 1, 2, 1970.

————. 1973. *Hoodoo-Conjuration-Witchcraft-Rootwork.* Memoirs of the Alma Egan Hyatt Foundation. Hannibal, Mo.: Western Publishing, Inc. Vols. 3, 4.

————. 1978. *Hoodoo-Conjuration-Witchcraft-Rootwork.* Memoirs of the Alma Egan Hyatt Foundation. Hannibal, Mo.: Western Publishing, Inc. Vol. 5.

Jackson, Donald, ed. 1955. *Black Hawk: An Autobiography.* Urbana: University of Illinois.

Jacobs, Claude V. 1990. Healing and Prophecy in the Black Spiritual Churches: A Need for Re-examination. *Medical Anthropology* 12(4):349–70.

————. 1989. Spirit Guides and Possession in the New Orleans Black Spiritual Churches. *Journal of American Folklore* 102:45–67.

————. 1988. Benevolent Societies of New Orleans Blacks during the Late Nineteenth and Early Twentieth Centuries. *Louisiana History* 28:21–33.

Jacobs, Claude V., and Andrew J. Kaslow. 1991. *The Spiritual Churches of New Orleans: Origins, Beliefs, and Rituals of an African-American Religion.* Knoxville: University of Tennessee Press.

Johnson, Jerah. 1995. *Congo Square in New Orleans.* New Orleans: Louisiana Landmarks Society.

Johnson, Walter. 1999. *Soul by Soul: Life Inside the Antebellum Slave Market.* Cambridge, Mass.: Harvard University Press.

Joyaux, Georges J., ed. 1956. Forest's *Voyage aux Etats-Unis de l'Amérique en 1831. Louisiana Historic Quarterly* 39(4):457–72.

Kaplan, Carla, ed. 2002. *Zora Neale Hurston: A Life in Letters.* New York: Doubleday.

Kein, Sybil. 1999. *Gumbo People.* New Orleans: Margaret Media, Inc.

————. 1992. The Celebration of Life in New Orleans Jazz Funerals. *Revue Française D'Etudes Americaines* 51:19–26.

Kein, Sybil, ed. 2000. *Creole: The History and Legacy of Louisiana's Free People of Color.* Baton Rouge: Louisiana State University Press.

Kendall, John S. 1937. Old New Orleans Houses and Some of the People Who Lived in Them. *Louisiana Historical Quarterly* 20(3):794–820.

————. 1853. History and Incidents of the Plague in New Orleans. *Harper's Magazine* 7:797–806.

King, Grace. 1926. *New Orleans: The Place and the People.* New York: Macmillan.

Kmen, Henry A. 1972. The Roots of Jazz and the Dance in Place Congo: A Re-appraisal. *Yearbook, Anuario 8.* Institute of Latin American Studies, University of Texas, Austin.

———. 1969. The Joys of Milneburg. *New Orleans Magazine.* May:16–19, 46ff.

Labbé, Dolores Egger. 1997. "Helpers in the Gospel": Women and Religion in Louisiana, 1800–1830. *Mid-America: An Historical Review* 79(2):153–75.

Lachance, Paul F. 1992. The Foreign French. In Hirsch and Logsdon, 101–30.

———. 1988. The 1809 Immigration of Saint-Domingue Refugees to New Orleans: Reception, Integration and Impact. *Louisiana Historical Quarterly* 29:109–41.

Laguerre, Michel S. 1980. *Voodoo Heritage.* Beverly Hills: Sage.

Landes, Ruth. 1994. *The City of Women.* Introduction by Sally Cole. Albuquerque: University of New Mexico Press [orig. pub. New York: Macmillan, 1947].

Latrobe, Benjamin Henry Boneval. 1951. *Impressions Respecting New Orleans: Diary & Sketches 1818–1820.* Edited with an Introduction and Notes by Samuel Wilson, Jr. New York: Columbia University Press.

LeJeune, Emilie. 1919. Creole Folk Songs. *Louisiana Historical Quarterly* 2:456–58.

Levine, Lawrence W. 1977. *Black Culture and Black Consciousness: Afro-American Folk Thought from Slavery to Freedom.* New York: Oxford University Press.

Logsdon, Joseph, and Caryn Cossé Bell. 1992. The Americanization of Black New Orleans, 1850–1900. In Hirsch and Logsdon, 201–61.

Lomax, Alan. 1950. *Mister Jelly Roll: The Fortunes of Jelly Roll Morton, New Orleans Creoles and "Inventor of Jazz."* New York: Grosset & Dunlap.

Long, Carolyn Morrow. 2001. *Spiritual Merchants: Religion, Magic, and Commerce.* Knoxville: University of Tennessee Press.

Macdonald, Robert R., John R. Kemp, and Edward F. Haas, eds. 1979. *Louisiana's Black Heritage.* New Orleans: Lousiana State Museum.

Maduell, Charles R., Jr. 1969. *Marriages and Family Relationships of New Orleans, 1830–1840.* Hébert Publications. Notarial Archives.

———. 1969. *Marriages and Family Relationships of New Orleans, 1820–1830.* Notarial Archives.

Malone, Jacqui. 1996. *Steppin' on the Blues: The Visible Rhythms of African American Dance.* Urbana and Chicago: University of Illinois Press.

Martin, Joan M. 2000. *Plaçage* and the Louisiana *Gens de Couleur Libre:* How Race and Sex Defined the Lifestyles of Free Women of Color. In Kein 2000:57–70.

McConnell, Roland C. 1979. Louisiana's Black Military History, 1729–1865. In Macdonald, Kemp, and Haas, 32–75.

———. 1968. *Negro Troops of Antebellum Louisiana: A History of the Battalion of Free Men of Color*. Baton Rouge: Louisiana State University Press.

Medley, Keith Weldon. 1996. The True Story of the Supreme Court Cast of Plessy vs. Ferguson. *New Orleans Tribune*, May, 12(5):8–13.

———. 1996–97. When Plessy Met Ferguson. *Cultural Vistas*, Winter:52–59.

Mikell, Gwendolyn. 1983. The Anthropological Imagination of Zora Neale Hurston. *Western Journal of Black Studies* 7(1):27–35.

Mohar, Angela. 1995. Milneburg—The Lakefront's Golden Era. *Preservation in Print*. Part 1, vol. 22(6), August. Part 2, vol. 22(7), September.

Morton, Patricia, ed. 1996. *Discovering the Women in Slavery: Emancipating Perspectives on the American Past*. Athens: University of Georgia Press.

Mulira, Jessie Gaston. 1990. The Case of Voodoo in New Orleans. In Holloway, 34–68.

Murphy, Joseph M. 1994. *Working with the Spirit: Ceremonies of the African Diaspora*. Boston: Beacon Press.

Neville, Art, Aaron Neville, Charles Neville, Cyril Neville, and David Ritz. 2000. *The Brothers: An Autobiography*. Boston: Little, Brown.

Ochs, Stephen J. 2000. *A Black Patriot and a White Priest: André Cailloux and Claude Paschal Maistre in Civil War New Orleans*. Baton Rouge: Louisiana State University Press.

O'Neill, Charles Edwards, S.J. 1990. "A Quarter Marked by Sundry Peculiarities": New Orleans, Lay Trustees, and Père Antoine. *Catholic Historical Review* 76:235–75.

Osbey, Brenda Marie. 1990. Faubourg Treme: A Community in Transition. Part I: Early History. *New Orleans Tribune*, December.

Porteus, Laura. 1934. The Gris-Gris Case. *Louisiana Historical Quarterly* 17(1): 48–63.

Potter, Eliza. 1859. *A Hairdresser's Experience in High Life*. Cincinnati, Ohio: Privately published for the author.

Prejean, Sister Helen. 1993. *Dead Man Walking*. New York: Vintage.

Puckett, Erastus Paul. 1907. The Free Negro in New Orleans, 1803–1860. M.A. thesis, Tulane University.

Rankin, David C. 1977–78. The Impact of the Civil War on the Free Colored Community of New Orleans. In *Perspectives on American History* 11:379–416, Donald Fleming, ed. Cambridge, Mass.: Harvard University Press.

———. 1976. The Forgotten People: Free People of Color in New Orleans, 1850–1870. Ph.D. dissertation, The Johns Hopkins University.

Reddick, Laurence Dunbar. 1939. The Negro in New Orleans' Press, 1850–1860: A Study in Attitudes and Propaganda. Ph.D. dissertation, University of Chicago.

Redding, Joan. 1991. The Dillard Project: The Black Unit of the Louisiana Writer's Project. *Louisiana History* 32:47–62.

Reinders, Robert C. 1965. The Free Negro in the New Orleans Economy, 1850–1860. *Louisiana History* 6:273–85.

———. 1962a. The Decline of the New Orleans Free Negro in the Decade Before the Civil War. *Journal of Mississippi History* 24:88–99.

———. 1962b. Slavery in New Orleans in the Decade Before the Civil War. *Mid-America* 44(4):211–21.

Rickles, Patricia K. 1965. The Folklore of Sacraments and Sacramentals in South Louisiana. *Louisiana Folklore Miscellany* 2:27–44.

Rigaud, Milo. 1971. *Secrets of Voodoo.* New York: Pocket Books.

Robinson, William L. 1860. *Diary of a Samaritan.* New York: Harper Bros.

Rosenthal, Judy. 1998. *Possession, Ecstasy, and Law in Ewe Voodoo.* Charlottesville: University Press of Virginia.

Rousey, Dennis C. 1996. *Policing the Southern City: New Orleans, 1805–1889.* Baton Rouge: Louisiana State University Press.

Roussève, Charles B. 1937. *The Negro in Louisiana.* New Orleans: Xavier University Press.

Russell, William Howard. 1863. *My Diary North and South.* Boston.

Saxon, Lyle, with Robert Tallant and Edward Dreyer. 1998. *Gumbo Ya-Ya. Folk Tales of Louisiana.* New Orleans: Pelican Publishing [orig. pub. 1945].

Schafer, Judith K. 1994. *Slavery, the Civil Law and the Supreme Court of Louisiana.* Baton Rouge: Louisiana State University.

———. 1987. "Open and Notorious Concubinage": The Emancipation of Slave Mistresses by Will and Supreme Court in Antebellum Louisiana. *Louisiana History* 28:165–82.

———. 1981. New Orleans Slavery in 1850 as Seen in Advertisements. *Journal of Southern History* 47(1):33–56.

———. 1980. The Immediate Impact of Nat Turner's Insurrection on New Orleans. *Louisiana History* 21:361–76.

Schultz, Christian. 1810. *Travels on an Inland Voyage,* vol. 2. New York: Isaac Riley.

Senter, Caroline. 2000. Creole Poets on the Verge of a Nation. In Kein, 276–94.

Schweninger, Loren. 1989. Antebellum Free People of Color in Postbellum Louisiana. *Louisiana History* 30:345–64.

———. 1979. A Negro Sojourner in Antebellum New Orleans. *Louisiana History* 20:305–14.

Sered, Susan Starr. 1994. *Priestess, Mother, Sacred Sister: Religions Dominated by Women.* New York: Oxford University Press.

Smith, Michael. 1992. *Spirit World. Photographs and Journal.* New Orleans: Pelican Publishing Co.

Smith, Theophus H. 1994. *Conjuring Culture: Biblical Formations of Black America.* New York: Oxford University Press.

Tallant, Robert. 1998. *Voodoo in New Orleans.* New Orleans: Pelican Publishing Co.

Teish, Luisah. 1985. *Jambalaya: The Natural Woman's Book of Personal Charms and Practical Rituals.* New York: HarperCollins.

Thompson, Robert Farris. 1983. *Flash of the Spirit: African and Afro-American Art and Philosophy.* New York: Random House.

Thornton, John K. 1998. *The Kongolese Saint Anthony: Dona Beatriz Kimpa Vita and the Antonian Movement, 1684–1706.* Cambridge, UK: Cambridge University Press.

———. 1987–88. On the Trail of Voodoo: African Christianity in Africa and the Americas. *Americas* 44(3):261–78.

———. 1984. The Development of an African Catholic Church in the Kingdom of Kongo, 1491–1750. *Journal of African History* 25:315–45.

Toledano, Roulhac, and Mary Louise Christovich. 1980. *New Orleans Architecture,* vol. 6: *Faubourg Treme and the Bayou Road.* New Orleans: Pelican Publishing Co.

Toledano, Roulhac, Sally Kittredge Evans, and Mary Louise Christovich 1974. *New Orleans Architecture,* vol. 4: *The Creole Faubourgs.* New Orleans: Pelican Publishing Co.

Touchstone, Blake. 1972. Voodoo in New Orleans. *Louisiana History* 13(4):371–87.

Vandal, Giles. 1983. *The New Orleans Riot of 1866: Anatomy of a Tragedy.* Lafayette, La.: Center for Louisiana Studies.

———. 1981. The Origins of the New Orleans Riot of 1866, Revisited. *Louisiana History* 22:135–65. Spring.

Vella, Christina. 1997. *Intimate Enemies: The Two Worlds of the Baroness de Pontalba.* Baton Rouge: Louisiana University Press.

Vincent, Charles. 1979. Black Louisianians During the Civil War and Reconstruction: Aspects of their Struggles and Achievements. In Macdonald et al., 85–111.

Wafer, Jim. 1991. *The Taste of Blood: Spirit Possession in Brazilian Candomblé.* Philadelphia: University of Pennsylvania Press.

Walker, Alexander. 1858. *Life of Andrew Jackson.* New York: Derby and Jackson.

Ward, Geoffrey C., and Ken Burns. 2000. *Jazz: A History of America's Music.* New York: Alfred A. Knopf.

Wilson, Samuel, Jr., and Leonard Huber. 1963. *The St. Louis Cemeteries of New Orleans*. New Orleans: St. Louis Cathedral.

Wilson, Samuel, Jr., Patricia Brady, and Lynn D. Adams. 1999. *Queen of the South, New Orleans, 1853–1862: The Journals of Thomas K. Wharton*. New Orleans: Historic New Orleans Collection and New York Public Library. Plus Video.

# At the End:
# In Recognition and Respect

M y gratitude to the following people is immense. To those of you listed below, please accept my respect, know how much I treasure your advice, support, and wisdom. You are not responsible for mistakes I've made—only for the good things you made happen.

For professional competence, practical assistance, and timely advice, I wish to thank Dr. Emily Toth, writer and scholar, Louisiana State University; Dr. Jeffrey Ehrenreich, chair of my department and anthropologist-extraordinary; Dr. Sybil Kein, Creole poet, musician, writer, translator; Dr. Albert Kennedy of the Herman and Ethel Midlo Center, University of New Orleans; Sallie Ann Glassman, community leader and priestess of Vodou; Pandora Laba, editor and writer; Seetha Srinivasan and the staff of the University Press of Mississippi; the members of my Sorta Zona Rosa Writers' Group: Gillian Brown, Lynn Byrd, Bonnie Fastow, Alice Kemp, Beverley Rainbolt, and Joyce Zonana.

I want to acknowledge three women who bring Marie Laveau to life: Barbara Trevigne, Creole, community scholar; Carolyn Long, independent researcher; and Dr. Ina Fandrich, philosopher and scholar.

The librarians and archivists of Louisiana are a national treasure. I would like to thank Marie Windell, Florence Jumonville, John Kelly, Ronald Saskowski, Sybil Boudreaux, Coralie Davis, and Connie Phelps at the Earl K. Long Library, University of New Orleans; Pamela Arceneaux and Sally Stassi, Historic New Orleans Collection, Williams Research Center; Mary Linn Wernet and Catherine M. Jannik, Cammie G. Henry Research Center at Northwestern State University in Natchitoches, Louisiana; Kathryn Page, Louisiana State Museum, Historical Center, New Orleans; Sally K. Reeves and the staff, New Orleans Notarial Archives Research Center; Bruce Abbott, Louisiana State University Medical Center Library; Charlene Bonnette, State Library of Louisiana, Baton Rouge; Jennifer Lushear, New Orleans Pharmacy Museum; and Dr. Charles E. Nolan and Anthony Tassin,

Archdiocesan Archives, Catholic Archdiocese of New Orleans. At Tulane University I want to acknowledge Dr. Wilbur E. Menerary and Kenneth Owens in Special Collections, Howard-Tilton Library; Brenda Billips Square, Amistad Research Center; Alma Freeman of the Hogan Jazz Archives; and Patsy Copeland and Mary J. Holt of the Rudolph Matas Medical Library.

The dedicated staff members of the New Orleans Public Libraries deserve special thanks. Irene Wainwright, Greg Osborn, Wayne Everard, and Colin Hamer of the Louisiana Division provided extensive assistance and answered innumerable questions. Two writers for the contemporary *New Orleans Times-Picayune* have supported me at every step: Dayna Harpster and Susan Larson. For professional, technical, and artistic assistance, I thank Joseph Ayers, artist; Dr. Ahmad Massasati, geographer; Carol Peeples, artist; Michael P. Smith, photographer; Celeste Conefry, translator; Addy Morales, graduate researcher; Dr. Randolph Bates, writer; Dr. David Beriss; and Ernest Mackie. Katy Moran took notes for me in the Pharmacy Museum and got us into Galatoire's for lunch on the Friday before Mardi Gras.

To old friends and to friends I've made in the course of this research—in appreciation—Kay Tiblier, Marcia Bennett, Delia Anderson, Orissa Arend, Richard Saxer, Vivian Kahn, Corinne Barnwell, Ann Edwards, Carol Gelderman, Macon Fry, Joan Halperin, Harley Kutzen, Melanie McKay, Chris Wiltz, Toni Wendel, Alvina Haverkamp, Ann Gussow, Carolyn Kolb, Caryn Cossé Bell, and Robert Meiers.

For the inspiration and blessings of the spirits that each of you brought to this project, I would like to thank Alicia Gates, Lorrie Brilla, Shelley Masters, Ed Brown, Linda Waters, Robert Lee Morris, Linda Barbour, and especially Christy Merritt and Kristena West. In the same spirit, I offer my abiding respect and gratitude to the late Joseph Logsdon, professor of history at the University of New Orleans; Sister Adeline A. Sanford, Bethel African Methodist Episcopal Church, Briton's Neck, South Carolina; Father Jerome Ledoux, St. Augustine Church, New Orleans; and Dr. Michael Harner, Foundation for Shamanic Studies.

And, last, I owe eternal gratitude and love to my parents Hugh and Moselle Coonfield whose religious values and Oklahoma faith continue to light my path; my brother and sister-in-law, Hugh and Heidi Coonfield of Salem, Oregon; my brother and sister-in-law, Ted Coonfield and Meg Nightingale of Portland, Oregon; and my precious daughter, Marlowe Ward. Now and forever—you are the best and the brightest of my life. So Be It.

# Index